THE ROPES TO SKIP AND
THE ROPES TO KNOW

WILEY SERIES IN MANAGEMENT

THE

ROPES TO SKIP

Studies in Organizational Behavior

AND THE

ROPES

TO KNOW

FOURTH EDITION

R. RICHARD RITTI

THE PENNSYLVANIA STATE UNIVERSITY

JOHN WILEY & SONS, INC.

NEW YORK • CHICHESTER • BRISBANE • TORONTO • SINGAPORE

Acquisitions Editor	Timothy J. Kent
Marketing Manager	Debra Riegert
Production Editor	Jennifer Knapp
Designer	Laura Nicholls
Manufacturing Manager	Andrea Price
Illustration	Jaime Perea

This book was set in Bookman Light by V&M Graphics and printed and bound by Courier Stoughton Inc. The cover was printed by Phoenix Color Corp.

Library of Congress Cataloging-in-Publication Data
Ritti, R. Richard.
   The ropes to skip and the ropes to know : studies in organizational behavior / R. Richard Ritti. -- 4th ed.

   p.   cm.—(Wiley series in management)
   Includes bibliographical references.

   ISBN 0-471-58593-9 (pbk.)
   1. Organizational behavior.   I. Title.   II. Series.
HD58.7.R57 1994
650.1--dc20

                                                93-19785
                                                    CIP

Printed in the United States of America

10   9   8   7   6   5   4   3   2   1

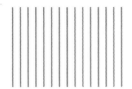

Foreword

Those of you who read this foreword might be interested to know that this fourth edition of *The Ropes* is being published over 15 years after the appearance of the initial version. What accounts for this longevity? My answer: Students and professors who use *The Ropes* see in it a reflection of their own experience in organizations, and *The Ropes* helps them to learn from those experiences.

And what accounts for this peculiar quality of the book? My answer again: This isn't fiction, these things actually happened. Or, in the words of a well-known humorist—I AM NOT MAKING THIS UP! Now, as you read *The Ropes*, some of you are going to say, "Now wait a minute, you're not trying to tell me that *this* actually happened." My answer: You bet, although I certainly have changed names and venues to protect the innocent (or guilty).

Just pick up any old issue of *The Wall Street Journal*, or some other credible business journal, and direct a critical eye to those little human interest items. You'll be rewarded; count on it. In fact, I have included a baker's dozen of these in this issue. And here . . . here's one hot off the press. Could I have made this up? It's about GM's Purchasing V.P., a Spanish national who is being hired away by Volkswagen AG.

- He sees America as a declining civilization. Too much golf and french fries consumed by executives.

- He has published a booklet for his agents prescribing the proper executive diet for them to follow. Its title? *Feeding the Warrior Spirit*. I AM NOT. . . .

- He's developed a program for cutting purchasing costs—PICOS. What does it stand for? *P*urchased *I*nput *C*oncept *O*ptimization with *S*uppliers.

In fact, the executive being portrayed has been judged by results to be extremely effective at his job. "Flamboyant," yes; "fanatic," yes; but also effective. Perhaps his is the only way, it is speculated, to rouse the sleeping giant.[1]

My point is that to understand the nature of human organization we need to understand it *as* just that, human. And this proves not only useful, but interesting.

I'd like to take the opportunity now to thank publicly those readers who from time to time send me letters, and even trial episodes for *The Ropes* that they have written from their own experiences. I find these to be enormously gratifying, although I have yet to find a way to weave them into the fabric of *The Ropes*. I also apologize to all for being a lousy correspondent.

Finally, I want once again to acknowledge some people who have been important to me in developing this book. Bill Whyte, my first mentor, taught me the value of clear exposition. I remember— though I am sure he does not—a key incident. I brought him a paper to read, to criticize. A man of few words, he glanced up at me, before reading a word, and asked, "Is this the best you can do?" What he meant was, Don't ask me to do *my best*, if you haven't been willing to do yours. Touché. I'd like to say that I took it back and polished it up a bit. Truth to tell, I don't remember. But the lesson I have never forgotten. Fred Goldner, a long-time colleague with a remarkable ability to perceive the "other side" of organizational life, has been a major contributor to the ideas expressed here. My buddy, Stu Klein, has done invaluable service as a supporter and intellectual policeman. "Listen, Ritti, now you've gone too far. You don't even believe that yourself!"

I would like to express my gratitude to the following reviewers who extended valuable feedback on the previous edition of *The Ropes*, as well as on the manuscript for the new edition: Richard Sebastian, St. Cloud State University; Carol Steinhouse, Indiana University; Ann Copay, University of Illinois; Edward Cahaly, Boston College; Jane Seebler, Oregon State University; Charles Dauds, DePaul University; and Joseph Dobson, Western Illinois University.

To Steve Kerr I owe a debt of thanks that is impossible to repay. As rejection letters piled high, Steve was the only editorial consultant with the courage of conviction to say, "I don't care if there is no apparent market for this manuscript. I like it. Let's publish it." A vote of appreciation is due as well to Ray Funkhouser for his encouragement and participation in the writing of the first edition. The snappy title of this text is his invention.

R. Richard Ritti

Contents

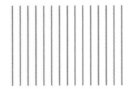

Prologue

The announcement reads, "Franklyn Named to New Corporate Post." Young men and women—and some not so young—gather around The Company bulletin board to read the details.

> The office of the President announced today that Ben W. Franklyn has been named to the newly established office of Corporate Director for Safety Programs. Mr. Franklyn moves from his post as plant manager at Portsmouth.
>
> M. M. Marsh commented personally on this appointment. "Over the years I have seen a growing and essential need for us to develop a comprehensive, hard-hitting approach to safety. In appointing Ben Franklyn to the new post of Corporate Director for Safety Programs, I am giving my personal support to this important effort. Mr. Franklyn's long years of association with every phase of our manufacturing effort make him admirably qualified to drive this important program ahead."
>
> Replacing Mr. Franklyn at Portsmouth will be Edward Wilson Shelby IV. Shelby will hold the position of Acting Plant Manager with specific responsibility for the development of our new Expandrium program. Ted Shelby has been staff assistant to the President, responsible for financial control systems.

The gathering digests this announcement with an assortment of mumbles, grunts of approval, some envy, and some questions.

"But what does *he* know about safety?" one young man asks his companion. "It doesn't seem right to me. With all that responsibility—Corporate Director—you'd think they'd have picked someone with real professional experience. Just doesn't make sense to me."

Over to the side a greying but still youngish man is shaking his head. The greeting tag stuck to his lapel reads, "Hi . . . call me *Stan.*"

"Poor Ben," he is thinking, "wonder what he did this time?"

"What do *you* think, Stan?" The young man addresses him in keeping with the tag. "Isn't that a lot of responsibility for somebody without any *real* background?"

"I take it you're new with us, Jimmie?" ("Hi . . . call me *Jimmie*.") "Well, don't worry about it. Mr. Marsh and our other top executives know what they're doing. Do you think they'd be where they are if they didn't?"

Stanley is giving Jimmie a ritual answer, of course. For, in fact, Stanley could tell Jimmie exactly what is happening, but that is not the way the game is played in The Company.

First of all, read that announcement again, carefully. Notice the "named to" instead of "promoted to." Also, it is a "newly established" office. That's significant, too. Why *now*? Surely we haven't just discovered the need.

Now read down a little bit. Ted Shelby is "Acting Plant Manager." You would have thought the communications people would have massaged that one a little more. Of course, it *is* possible that The Company needed a Safety Director so badly that they couldn't wait to find a permanent replacement—but, well, you get a feel for these things. Also, the "specific responsibility for, etc, etc . . ." For that line read, "The new Expandrium program is SNAFU."

Obviously, Shelby is Marsh's hatchet man. Financial control people always are, and Shelby comes right out of Marsh's office. He doesn't know a damn thing about manufacturing and never will—because he's one of the "new breed."

And don't let the Corporate Director business fool you either. Corporate Directors (of given varieties) come and go, but plant managers are crucial—though the ring of the title is not as exotic.

So what Stanley might have told Jimmie is simply this.

"Look, Ben Franklyn has served The Company faithfully and well since he started as a machinist's apprentice at sixteen. He's tough and capable, but the business has passed him by. It looks to me like Ben got into some kind of hassle with the big boys over this new Expandrium line. And when Ben gets it in his head that he's right, he's not about to back off.

"This time Marsh has finally had enough. Ben's about three or four years from retirement, so Marsh is going to ease him out of the way with a face-saving corporate directorship where he can't do any damage. Ben doesn't know a damn thing about anything but manufacturing, so you can't just turn him loose in the china shop.

"But the rest of those poor bastards at Portsmouth are in for real trouble. Marsh wants that Expandrium line on time, and Shelby is out there to wield the axe. In other words, heads will roll. And that's where the acting manager part comes in. You can't go in there and rough up the troops, then expect them to love you. So when the dirty work is done, Shelby will be lifted. Then a permanent manager will be named to secure the peace."

There you have Stanley's exegesis of a corporate announcement. And I would have to say that he is right on target. Stanley's ability to read the corporate tea leaves is the product of hard-won experience, the experience I am going to relate to you here. For what you are reading is a textbook, a serious text, though it may not appear to be nor read exactly the way you might expect a text to read. Yet, it is nothing less than a text on organizational life. More specifically, it deals with organizations that constitute America's greatest institution—business. It is an instruction manual for the novice, for the junior executive, and for those in the September of their careers. For each there is a different function. The novice learns what to expect, how to interpret the ritual events of this new undertaking. The junior executive finds confirmation of early observations, plus valuable lessons about future activities. And those in the golden years of their careers will find either a comforting affirmation of rightness of thought, or perhaps an unhappy revelation on a fall from grace.

Yet this is a book primarily for the beginner whose career is yet to unfold. With the lessons of these pages, you will quickly understand what is taking place, and you will be able to translate symbol into meaning much as a dream analyst does for a patient. That this is a painless and rather pleasant way to get to "know the ropes" is simply added merit.

OUR CHARACTERS

Inasmuch as this book is a series of allegorical stories and cautionary tales, the cast of characters does not, strictly speaking, constitute a reflection of real life. Our characters are few, and none is truly an individual but a representation of a type. You may occasionally feel the book is disjointed, as when the mail boy in one sequence is a mill hand in the next. But the organizational characteristics of the positions are similar in many ways, as are those of their occupants. So why invent a new character? Put another way, there may be inconsistencies in positions but not in social roles.

Mr. Marsh is the universal executive, the top man in The Company (an allegorical corporation).

Bonnie is our secretary, at once innocent and all-knowing, understanding though not truly conscious of the power of her position.

Our main character is *Stanley*, the universal subordinate. In our opening chapter, he has graduated recently from The University and is just launching his career. Here, we chronicle Stanley's ago-

nies and triumphs as he learns the ropes. Later we will find him at
various stages in his development as a corporate employee, never a
failure, never outstanding. For Stanley is Everyman, both sinew and
fat in the corporate body. You ask, "Stanley who? Doesn't he have a
last name?" Answer—no. Stanleys and Bonnies just don't have last
names in The Company. Nor does Mr. Marsh have a given name.
Nonsense, you say? Well, try this experiment. Pretend you are looking for your mail clerk (who, by the way, may be older than you).
Find out the clerk's last name and ask one of your friends, for
example, "Say, have you seen Mr. Szekely?" Your friend will look at
you blankly. "Who? No one by that name here. Where does he work."
  "Mail room," you will say.
  He says, "No such one, only Jimmie."
  "Yeah," you say, "Jimmie, Jimmie Szekely."
  "Well, why didn't you say so?" etc., etc.
  Now try the equivalent thing asking about Mr. Marsh.
  "Mason been through lately?"
  This last exercise will also prove informative and undoubtedly
more interesting. Things in The Company are ordered and orderly.
We keep track of who's who in small but meaningful ways. And so it
is that Mrs. Mason is Mr. Marsh's secretary, and Bonnie is the secretary for Department D.
  Lesley is, so to speak, Stanley's twin in The Company. Lesley's
main problem in the corporate world is to convince the Shelbys and
the Franklyns that she's really serious about her career.
  A third Stanley and Lesley counterpart in The Company's management ranks is *Claude*, a graduate of the Polytechnic Institute
and one of The Company's first "Equal Opportunity" professional
employees. Like Lesley, Claude has certain barriers to overcome as
he moves up The Company's career ladder.
  The Executives and corporate staff of The Company are in New
York, an allegorical city. People in The Company refer to corporate
headquarters simply as "New York." And here we find *Edward W.
Shelby IV*, our universal staff manager. His intermediate position is
indicated by the fact that he has both first and last names. Ted
Shelby is there to advise and devise. As far as he is concerned, the
key to a successful business is to apply the most modern management techniques. He cannot believe that anyone without an MBA
(including, some suspect, even Mr. Marsh) could possibly know anything about running a company.
  Out in the Plant (wherever it might happen to be) we find
Ben Franklyn, the universal line manager, Ted's antithesis in the
dialectic of corporate existence. Ben's job is to get things done.
  Ben has come up through the ranks and has been with The
Company forever. As far as he is concerned, the only important
activity in a business is getting the product out the door. He cannot

believe that anybody who has not been a foreman could possibly know anything about running a company—except Mr. Marsh and the "Old Man" (Marsh Senior who gave Ben his first promotion to foreman).

Kerry Drake is Ben's counterpart in the professional ranks of middle management, running things in design, finance, or production. Kerry's given name is actually Junius. As a boy he was called Skip, but that didn't seem appropriate in The Company. And then someone noticed his resemblance in a handsome, prematurely grey way to the comic strip character of the same name, and so he became Kerry to all. He's been down and up in The Company. Kerry will be a success, but he lacks the single-minded drive, self-interest, and strategic sense to make it to the top. His fundamental qualities are honesty, openness, and loyalty to The Company.

Finally, we have the universal consultant, *Dr. Faust*, chairman of The Department at The University. Faust is called in whenever there is some sort of problem and whenever times are good enough that nobody is watching budgets *that* closely. Occasionally, he will present a seminar or a training session. His major function is to sanctify with the aura of outside expertise that which has already been decided upon by the management of The Company. But make no mistake, Faust knows whereof he speaks. In fact, now and again he finds himself wishing he had the time to set down in writing some of his more "instructive" experiences.

THE FUNDAMENTAL THINGS APPLY . . .

The French have a saying, "The more things change the more they stay the same." Or, as Sam puts it in *Casablanca*, "The fundamental things apply as time goes by."

The cause for this reflection is my realization that it has been fifteen years now since the first edition of *The Ropes* appeared. A lot of things have changed, but the fundamental things of human organization have stayed the same. That's what *The Ropes* is all about: how people interpret symbols, about ritual events, about how people put meaning into events. It's about socialization and perception, about communication and power. And these things don't change. So to interpret that title phrase, the more those surface events change, the more we see yet again the play of those fundamental concerns of human organization.

So what are some of those things that *have* changed? Well, for one thing, every few years we seem to discover new technical principles that constitute the current formulae for "how to do it." A new motivational panacea, a revived form of participative management. We have seen job enrichment, management by objectives, "quality circles," Japanese management, downsizing, rightsizing. Some of these ideas are ephemeral, metaphorical mayflies of management. Yet others are immortal, resurrected from time to time as suits the need.

THE CHANGING ENVIRONMENT

But looking back over the years, what strikes me most is the different social and economic environments in which the various editions of *The Ropes* have been read. The 1977 edition, being read during the tenure of Jimmy Carter, was the product of the Nixon/Ford years. We had the "gloom and doom" syndrome. The Iranian hostage crisis, "stagflation," and short-term interest rates over twenty percent. (You could look it up!) The symbol of the futility felt during the Carter years was the widely circulated story of how the president had been the victim of an assault by a vicious rabbit—the "attack rabbit."

The second edition came out in the middle of the first Reagan term. Hey, things weren't that great. While we were waiting for supply-side economics to kick in, David Stockman was coming to the realization that the dollars needed to reduce the federal deficit—as promised—weren't going to be found in the likes of the budget for the National Endowment For The Arts. It's worth noting that in mid-1982 the DJIA stood at just about 800! Nonetheless, inflation was being brought under control, "deregulation" was proceeding apace, and things were starting to look up economically.

The third edition arrived in the full flush of what some small-minded souls called the "greed years." Junk bonds were flying, thirty-year-olds were wondering why it was taking so long to make their first million. IBM had reported its best year ever (also a record number of employees). The official line was that this was the work of the supply-side revolution. More orthodox nonbelievers pointed to record military spending and invoked "military Keynesianism" to account for the newfound largess. Oh yes, and the DJIA would shortly reach a level representing a fourfold rise from its second edition level. Finally, 1988 saw the landslide election of George Herbert Walker Bush, pledging "read my lips . . ." Listen, things were GREAT.

As I write this in what is to become the 1994 edition, things are NOT so great. For one thing, the country is spending about half its income simply to finance a humongous hangover from the go-go years. Michael Milkin, he of junk-bond fame, has done some time, as has a kingpin of the Savings and Loan (S&L) scandals. President Bush, held responsible for a protracted economic downturn, took on the Carter patina and was shot down in flames. Meanwhile, an off-again on-again candidate businessman with zero political experience got about 20 percent of the presidential vote. And even though short-term interest rates are less than a fifth of the first edition record, nobody is taking. IBM is talking for the first time in its history about honest-to-God *layoffs*, and in any event is planning on cutting it's work force by 40,000 in this business year. Downsizing with a vengeance is the order of the day.

WELL . . . ?

So what would you have me make of this, you ask? I guess the first thing would be that environments *do* change a lot, and that over the years The Ropes has been read in its various editions in a variety of environments, both harsh and beneficent. The contemporary reader might be lead to observe that things will never be the same, but *The Ropes* has a different message: the fundamental things apply.

Here's an illustration. At the opening of the decade of the seventies, business pundits were heralding the arrival of the "new breed" of managers, student radicals from the late sixties and early seventies. They were to put a new face on business, bringing a heretofore absent "social consciousness" to management. And it's true, I have attitude survey data from the Columbia University MBA class of 1970 that would do justice to a cadre of socialist youth. So what did we get? Well, pretty much more of the same.

What's that? Not so fast, you say. What about those things that *are* changing? And isn't it a fundamental principle of open systems that they adapt to changes in their environment?

Granted. But that's not my point. Yes, from a technical/rational perspective we see change, and right now we see a rash of downsizing—ah, I mean rightsizing. But from *The Ropes* perspective, that's just half the story, and not the most interesting half at that. From a cultural/interpretive perspective, we see much *the same* face of organizational behavior acted out on a different stage. That's my point. The symbols may be different, and the rituals may be carried out in a different context, but their meaning is the same. Performance appraisal, for example, may be infused with a new urgency as a rational tool, the technical key for intelligent "rightsizing," but its ritual and ceremonial meaning are utterly unchanged—it's a way of legitimating management use of power. The fundamentals, the constants of organization, are rooted in human culture.

THE PARABLE OF IBM

I can think of no better example than a trio of heretofore outstandingly successful organizations, DEC, IBM, and Wang, which, for very similar reasons, have suffered greatly as this edition goes to press.

Their stories are similar. Organizations with cultures finely tuned to an environment that ceased to exist and a management unable or unwilling to abandon that culture.

Where was the computer industry at the time of the 1977 edition? The above-mentioned three were doing very well. IBM had over three-fourths of the mainframe market and could have had more were it not for anti-trust worries. DEC had the "techie" market, and Wang had a specialty applications business. All systems were completely "proprietary," customers ran IBM operating systems on IBM hardware, and so forth. What a mainframe should cost was what IBM charged. IBM's product development was geared to a five-year recovery of investment cycle. Customers would see only incremental improvements in the interim. And given the staggering investment in plant and personnel required, you simply couldn't go head-to-head with IBM in a business that IBM wanted. From a business perspective, the personal computer was a curiosity, championed by techies and visionaries.

Things hadn't changed a whole lot when the 1982 edition rolled around. IBM had introduced its PC almost as an afterthought and was amazed by its popularity among business users. Ken Olson of DEC wondered publicly why anyone would want such a thing as a PC. But in its inadvertence, Big Blue had done an unaccustomed thing. The IBM PC had been cobbled together from off-the-shelf components, with published technical specifications (an open, not a proprietary architecture), sporting a crude Disk Operating System patched together by a Seattle computer nerd and entrepreneur, and one of his buddies. Who knew? Anyone who has ever used that first-ever PC can readily understand why it didn't figure big in IBM's cosmic scheme of things. The PC didn't do many things, didn't do them very fast, and didn't do them very well. But it was just this rudimentary quality that was like catnip to a budding generation of techies who, for the first time, had *unlimited* access to their very own computer. As we say, the rest is history.

The 1987 *The Ropes* witnessed a sea change in the world of IBM and DEC, but not in their management cultures. "Out there" now were legions of talented PC programmers, producing word-processors, spreadsheets, database managers, everything imaginable, and all with ZERO overhead. Each was looking for their one chance to make it big, and some did. A cottage industry had been born. On the hardware side, reverse engineering had made the PC "clone" a reality. The IBM defacto industry standard was IBM's no more. IBM tried to recover using its tried and true strategy, a new and thoroughly proprietary PS/2 to be accompanied by OS/2.

Yet from IBM's perspective, it had just wrapped up it's biggest year. Who on the Corporate Management Committee was prepared to listen to a corporate Cassandra foretelling woe and disaster in just a few short years? As T. J. Watson, Jr. told the *Wall Street Journal* in December 1992, when something is making the money that the mainframes were, it's pretty tough to forecast a disaster.

So where are the three in 1993? Wang is belly-up in Chapter 11. Once a 3 billion dollar business and Wall Street darling, Wang never saw what hit it. Ken Olsen of DEC, forced out by the board of trustees, may not yet know why anyone would want a personal computer. The new CEO has broken DEC into a number of smaller, individually accountable business units, in emulation of IBM. Big Blue, battered by Wall Street, is trying finally to reinvent itself. Tens of thousands of employees, no longer required to sustain a proprietary business, are being "separated," perhaps finally to be fired. Those of you reading this in 1994 and 1995 will know a lot more than I about the ending of the story. Yet this much is certain: the IBM and DEC of the 1980s will be no more.

What happened? Is it true that you really can't "teach elephants to tapdance?" In hindsight, these organizations, at least DEC and IBM, should have started doing five or six years ago what they are scrambling to do now, streamline and decentralize, and abandon proprietary products as their core business strategy. But in the midst of unprecedented success, and with a management thoroughly imbued with the culture that lead to that success, how could they? The environment "enacted" by IBM management saw the PC problem as flowing from the *abandonment* of the proprietary strategy that had worked so well, and that they knew so well. Consequently, the PS/2 and OS/2.

But why hadn't these organizations diversified more? Simply because their core business was so much more profitable than any other business they could invest in. So who would have listened to someone in 1987 saying, "Repent, the end is near!" Exactly, nobody.

I'm running out of space, so you can finish the analysis of the business problem that occurs when 40 percent of your product cost is overhead, and your competitors are surviving on a 6 percent profit margin. The lesson for *The Ropes* reader is not who is responsible, but *what* is responsible. And that is the culture of the organization. The enormous force of how a collectivity of individuals understands and interprets what is taking place around them, and how this force constrains all to interpret events in similar fashion. Could the executives of these organizations have done it differently? Ask yourself how it is that these very bright and very hardworking people could get it so wrong. If you understand that, you'll understand a very great deal.

PART ONE

ENTER THE MEN'S HUT

CORPORATE CULTURE AND SOCIALIZATION

PERSONAL INTRODUCTION

The aim of this text is to introduce you to a different way of looking at organizations, to "learn the ropes" through an analysis of the myths, folkways, and rituals that constitute everyday organizational life. And so the stories, though in themselves isolated incidents, are chosen to represent a larger truth of organizational life, a truth that can be discovered through analysis of the cases.

Some readers draw the conclusion that these stories exemplify what is wrong with organizations, that *The Ropes* is about incompetence or immorality in management, and that the cases are here to open up discussion on how to "do it right."

Now I do admit that people in organizations do screw up and that many would benefit from a more rigorous application of sound management principles. But that's only half the explanation, only one side of the organizational behavior coin.

TWO PERSPECTIVES ON ORGANIZATIONAL BEHAVIOR

It seems to me that there are at least two ways of looking at behavior in organizations. The first, the majority viewpoint, is the technical/rational one. The second, certainly a minority viewpoint, is the cultural/interpretive one. To oversimplify a bit, the technical/rational perspective analyzes a case situation to understand better what went wrong and how to do it right according to the principles developed by the study of human behavior in organizations. So, for example, ineffective leadership behavior is analyzed with a view toward eliminating poor practice. Some call this the "machine metaphor."

The cultural/interpretive perspective is more difficult to explain. In fact, you may not fully understand the "culture metaphor" until you have finished this text. But, essentially, it is this: there is a tendency for all of us to forget that organizations are social groupings of human beings, not machines. And we are especially likely to forget this in a learning environment that emphasizes a rational, technique-oriented approach to problem solving.

But human societies, of which organizations are obviously a part, have rules of their own that have little to do with the technical concerns of efficiency and effectiveness. These rules are usually referred to under the broad term "culture" and have everything to do with our understanding of the *meaning* of human events in organizations—how we *interpret* them. Take that leadership example given earlier. The cultural/interpretive perspective would analyze the situation in terms of the meaning of effectiveness in the given context, and why people attribute ineffectiveness to the leader rather than some other feature of the situation. This analysis would have to proceed from entirely different concepts rooted in our society and the organization's culture.

Perhaps the best example I can give at this point is that Company announcement Stanley has just finished reading. How are we to understand what is going on without some reference to the culture of The Company? Franklyn is not being moved to safety director for technical reasons or because someone is mistaken about his qualifications. No, the move has been carefully considered, and the "communications people" have given a great deal of thought to just how that announcement should read. The only way to understand properly what is going on is to recognize that this is one of the many rituals of Company culture. It is intended, in this case, to preserve the integrity of the management's structure of authority. That is, a great deal of effort goes into maintaining the image of those in authority as being there by way of superior competence, and therefore deserving the unquestioning obedience of subordinates.

My belief is that both these perspectives are valid, indeed, *necessary* to the understanding of organizational behavior. We should avoid that all too human tendency to take sides, to feel that if one perspective has merit, then the other must be wrong. This said, I now note that *The Ropes* is presented primarily from the minority viewpoint, the cultural/interpretive perspective. My reason is that the majority viewpoint is already well represented and presents only one face of the coin. Without the complementary cultural perspective, some situations will defy analysis and comprehension. From that perspective, I hope you will be able to see that some things that strike you as silly or inefficient are culturally necessary for the preservation of continuity of human organization.

CORPORATE CULTURE AND ORGANIZATIONAL CULTURE

In the pages that follow, the terms "corporate culture" and "organizational culture" will both be used. Although they are interchangeable in some contexts, they refer to different things. Corporate culture is the more general of the two, referring to the interpretive systems commonly shared by corporate organizations in "Western" societies. Organizational culture refers to the interpretive system of a particular organization, for example, the culture of the IBM organization. Thus, a given organization shares a common corporate culture, but also has elements of its own, its own particular myths, rituals, and symbols. Consequently, the phrase, "the corporate culture of Procter & Gamble (P & G)," while encompassing both the shared and particular elements, is generally intended to refer to those things that give P & G its distinctive way of doing business.

A bit earlier, we witnessed Stanley's interpretation of a Company announcement. How did he learn how to read the corporate tea leaves? That announcement certainly presented the important facts, but it gave none of the *interesting* ones. Indeed, it was deliberately written to conceal the interesting facts. Still, most Company old-timers would have seen exactly what Stanley saw. And that is because they understand the corporate culture of The Company.

Corporate culture? Well, a culture is a system of commonly accepted meanings and commonly held views about what constitutes proper beliefs, attitudes, and motives. That doesn't mean all that much to you? Then let's try a different approach. Use your own common sense definition of the term "culture."

Now then, what is the difference among Hare Krishnas, IBM, and Hell's Angels? Immediately evident are: orange robes, shaven heads, and sandals; three-piece pin stripes, shaven faces, and polished cordovans; black leather jackets, beards, and jackboots. Then, to accompany these obvious differences, each of these organizations (for that's what they are) entertains very different ideas about proper beliefs, attitudes, and motives, not to mention behavior! So maybe they are a better illustration of organizational culture.

Just how do you learn a corporate culture? The answer: through the process we call *socialization.* (No, no more definitions. Just another illustration.) Consider this: how does a child learn the social role of wife and mother? Well, mostly by watching. And if the child is a girl, by being given a doll or similar toys to "practice" with. Oh yes—boys are given dolls, too, sometimes. But more than likely the dolls are G.I. Joe, Rambo, or some such. Boys are also given footballs and encouraged to bash each other's brains in. More socialization. Girls, at least in the past, were discouraged from doing tomboyish things, boys sissyish things. Not that it always worked, mind you. But the point of all this is that socialization is much more what is done than what is said. You may be told that this is what girls do and this is what they don't do, but seldom will you receive a detailed explanation of just why this should be so.

Somewhat later, having mastered the rudiments of the prevailing culture, each will undertake learning the mysteries of successful interaction with the opposite sex. Again, socialization involves learning proper behavior as well as proper beliefs, attitudes, and motives. And again, socialization proceeds through observing the behavior of others, even by watching TV! Unfortunately, major learning experiences commonly take the form of painful mistakes. Novices find themselves in social situations in which they have no experience, or in situations they have misinterpreted as similar to something they do know. They proceed to do something utterly wrong and, occasionally, painfully humiliating. That is why being a teenager is a most difficult time.

Learning a corporate culture is a process similar to a teenager's learning to deal with the opposite sex. First, as teenagers, we have to learn new rituals and what they mean—things such as who opens the door for whom, and when—and more recently, why not to. What are the appropriate gifts for whom and on what occasions? And perhaps most important, we have to learn the meaning of symbols and symbolic communication. Indeed, there are many ways to say no, some of which mean yes.

Symbols and rituals abound in our larger society. The function of ritual is to give concrete expression to deeply held cultural values. A baptism, funeral, Holy Communion, or Bar Mitzvah celebrates the fundamental social importance of birth, death, or passage into adulthood. And, of course, getting yourself dragged from the site of an environmental protest and thrown into jail is what else? Ritual gives objective meaning to strongly held beliefs.

Socialization into a corporate culture is the process of learning its symbols and rituals and how to interpret the meaning of events within this framework. That corporate announcement of promotions and transfers is a ritual event. As such, it gives concrete meaning to strongly held beliefs about corporate rationality. People are promoted because they have earned it and deserve to be, and they are always properly placed. How do we know? Because top management says so, and "they wouldn't be there if they didn't know what they were doing," a ritual equivalent of *Amen*.

Another comment about organizational culture: about 5000 years ago, a mere grain in the sands of time, my ancestors (and possibly yours) were painting themselves blue and dancing around bonfires, waiting for the rising moon to pass directly over the peak of the third monolith as foretold by the priests. Now, the priests were quite clever about these things. As major figures in preindustrial society, they established their position of power by foretelling events and suggesting that they had indeed arranged them. This suggestion of being in league with the mysteries of the world naturally carried over to other worldly affairs. And so, in taking credit for the inevitable, they solidified their position in the status hierarchy. Many contemporary management rituals, I believe, serve precisely the same function!

A second type of ritual is exemplified by the rain dance. Now, being modern and quite sophisticated about these things, we know that whatever the amount and quality of dancing, it is unrelated to future rainfall. Still, there is value to the ritual, if only indirect. First, the belief that you are doing something about a dangerous situation relieves anxiety. Furthermore, such belief restores the motivation to get on with related work such as preparing the fields for new crops. In later examples, as before, I hope to illustrate that corporate cultures are replete with such rituals, prime examples being the performance appraisal and much of strategic planning.

About the function of myth in corporate culture: myths are accounts of the origins of things and "unquestioned beliefs about the practical benefits of certain techniques and behaviors."[1] Myths are accounts of where we come from, why we are as we are, and why we do what we do. Corporate myths are not necessarily false, but are certainly embellishments of the truth. In every corporate job I took as a young man there was a commonly held view that "we take only the top 10 percent of the graduating class." Before long I began to realize that 10 percent really goes a long way.

A myth of IBM (which, apparently, is largely true) includes the legend that "big blue" got into the big time by not laying off workers during the Great Depression of the 1930s. Rather, IBM kept its workers churning out business machines on faith that the economy would improve. And then, virtue rewarded, IBM just happened to be in the right spot at the right time in 1936, when the Social Security program needed lots of such machines—and right away! The function of this myth, of course, is to say a great deal about IBM, its integrity and its personnel policies. And so in forsaking its policy of no layoffs, IBM is abandoning one of the key elements of its corporate culture.

Let's say that by now you have been socialized into the culture of your corporation. You have learned to interpret the symbols and rituals, and you have internalized the myths celebrating the meaning of your corporation and its people. In fact, you have been promoted into MANAGEMENT. In preindustrial times, there was an institution akin to management called the "men's hut," a place of taboo, a repository of arcane and secret lore, accessible only to those who had been fully socialized into adulthood. The key event marking admittance to the men's hut was the "rite of passage" from childhood to adulthood, that is, to full acceptance by the tribe. The hut was a symbol of, and a medium for maintaining, the status quo and the good of the order. Secret knowledge about an organization and its members is necessary, as Erving Goffman points out, "to give objective intellectual content to subjectively felt social distance."[2] For, as subsequent examples will show, jealously guarded secrets and intimate participation in restricted circles often turn out to be either trivial or disappointing or both. The real prize is the attainment of membership, not the knowledge that objectifies that membership.

No organization functions as subordinates commonly understand it to function, and no organization could. A dramaturgy of rationality is necessary to maintain the allegiance of the faithful—recruits, lower echelons, the public. The principles of rectitude, fair play, and equality that support the faith of the mass membership are not always applicable to the sound conduct of the organization's affairs. Senior inhabitants of the men's hut know this well. And so one wonders if school superintendents believe in learning, or colonels in patriotism, or bishops in God as the faithful do. I suspect that, instead, these leaders hold allegiance to the school system, the army, or the church—which is a very different thing. Put another way, their allegiance is to a semisecret core of personal relationships, operational practices, and rituals that constitute the temporal body of the organization. The point is that management is to the modern corporate culture what the men's hut was to preindustrial culture.

In the stories that make up this part of *The Ropes* you will read about the processes of socialization into the culture of the organization. In particular, the next section looks at one of the basic psychological mechanisms affecting how human beings gather and filter information perception. We will see that perception plays an important role in how we form impressions of people and in how we interpret the everyday events of the corporate culture.

Section One

De Gustibus Non Disputandum Est

Socialization and Perception

Epigrams sum up the essence of human experience. They are a shorthand that ancient and modern cultures use to express their collective wisdom. "De gustibus non disputandum est," "Chacun a son gout," and "There's no accounting for taste" say precisely the same thing in three different tongues. They are uttered when their speakers are baffled by the speech, dress, or actions of those they expect to speak, dress, or behave differently.

The principle being invoked is actually the opposite of what is implied by the saying. In fact, there is a great deal of accounting for taste, and, as social animals, people are continually doing it. "Birds of a feather flock together" is more collective wisdom and makes the point directly.

The point is this: people like predictability and dislike uncertainty. In the everyday course of our work lives we would like to know in advance what to expect and how to guide our behavior. This is probably because we want to conserve our energy and attention for those events that are not everyday, for which we have to work out fresh solutions and behavioral repertoires. Consequently, if we already possess routines that experience has shown to function smoothly in everyday situations, well . . . if it ain't broke, why fix it? Similarly, through the process of socialization into the organizational culture we develop "trustworthy recipes for thinking as usual," handy scripts for producing and interpreting behavior in everyday situations.[3] So people really don't have to think much about what they are doing in everyday situations, they just follow the recipe. These recipes also provide implicit explanations for events. And these explanations in turn are embedded in the cultural contents of myth, symbol, and ritual.

This is where social perception comes in, shaping the interpretation of behavior and events within this cultural framework. Perception? What we believe we see—what we perceive—is not actually what is there, or what is happening. We unconsciously patch it up, distort it, or add to it to make what we see consistent with our other perceptions or with our past experience.

Here are two related but different examples from the physical world to illustrate the principle. The perception of color depends very much on the color context, or field, surrounding the object. Using this principle, French impressionist painters depicted the color green by alternating tiny dots of yellow and blue, which, when viewed from the proper distance, are perceived as solid green. And here is an experiment you can try yourself. Rig up a series of five cylinders, cans of different sizes but like shapes, and load them so that their weights are identical. Now judge their weights subjectively, picking them up by an identical handle attached to the top of each. What you will perceive is that the big one is the lightest and the small one the heaviest. Why? Because from past experience you unconsciously expect the big one to weigh more; when it doesn't, your perception is "less than it ought to" compared to "more than it ought to" for the small one. Another context effect.

Now let's move to social perception. A well-known early experiment in social psychology that can be run in several variations involves showing a picture briefly to an "experimental subject," and then having this person tell another what was seen. The second then reports to a third, and so on. The picture shows a poorly dressed white man with a straight razor in one hand making a threatening gesture at a well-dressed black man. But when the final participants (all white) are asked what the picture showed, many report the razor in the hand of a poorly dressed black threatening a well-dressed white.

The principle is simple. As the communication passes from person to person, participants become increasingly uncertain about the details of the original picture. Therefore, when asked to report the facts, they call on their own store of facts, prejudices, and stereotypes to fill in the details. They consequently arrive at a coherent (though erroneous) account of what was seen.

So the social perception of organizational events is influenced by context, just as is physical perception. But the context for social perception includes all our past organizational experience, including beliefs, stereotypes, and those trustworthy recipes for thinking-as-usual. Thus the tendency is to make what we "see" accord with what we "know." And in doing this we typically, consciously or unconsciously, ignore, distort, and invent facts to make the observed situation consistent with "what we all know" about our organizational culture. Ignore: "That couldn't have happened, I must have been mistaken." Distort: "Well, she may have been right, but she certainly used an awfully bitchy tone." Invent: "I am certain that's what Mr. Marsh said. It couldn't have been otherwise."

These perceptual mechanisms are the keys to sustaining the integrity of organizational cultures. Most often, what we perceive accords very nicely with what we believe. These mechanisms are also key to the related processes of impression formation and impression management. Impressions that we form of others in our organizations are important elements in our trustworthy recipes for thinking-as-usual. We feel that we need to understand others, their beliefs, attitudes, and motives, to manage our work relationships appropriately.

But the fact is that, in organizational life, woefully uninformed judgments about others have to be made. We get to know few people well, especially in large organizations with planned geographical mobility. Consequently, the facts do not always have a chance to "speak for themselves," and other bases for judgment are sought. More often than not, the basis is in what Erving Goffman has termed the "presentation of self." And here is where speech, dress, and manner come in, and why symbols and ritual are so important. The need for presentation of self in organizational life also explains why people attach so much importance to symbols of high status— the rug on the floor, the window, the corner office.

Impression management is important in shaping relations among superiors and subordinates. Superiors project the image of the generalist, knowing the stuff of many specialties, but *only* enough to make the necessary decisions. The superior must display an appropriate sense of urgency. The superior's manner must be crisp and hard hitting. Why so? Because few know, and fewer still are able to appraise the merit of the work that has actually been done. Hence, the impression may be more important than the work activity itself. Subordinates, in turn, must project the image of restrained dependability, a willingness to learn, and a recognition that simply doing the work is not as important as providing the initial structure, making the decision. At bottom, the art of impression management is one of providing the proper cues so that the perceiver will ignore, distort, or invent "facts" that provide a true image of what is desired.

Of course, the kind of impression management talked about here is not limited to The Company. People everywhere dress, speak, and act in ways that they believe convey important facts about themselves. Thoroughly middle-class "Marxist" professors show up at conventions in blue denim shirts and jeans (solidarity with the workers). Various personal service workers affect the white smock— even optometrists, though the functional requirement of sterility may be lacking. Check out those old 1960s and 1970s Sci-fi movies sometime. Your basic "bent scientist" at the computer *always* wears the white lab coat. And, as described at the outset, you don't need two guesses to tell the Hare Krishna from the IBMer.

The chapters that follow illustrate the points just made concerning socialization, perception, and impression management and show how these relate to the myth, symbol, and ritual of the organizational culture of The Company.

Hi, Call Me _____

Every summer, The Company has a Company Picnic. It is similar to a picnic, a time when families and friends drive out into the country to spend a pleasant day; but there is an important difference. The Company Picnic is not for the purpose of having a pleasant day in the country; it is always held in a big park in the middle of town. If anyone has a pleasant day that is just fine, but incidental to the purpose of the event.

The Company Picnic is a genuine ceremonial rite. It is a day for setting aside the usual roles and relationships among Employees. Executives shed their corporate uniforms and spend the day on display for the faithful. Ben Franklyn proves to be surprisingly human, and Edward W. Shelby IV has memorized the first names of the entire top management. Perhaps he will come across some opportunities provided by the camaraderie of The Picnic. And Stanley, Lesley, Claude, and Bonnie are expected to talk quite casually and openly to anyone, about anything.

For this is a day for renewing belief in The Company and reaffirming the values it stands for. The Company as family is the theme of the day, with this sentiment embodied in the sticky-back tag that all attendees are given when their name is checked off the sign-up lists. The tag says: "Hi, Call Me _____," and everyone from Mr. Marsh to Jimmie Szekely writes in their *first* name and sticks the tag on the front of their sport-shirt. When the tag is securely attached, everyone collects a hot dog and a paper cup of beer and dutifully mingles.

I noticed Stanley mingling over on the horseshoe courts, playing a game with a man considerably older than himself. Stanley had been with The Company for about a year. Like most newcomers he started at one of the outlying locations but had recently been transferred to "new responsibility." He was now working out of Company Headquarters in New York. (New York, of course, occupies a place in

Company legend analogous to Camelot—those in outlying areas are simply told by their superiors, by way of justification, that "the people in New York want this," or more simply, "New York wants this.")

I hadn't seen Stanley for quite a while, but I had run into him several days before, just in time to tell him that, since he was in town for The Company Picnic, he really ought to go. Stanley obviously had gained considerable self-confidence and a sense of importance from his "new responsibilities;" in fact, he had a tendency to overdo it.

As I approached the horseshoe courts, it was clear that he was overdoing it today. Although not an extrovert by nature, Stanley was always willing to give it a try. After all, isn't it the outgoing guy who gets ahead? Of course, it didn't hurt that he had been near the beer tap all afternoon.

"Yes, I was transferred to New York about two months ago," Stanley was saying. And the emphasis he placed on *New York* revealed how impressed he was with this. Stanley still retained his "plant mentality." Clankety-thud. His last toss knocked away his opponent's leaner, replacing it on the stake. From closer up, the older man was a rather distinguished looking, silver-haired fellow.

I don't think Stanley took notice of this. "I was out at Pawtucket before that, but now I'm working out of the home office here, got a project going in Portland." Clank. Another ringer for Stanley. He is playing a good game of horseshoes.

"Portland, eh?" said his opponent. "Then you're with the sales force?"

"The *sales* force?" said Stanley. "Oh, hell, no! Listen, don't you know about the Expandrium processing line we're installing in Portland, Maine? I've got full responsibility for getting it on stream."

"I guess I hadn't heard about that one . . . ," his opponent paused and looked at Stanley's name tag, ". . . Stanley."

"You'd think," said Stanley, as he tossed another ringer, "that in The Company people would have a better idea of what's going on. One thing I've learned, and I'll pass it along for what it's worth, if you don't know what's going on, you'll never get anywhere in this outfit."

"I won't argue with you there," said the older man.

Stanley tossed another ringer. "That's the game!" he said. "You know, horseshoes isn't as hard as it looks."

"Takes some practice." And looking at Stanley's name tag again, "Thank you for the game, Stanley."

"Don't mention it, see you around," said Stanley.

"It's nice to see you being so democratic here today, Stanley," I said.

"Well, I don't see any harm in talking with workers," said Stanley. "They probably don't get much of a chance to talk to management people man-to-man."

"You don't know who that *was*?" I asked him. Come to think of it, if Stanley had known, he might have acted a little differently.

"I looked at his name tag once, but I don't remember what the name was," said Stanley, "Why? Who was it?"

"That, Stanley, just happened to be Mr. Marsh!"

Stanley blanched, dropping two handfuls of horseshoes on his feet. Yet I doubt that he noticed. He was more interested in the whereabouts of that distinguished gentleman he'd just trounced in his first game of horseshoes. What should he do, what *should he do*?!

Did Stanley blow it here? Is his bright career nipped in the bud? Will the edict come rolling down from on high, "Send him to Petaluma?"

No, of course not.

There are several reasons why no ill will befall Stanley, no matter what he might say to Mr. Marsh in this situation. In the first place, this is a ritual—a time when the great men leave the men's hut and mingle with the tribespeople. Mr. Marsh must show personal interest in each and every person he encounters. He assumes that all know him and that he is performing a duty similar to that of a prince of the church going among the faithful—that is, to be touched and rejoiced in. His common clothes are only part of the ritual, for his presence remains. And in spite of what his tag says, he is still Mr. Marsh.

Stanley's anguish is really unnecessary and is the result of a basic error that he is making. He grossly overestimates his own presence. He sees the world, and particularly The Company, from a very egocentric viewpoint. Whatever interest Mr. Marsh might have shown in anything that Stanley said or did was nothing more than rote role behavior, which Stanley mistakenly interpreted as genuine interest.

The other reason nothing will happen to Stanley is the fact that there is but one Mr. Marsh, and the thousands of Stanleys know who he is, or will soon find out. But Mr. Marsh doesn't know who *any* of the thousands of Stanleys are. In truth, there is virtually no way that Stanley could either make it or blow it on this occasion, for the picnic is a solidarity ritual, a gathering of the clan, a reaffirmation of belief. What anybody actually says or does in this context makes little difference to anybody else.

Some day, perhaps, Stanley will move up high enough in The Company that his behavior on these occasions will indeed be significant. But it will not be so much for the way he deals with the Mr. Marshes of that day as for the style he uses in meeting the faithful. Even then the judgment will be based on how well he carries out the ritual of "The Company as family."

The Power Of Positive Thinking

2

His first days with The Company were days full of new experiences for Stanley, and sometimes these were not pleasant experiences. Like most new hires, Stanley had lots of book knowledge, but precious little understanding of the ways of the corporate world generally, and of The Company particularly.

"Where in the hell is he?" Ben Franklyn's bellow reverberated through the building. Stanley's first impulse was to answer back, "Over here," but he caught himself. He knew Ben was referring to him, and he knew that everybody else a hundred yards in each direction knew it too. But for the life of him, he couldn't figure out what he'd done.

A minute or two later Ben Franklyn came into Stanley's office, where Stanley had been sitting all along (Ben could have found him without all the bellowing, but then Ben liked to bellow.)

"What in hell have you been doing in B Building?"

"Nothing, since the crew finished installing those overhead pipes," replied Stanley "Is there a problem?"

"Let's take a walk over to B, I want to show you something." Stanley tagged along after Ben, still bewildered. There was certainly nothing wrong with the overhead pipes, so what could it be?

Ben pointed up at the overhead pipes and growled "What *is* that stuff?" Ben knew, of course, but that wasn't the point.

"You've never seen Insuban?" said Stanley innocently. "Insulating material. The specs called for those pipes to be insulated, so I ordered the best stuff I could find."

Ben is just about purple. "Insuban?" he fumed. "*Expandrium!* Ex-pan-dri-um! That's what *we* make!"

"For insulation?"

"Damn right, for insulation and a lot of other things you've never thought of. And we *will* use it. For chrissakes if *we* don't use it, then who the hell else will?"

24

"Well, we can't take it down now," said Stanley. "There's a lot of money up there on those pipes. I guess it's too late."

"Oh no it isn't. You can get yourself hold of some Expandrium paint and have somebody go up there and cover that stuff up. Now! Right away! Before somebody sees it!"

"So I had it taken care of," Stanley is telling me later, "but how come Franklyn's getting so excited about something like that? Who the hell is ever going to look at what's on those pipes? And who in the world would care!"

Stanley, in reliving the story, is getting heated up all over again. "Who ever heard of insulating anything with Expandrium anyhow? Man, I'm an engineer, not a salesman! That's not the kind of thing I'm supposed to worry about!"

Scarcely a few weeks had passed when Ted Shelby, one of Mr. Marsh's staff assistants, announced that the Chairman himself would be touring the now-finished project that week. Stanley, as Assistant Plant Engineer, would accompany the touring party to provide "technical backup," to answer questions that might arise on details of the new construction. The occasion was to mark the official opening of the B Building facility and, incidentally, give Mr. Marsh an opportunity to impress upon members of the board of directors that The Company was indeed a dynamic outfit.

So it is that Chairman Marsh and board members, Ted and Stanley, all properly outfitted in hardhats and safety glasses, are clambering along the elevated catwalk that runs the length of the building. "Good view of the entire show from here, Ted," comments one of the influential board members. "Say," he says, pointing to Stanley's disguised overhead pipes, which are right in front of his nose, "Isn't that Expandrium insulation? I don't believe I've seen that application before."

Stanley, seizing the moment, cuts in politely, "Well, sir, it's always been our material of choice in The Company. Fact is, we're finding new uses for Expandrium almost every day. We see it this way—when your own outfit makes the best product, you go with it."

Mr. Marsh could be seen nodding vigorously at Stanley's explanation. And later, just after the group breaks up, but before Stanley is out of earshot, he turns to Ted. "Good show, Ted. You know, I wish more of our people would understand, like young what's-his-name there does, that every one of us is a salesman for The Company."

Cleanliness Is
Next To . . . ?

Stanley met Lesley for the first time when each had been with The Company only a matter of months. Stanley had just become Ben Franklyn's engineer at the Pawtucket Rolling Mill. Lesley, a trainee in technical sales, was aiming for a position as a manufacturer's representative. A manufacturer's representative? The Company made its own Expandrium fabricating machinery because that was a specialized business. So to make sure that these machines were installed correctly and functioning well, The Company had its own group of technical sales people—manufacturer's representatives.

Les and Stan had spoken to each other a few times as each went about the day's tasks. Today Stanley decided to make her acquaintance. Les was sitting at the far table of the mill cafeteria poring over her manufacturer's manual in her slightly nearsighted squint.

"Um, mind if I sit down? I'm Stan."

"Lesley. Hi."

"You're new here, aren't you? Just in the past few days?" Stanley pressed on, "What department do you work in?"

"Oh, I'm not really *here*. I'm out of the New York sales office. I'm a technical sales trainee," said Les, still a little impressed by her good fortune in landing the job.

"Uh, then, what . . ."

"What am I doing here in the mill?"

"Yeah."

"You know, actually, I'm not too sure myself. I guess what I'm supposed to be doing is . . ." Les went on to describe her job. It seems that whenever a piece of Expandrium processing equipment went "down" for a day or so her job was to give it a thorough inspection: check for worn parts or stress fractures—almost anything that might be out of whack. This was done exactly as outlined in the official step-by-step maintenance procedure set forth in the manual she had been given—"the bible," as it was called by the New York staff. When the maintenance check was completed to her satisfaction, she supervised start-up, checked samples of product, and generally made sure that everything was okay.

"Only think I *can't* figure out, really, is why *I'm* supposed to be doing this. The guys you've got right here in the mill have been doing this stuff a lot longer than me, and I just know there have to be some shortcuts in this business. Why even now I can see that there are only a few spots where there's ever going to be any . . . Would you *mind* moving that cup?! Oh, look! . . ." Lesley had been so caught up in describing her job that she hadn't noticed Stanley's coffee cup sitting on the open page of her "bible." And there, right in the middle of the page, larger than life, was a wet, brown ring. As she scrubbed at the offending trace with a napkin, Stanley tried to apologize but only made matters worse.

"Honestly, Les, I don't see why you're so upset. It's just an old manual."

"A *new* manual," came the tart reply.

"New, old, so what? You can still read it, can't you? Look I really *am* sorry. I just don't see . . ."

If Stanley had paid a bit more attention to the manual he might have seen why Lesley was so agitated. For one thing, he would have seen that the manual was encased in a neat plastic cover that Lesley had fashioned herself. And look at her. Her coveralls were smeared with grease to be sure, but she was the essence of neatness and organization: blond hair pulled back into a bun—all business.

"Oh, I guess you're right, Stan, maybe I am getting upset about nothing. But I think this manual's pretty important to them. You know, they replaced the first one after just one month. And—I still don't understand this, but I got kind of a long 'Dutch uncle' talk about how maybe I hadn't been paying enough attention to the manual. But how could they know? As a matter of fact . . ."

"Sure, I *do* see," Stanley broke in, "*that's* the problem. I think I know the answer, Les. Listen, you're so worried about keeping that thing in its pristine state—but that's just the problem."

"Sure." Lesley was unconvinced.

"Now wait, you'll see. When I was in the service I spent some time in the motor pool. Now I know it's different, but it's the same thing, I think. My first assignment was to the routine maintenance section. Every six months or whatever we were supposed to put each vehicle through a complete maintenance check. Just like you —everything exactly like it says, step-by-step. And just like you I found out that there's never anything wrong with most of the parts. Pretty soon you find out most of the places where the trouble's likely to be. So the first day on the job, one of the older guys, a sergeant, stops me and says, 'Don't worry about that, kid, we'll never finish if you do all that stuff.' I started to object and he says, 'Shut up and just do what I tell you.' But what if the CO finds out, I say. 'Don't worry, he won't,' he says. And with that he takes my brand new maintenance manual, open to my procedure, throws it in the grease on the floor and tromps on it with his GI boot.

"Hey wait, I say, what are you doing to my manual? If you've a gripe, take it out on yours. Then he says, 'I already have. Listen, kid, after you've been around here a while, you'll smarten up. How do you think they check to see if you've done it all by the book, anyway? Think about it. They know that we don't do every different job often enough to have it all down pat, so we have to check the manual as we go. And if you do that, well, certain pages get dirty, greasy, dog-eared, and everything. There's a lot of wear and tear when you, er—follow the book like you're supposed to. And pretty soon you're going to find out that every month they issue a new manual—a *nice clean* new manual. Get the idea?'"

So that's how Lesley finally figured out what the problem was. The Company figures that it is important to have some measure of performance for all its people. And Lesley's no exception. But The Company isn't about to assign someone to look over her shoulder every minute to make sure that she's following the detailed maintenance procedure. No, they have a better way. They look at the tell-tale tracks on the "bible." Coffee ring here, good; she's been studying that particularly tough section. Grease? Okay. Edges of these pages worn? Yes. And so, in taking great pains to keep her "bible" in its "pristine" state, as Stanley called it, Lesley had actually been providing evidence that she hadn't been doing her job.

And what was that job? Not maintenance, no, of course not. Her real job was to learn exactly where and how problems were likely to arise in every special piece of Expandrium processing equipment manufactured by The Company. She had to be thoroughly familiar with each part and recognize any sign of trouble instantly. But, you say, if that's the case, then why didn't The Company just tell her that? Now that is a tough question to answer in just so many words. Look at it this way. It's basically a question of motivation. It's just possible that you may learn some things better by thinking that people are depending upon you to do something else. The lesson: things in The Company aren't always what they seem, and often they work better that way.

Look Of A Winner

L ooking up from my word processor, I see that it has begun to snow. A bitter nor'easter is swirling in over the harbor, kicking up puffs of foam. A good day to be indoors, I think.

But there are some of us who are not so lucky as to have the choice—Stanley, for one. So it was on a day just like this one, some years ago, that he had one of his earliest instructive experiences. Stanley had been with The Company for several months. New experiences were cascading over him, many of them difficult to evaluate. On such occasions he would seek out his former mentor, Dr. Faust—consultant to The Company—and ask for interpretation. Faust, for his part, seemed to enjoy the role.

"It all started out innocently enough, I suppose," reflected Stanley. "I was in New York for a week to go to this 'systems procedures' seminar for all new plant people. One day it was really cold, windy, just miserable weather. The warmest thing I had was this old Army overcoat and headgear. But I figured, what the hell, who cares what you look like for one day? So I walk into the Headquarters building where this seminar is being given, and the first thing I know this older guy gives me this fishy look. Then he says, 'Can I help you? Who do you want to see?' So I say, 'It's okay, I work here.' While we're waiting for the elevator you can see him kind of working up to something, and finally he says, '*You* work for *The Company*?'

"I tell him I do, and then after a while he says, 'Don't you think it's a little risky to dress that way?'

"Now I'm starting to get the picture. But even if I weren't, he gives it to me in detail as we ride up the elevator. 'People in The Company don't dress that way,' he says, 'and if you ever want to get anywhere, son, you'd better think it over and change your ways.'"

"Interesting," said Faust, puffing as always on his pipe. "I suppose he was one of the old-timers."

"I don't know," replied Stanley, "but wait, I'm not finished yet. I go up to the seminar room and take off my coat. Now I've got this wool checked shirt, you know the kind. No room for a jacket under the overcoat, and just a shirt and tie isn't warm enough, so I've got this shirt on.

"Things go okay until we break up into work groups. Everybody introduces himself and someone says to me, 'Where do you work, Stan?' So I say, 'The Company, just like you.' The guy says, 'Come on, you're kidding me. *You* work for The Company?'

"Now he's a young guy, but he sounds just like the older guy. So he starts laughing, I mean uncontrollably. Then he says, 'Hey, this guy works for The Company, he really does, can you believe it?'

"Well, this breaks them all up. They all sit there, sort of pointing their fingers at me and saying, '*He* works for *The Company!*'

"I won't drag it out any longer, but what I want to know is what the hell do *they* care? How come they get so excited about something like that?"

Faust paused to ensure that Stanley was indeed through. Then, repeating the obvious he said, "Yes, they do care . . . But don't misunderstand, they weren't mocking you. They simply were amazed.

"Why should they be amazed?" Faust continued, giving words to the thought that had formed in Stanley's mind. "They were amazed because they had never seen anything quite like that before."

Faust puffed his pipe in silence for a moment to give proper emphasis to his next metaphor, then he went on.

"They were amazed in the same sense as a savage who has just seen the violation of an ancient taboo without retribution from the gods. It is amazing and a little frightening, and it also suggests that the one committing the violation may be just a bit special. Beyond this I can't really explain anything more to you except by way of example."

Stanley prepared himself for one of Faust's Socratic exercises. "Now consider this situation and tell me what you think is going on," said Faust. "Think carefully about it, and tell me why you retain or discard the possible explanations."

Faust went on to describe a meeting involving a dozen or so lower and middle management people at The Plant. They were working out a long-range manufacturing automation strategy of great consequence for the entire Company. All were suitably attired (coats and ties) save one man who had on an old, grease-stained flannel shirt. His sleeves were rolled up to elbows, exhibiting a muscular pair of forearms.

"Well?"

Stanley thought. "I guess you want me to account for the guy in the flannel shirt," he replied.

"Precisely," Faust puffed slowly.

"It wasn't just that he didn't have time to change, because then you wouldn't have asked me to explain it."

Faust nodded in acknowledgment.

"And I guess since they're all management people he'd have to know better."

Another nod.

"Does he dress this way all the time?"

"Almost invariably, except when he travels to New York."

"Then he's trying to prove something?"

"That is essentially the question I have posed to you, not the answer," Faust intoned.

"Okay, okay. Then he's advertising that he's something special. But what? Yeah. It's that he's not *just another* middle management guy. He's something else, and . . . and more."

Faust gave no visible encouragement, but Stanley felt he was getting somewhere.

"Yeah, the grease . . . the arms. Here's a guy who knows not only management, but knows The Company right where it lives, the manufacturing floor. Gets along with everyone, too. I'll bet." Stanley could hardly contain himself as new inferences raced through his head.

"Go on."

"He's so good that he doesn't have to give a damn about wearing a stuffy old shirt and tie, except when he goes to New York . . . and that's good, too, because that way he gets to show that he can suit up when he wants to." Stanley actually felt himself developing a deep admiration for this phantom of his imagination. "Now I'll bet . . ."

"Enough, enough." Faust held up his hands. "You now feel that you know this fellow, don't you? And I've told you almost nothing about him. You yourself have supplied the details from what you know about The Company, and through logic and deduction. And so, of course, do all the others. This is the point I wished you to see."

Faust continued. "You must understand that none of us knows another very well, especially in organizations such as The Company. We continually call on our store of knowledge about the world and our sense of what is and what is not reasonable in order to interpret what is going on about us.

"We seem to have a need for consistency that compels us to come up with reasons for what at first appears to be unreasonable. So each will create for himself a phantom endowed with qualities and capabilities to fit the image received.

"That is part of the reason your friends got so excited about your appearance. Each believes The Company is a superior company and fittingly hires superior people—and, by George, they ought to look that way."

"I understand," said Stanley. "But let's get back to your example. If what you say is true, then why doesn't *everybody* manufacture a personal image?"

"They do," said Faust.

"Now, wait a minute, you said . . ."

"No, *you* wait a minute." Dr. Faust punctuated his command with a thrust of his pipe stem at Stanley. "And think before you talk. I said that everyone presents an image to others that is to some extent calculated and shaped. In large measure, these presentations of self are consistent and raise few questions. Managers look like managers, workers like workers, and so on. I presented an extreme case—ah—for heuristic purposes."

"No, what I meant was, because there seems to be some advantage in it, why doesn't everybody pretend to be something he isn't?"

"When did I say anything about pretense?"

"Sure you . . . ," Stanley caught himself. "I mean, isn't this guy pretending to be something he isn't?"

"Did I say that?" The tone of Faust's query conveyed the answer. "What I pointed out, quite simply, was only that *you*, not I nor he, had supplied the details as to his status in The Company, his ability, his social relations with the mill hands, and the like. In fact, I doubt if any pretense is involved, as I understand the word. Obviously, this man is acting out something he *wants* to be. And I doubt that this could be done convincingly through sheer calculation. At one level of consciousness, even charlatans must believe that, indeed, they are doctors or psychologists, or whatever else." Faust was no longer speaking directly to Stanley.

"After all, in an existential sense, which of us knows what he *really* is. Which is more real, what we pretend we are, what we think we are, what we are afraid we are, what others think we are?"

Faust suddenly remembered Stanley and returned form the cosmic realm to the situation at hand.

"No, I don't think this is calculated behavior—quite the opposite. I am quite sure that this fellow would not be able to articulate what he was doing. His pattern, his display has more or less evolved because it 'feels right,' and because he likes the things that happen to him in this mode. He likes the questions people ask, the inferences that they draw. What they make of him is what he wants to be. And who are we to deny that this is what he really *is*?"

Just In Case

With the CATCH-UP program (Company Approach to Technical CHange and UPdate) getting into full swing, just about everyone on The Company's staff was busy preparing presentations describing the benefits to be had from the project they were proposing. Project proposals were Dr. Faust's bread and butter, and he did not take them lightly. This was one area in which he had turned art into science—and one of the axioms of his science was something he termed "contingency management." That is, he left nothing to chance, practicing endless dry runs of his presentations to insure that all problems (or contingencies) had been anticipated, and that the proper responses had been concocted—just in case.

Thus it was that one day Dr. Faust invited Stanley to "react" to the presentation of his proposal for the "Subordinate Readiness Program for Professional Personnel."

"You understand," he explained, "that I want you to be as critical and nit-picking as possible, so as to—ah—simulate the type of reaction we can expect from the management review committee."

"Right," said Stanley. "Fire away."

Now you might have thought that Dr. Faust would employ the latest "multimedia" computer driven technology for his presentations. But such was not the case. Faust disdained such things for intimate gatherings like that of the corporate management committee. The technology of the easel chart had the singular virtue of placing himself as the primary focus of attention. Furthermore, surreptitious notes lightly penciled in the margins and invisible to the audience, provided the aura of an overwhelming grasp of the ancillary facts of the situation. Better still, these were the fallout from many previous dry runs, and thus anticipated likely questions from the group. And there were other reasons, too.

Stanley watched as the cover sheet was removed from the presentation easel, much as a painting by a leading artist might be unveiled for the first time. But what the . . . ? Given the importance Faust placed on "the presentation," and the amount of time he had spent on this particular one, Stanley was completely taken by surprise.

There, boldly sitting on the easel, was a crude, hand-lettered chart entitled: "SUBORDINATE READINESS PROGRAM—PROFESSIONAL PERSONELL." Obviously, Dr. Faust had done it all by himself. And it hadn't been just dashed off, either, but elaborately, painstakingly constructed. It bordered on illegibility. It was crimped up against the right-hand margin as though Faust had run out of room and had to compress the second half to get it all on the board, and there were several blatantly misspelled words—"personell," "permanant," and others. But not, Stanley noticed, "mnemonic." Words like that were invariably spelled correctly.

"Um, Dr. Faust, when you have your charts put in final shape by the graphics department, make sure to remind them to correct the spelling of 'personnel' and 'permanent,'" Stanley noted diplomatically.

"These charts *are* in final shape, unless of course, you come up with something new," Faust said decisively.

"But they don't look very, er, professional," suggested Stanley. "Won't they make a poor impression?"

"Precisely!" Dr. Faust declared. "A poor impression, but . . . a proper one as charts."

"Huh?"

Dr. Faust paused to light his pipe. "Look at it this way. There will always be a skeptic in the group (probably a financial officer) who doesn't understand the—ah—necessity of the consultant's function. And this person will inevitably say, 'Faust, with the money you put into those charts, I bet we could have declared a stockholders' dividend. What's all this going to cost, anyway?' Well, that is the type of question one likes to avoid, as it only distracts from the matter at hand. So, one avoids having his charts look too—ah—professional. In point of fact," he added, "doing the charts up this way, by myself, cost The Company a bit more than it would have cost to send them to the graphics department."

"Okay, I understand that feature," Stanley allowed, "but don't you think you've overdone it? I mean, look, if you can correctly spell 'mnemonic,' I know you can spell 'personnel' and 'permanent.'"

"Of course I can . . . but *he* can't."

"Can't what?"

"Can't spell 'mnemonic.' That's why one has to choose words like 'personnel'—he'll spot that one right away."

"Who is He?"

"Who else but Franklyn? He always feels honor-bound to put in his two cents', to find something wrong. It doesn't matter to him what it is, as long as he can take you to task on something. The first chance that comes up, he'll say, 'Faust, they ought to send you doctors back to grade school for reeducation. Personnel has two n's, not two l's.' I will be slightly embarrassed, of course, but now he'll quiet down. Otherwise, he would continually interrupt the presentation."

Contingency management, thought Stanley. Faust continued with the presentation. After a couple more charts Stanley said, "Could I interrupt?"

"Certainly," said Dr. Faust. "Do you find something amiss?"

"Well, I don't know," said Stanley, "but it seems to me that the feature of the program you just explained doesn't have any real application here—no value at all to The Company that I can see. In fact, it looks suspiciously academic."

"Interesting that you should see it in that light," said Dr. Faust. "Is there anyone in particular who you think might object to this feature of the program?"

"Why, Kerry Drake, of course," said Stanley. "You know how he feels about . . . " As Stanley says these words, Faust's next line flashes through his mind before he can open his mouth.

"Precisely! That will take care of Kerry. Oh, I won't give this up easily, of course. But I'll agree reluctantly to let it go, and Kerry will feel that he has cut his share of 'fat' out of the program."

Two more charts, and Faust is through with his presentation. He flips up the final page, and Stanley is surprised to find a new title page beneath it: "SUBORDINATE READINESS PROGRAM—PROFESSIONAL PERSONNEL: FINDINGS AND CONCLUSIONS."

"What's that?" asked Stanley.

"Don't pay any attention to that," said Dr. Faust. "I just did it up in advance. I won't actually use it for several months."

"But how can you have the findings and the conclusions already?"

"No problem," explained Dr. Faust. "I already know what I have to find." He noticed the suspicious look Stanley was giving him. "Oh, have no fear, the study will be done. But with subordinate readiness, as with so many things, ultimately it is a matter of judgment: how 'ready' is 'ready?' I can guarantee you that after we finish interviewing all our plant managers and executives, plus our top professional personnel, we'll find that they aren't 'ready.' We will thus come up with the findings and conclusions here in the charts."

"You're sure this isn't some kind of cheating?" asked Stanley.

"The naive observer might come to such a conclusion," admitted Faust, "but you must understand that in all my experience I have yet to encounter a group of professional people who were at an acceptable level of 'readiness.' No large organization rates highly with respect to 'subordinate readiness,' and the higher in the corporate ranks one goes, the truer that is.

"But the crucial thing for you to understand is that Marsh wants this program badly. I wouldn't be here if he did not."

Again, Stanley was eyeing him suspiciously, so Faust went on. "Let me tell you about a distinguished colleague of mine. He was once making a presentation to Marsh and his aides. It happened that Marsh really believed in that particular product, and my colleague was expressing doubts. Marsh finally said, 'I can't accept that!' 'But,' my colleague said, 'those are the facts.' Marsh told him, 'Well, I don't like those facts. Get me some new facts.' And, you know, Marsh turned out to be right. He had understood the market potential of that product and wanted it so badly that he made it go, in spite of my colleague's 'facts.' After all, there are plenty of facts around, and one is free to select from them at will.

"So, you should see that my role as consultant here is to help Marsh get done what he wants to get done. He knows that I'm already sympathetic to The Company's need for a Professional Subordinate Readiness Program. This way, he knows that he'll have my report to back him up . . . just in case."

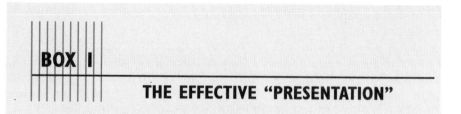

BOX I

THE EFFECTIVE "PRESENTATION"

As President Reagan's Secretary of Defense, Casper "Cap" Weinberger had been notably effective in gaining approval from Congress for major Pentagon budget increases during the decade of the 80s.

Look at the record.

- 1982—$222 billion requested, 216 granted. A 20 percent increase.
- 1983—$257 billion requested, 245 granted. A 13 percent increase.
- 1984—$284 billion budget presented, 273 requested after cuts, 262 granted. An eight percent increase.
- 1985—$305 billion requested, 284 granted. A seven percent increase.

Remember that all this was accomplished during a period of record and mounting budget deficits and of heavy pressure to cut all budgeted programs. The figures above represent over a 100 billion dollar budget increase since 1981, an increase equal to one-half of the mid-1980s yearly budget deficit.

How did he do it?

First, Weinberger himself understood well that the budget game is less a serious political contest than a ritual that allows Congress to appear to be behaving responsibly while in actuality protecting "pork barrel" defense spending programs benefitting their districts. He likens it to Japanese Kabuki theater, a highly stylized art form.

Next, the Secretary, as in Kabuki, had evolved the dramaturgy of the presentation into an art form, with the centerpiece being the easel chart. In one such presentation, he depicted huge soldiers with similar weapons, labeled "Reagan budget," dwarfing little soldiers and little weapons, labeled the "OMB budget." A winner for 1982.

Another favorite tactic is to offer conciliatory cuts in an already inflated budget. In 1983, while refusing to accept OMB engineered cuts, Weinberger offered his own. And where did the dollars come from? Actually, they didn't. He stripped billions from the budget simply by lowering the built-in inflation assumptions!

1984 followed a similar scenario in a confrontation with a familiar adversary, David Stockman. Naturally, the budget proposals had already been inflated with "cut insurance," and Weinberger then placated Congress by dollars cut through further reductions in the inflation estimate, lowering fuel price projections, and similar measures. No pain, big gain. Moral outrage was part of Cap's dramaturgy, this time, "we have reached the bone," he is quoted as saying.

The next year, 1985, was a congressional election year, so Weinberger stonewalled it, bluntly refusing to make any cuts and saying simply, "we need it all." Cap knew that incumbent Congressmen are remarkably timid about cutting funds for local pork-barrel projects when up for reelection.

For 1986, the Secretary presented a "scrubbed" budget, but yielded further to Congress by producing an additional $6 billion in cuts, this time through revised accounting procedures. Now down to the "bare minimum," Weinberger resorted to the "Washington Monument" ploy to forestall further cuts. In effect, cut my budget and I'll close the Washington Monument (or some other national shrine) because we won't have the funds to operate them.

Source: *Wall Street Journal*, March 1, 1985, p. 36.

The Sincerest
Form Of Flattery

In his early days with The Company, Stanley moved around quite a lot. He started at Pawtucket, went on to New York, to Portland, and finally to Portsmouth to be involved in building and modernizing some new facilities. Company policy required the operating management of the new facilities to be in on the construction phase, and so it happened that Stanley first came to work for Kerry Drake.

Drake is an interesting character. Totally dedicated to The Company, sincere and blasphemous, a stickler for detail and intolerant of incompetence, Kerry is capable of being both very human and unreasonably inhumane to his subordinates. Yet Kerry has a kind of charisma based on his technical competence, his obvious sincerity, and his dedication to the job. The self-image he likes to project can be summed up in two of his favorite slogans: "You have to fire a man a week to keep a healthy organization," and "I don't have time to separate the unfortunate from the incompetent." In point of fact, however, he seldom fires anyone (transferring them instead to a "more suitable opportunity"), and he puts a great deal of effort toward winnowing the unfortunate from the incompetent.

Kerry also takes care of his boys—and girls. If you work out with Kerry, your next step is a big step forward. People in management who know Kerry know that his people have the right attitude and can do the job. But Kerry is not one to suffer fools lightly.

And so it was that, early on, Stanley came under the sway of Kerry Drake as one of his assistants at the Portsmouth construction site. Kerry had a substantial management position with The Company, and Stanley was just a beginner; but because the construction group was small, Stanley and Kerry worked closely together. Also, quite typically, Kerry didn't give a damn if you were a V.P. or a sweeper. If you worked for him, you worked. Honest mistakes were okay (to some extent) but woe to the one who erred by oversight, sloppiness, or lack of application.

This was quite a heady situation for Stanley. He had visions of rapid progress to the upper echelons of Company management, and, in these visions, Stanley the Executive bore an uncanny resemblance to Kerry Drake. No, not in looks—but in manner, grit, determination, and unbounded intolerance of folly. Yes. That is the way it should be.

Occasions that one would expect to dampen this enthusiasm had quite the opposite effect. In one situation, for example, Stanley was Company spokesman in bid negotiations with a group of contractors. His responsibility was for presenting construction specifications to the assembled group and answering questions that arose. Typically, Kerry let his people do this while he observed how things were going.

"Finally, the successful bidder will have the responsibility for restoring all sites to grade, with backfill in accordance with specs as described in Section 1. Questions?"

Quite pleased with his success thus far, Stanley awaited the next challenge.

"It says here on page 21 that under no circumstances will contractors be allowed to use substitutes for Expandrium fittings. Under *no* circumstances? Will you guarantee availability?"

Stanley's answer was crisp and to the point. "The specs are clear enough here. I don't believe anything is left to guesswork. And, I believe the specs are quite clear on the issue of whose responsibility it is for the purchase of materials." (Quite right, the contractor.)

"Say, I have something maybe you could clear up for me," said another, pointing to a stack of blueprints on the table. "These gizmos here are blacked in on the drawing, but these aren't. Otherwise, they look the same to me. Does it mean anything? I don't think so, but I want to be sure."

Stanley thought a moment before answering. Fact is, he'd never noticed that before. It looked as if the draftsman had colored in a few just to give the idea, but didn't want to waste the time doing all of them. Sure, that was it. No sooner had Stanley conveyed this intelligence to the assembled group of contractors than Kerry was on his feet gesturing wildly.

"No, that is *not* so! This young man doesn't know what the hell he is talking about." And turning to Stanley after a brief explanation of what it did mean, "Keep your goddamned mouth shut when you don't know what the hell you are talking about. It's that kind of damned-fool talk that can cost The Company money."

End of quote.

You, of course, need no elaboration as to Stanley's feelings at that point. But was this the end of Stanley's admiration for Kerry? Not at all! Kerry was absolutely right. No place for that kind of thing in The Company. And that was the way to handle it, too. No nonsense. A promptly administered kick in the ass would serve the memory well. The fact was that, half consciously and half not, Stanley's behavior in all respects came to resemble Kerry's more closely.

Oddly, Stanley's results were somewhat different. When he sat down with the electricians and the "mechanical people" to knock heads together, well, somehow nothing happened. And after a few months Stanley himself noticed that no one paid particular attention to his edicts. Somehow, injunctions from Stanley like "you people said next week, and next week it's going to be. And if you can't bring it off, well, we'll just have to get someone in here who can. We don't have time to separate the unfortunate from the incompetent!" just didn't bring results.

Months passed and, mercifully, Stanley toned down. Actually, he became absorbed in the work he was responsible for and started to become quite good at it. Kerry was around less, traveling to various locations to pick up the "latest thinking," and was consequently less of an influence. The time had come for Stanley to understand what had happened.

"Little Kerry." Yes, over the previous year Stanley had been dubbed Little Kerry by the entire crew—and not by way of admiration. You see, Kerry himself wasn't exactly loved by his counterparts and coworkers in other divisions of The Company. But he had the authority of office and, more to the point, he was almost always right in technical matters; so he had their respect. Furthermore, you didn't get one of Kerry's "treatments" unless he was sure that you were wrong. And you probably knew it too.

The upshot of all this is that Stanley's Kerry imitation only served as a focal point for the resentment Kerry engendered. And "Little Kerry" was a legitimate target. Stanley didn't have the rank or expertise (or, let's face it, the grey hair) to pull off Kerry's act.

The lesson: behavior is perceived and interpreted within its context. Stanley could imitate Kerry's "moves," but not the interpretive context.

"Hi, Sweetie . . ."

I thought The Company was sending one of its technical guys over today," he whispered to his secretary. "We've go to get this baby on line *today*."

"Mister Toole, I believe this is the, ah—'guy' from The Company."

Chuck Toole, the Mill Master Mechanic at Another Company, was not prepared for that bit of information. "What!? You mean that, that . . . *that's* her?" nodding his head in Lesley's direction. "Christ Almighty. I though they were going to send someone over who could help us get moving, not some, some . . ."

Although Toole left the sentence unfinished, his sentiments were clear: not some cute little dolly out of customer relations, he was thinking. "What the hell, might as well get this over. Would you show Miss What's-Her-Name in please, Connie?"

Connie took Lesley's card and introduced her by name to Toole, who in customary fashion immediately took the proverbial bull by the horns. "I'm afraid there's been some misunderstanding here, Lesley. You see, I was expecting one of your technical guys." Without waiting for a reply, Toole plunged ahead in his assumption. "Understand, I've got no problem with the Company—I'm satisfied just fine with your service. But we're having this problem in getting the right finish on our impact extrusions . . . but, well, that's not your problem."

"Oh, yes, Mr. Toole, that *is* my problem," Les broke in firmly. "As a matter of fact I've spent most of the past month working on that problem. You see . . ." Lesley went on to explain that somehow or other The Company's design people had miscalculated the stress on the thrust bearing that centered the mandrel . . . .

Well, that's no concern to you. So here's what happened. She went out on the mill floor and expertly directed the millwright crew in the disassembly and replacement of the offending item. This done, she asked for a personal tour of the mill—said tour being part of her "game plan" for every new customer.

And here she really did a number on Chuck Toole and his counterparts at every other company. They'd stroll through the bays of heavy equipment, and Lesley would conduct a running commentary on the strengths and weaknesses of each machine, while asking a barrage of technical questions. She knew that many of the questions did not have ready answers, even from the mill's Master Mechanic. Title aside, he was more of a management person than a practicing technician. The effect was as you might guess. After her first visit, very few of her customers could really say that they liked this young lady very much, but they sure as hell were impressed.

But why was all this necessary, you ask? Wouldn't it be enough to do your assignment well and have that speak for itself? Lesley knew the answer to that one. Unfortunately, the answer was no. For when she first started out in this business she traveled with a senior representative, a middle-aged man. His standard routine was to get the task accomplished as quickly and simply as possible and then spend the rest of the visit socializing, swapping stories, talking sports or whatever he knew to be his customer's interests. And he was extremely effective. That's one reason Lesley had been assigned as his trainee.

But when she went out on her own, she learned very quickly that what worked for him didn't work at all for her. The first hurdle was that her customers, mostly middle-aged Ben Franklyn types, flatly refused to take her seriously as a technical expert. Of course, Ben evenhandedly found it difficult as well to take seriously "young college fellas" like Stanley.

Anyway, when Lesley completed the task as quickly and simply as possible, customers still refused to take her seriously. It was as though they had witnessed a trained chimpanzee performing a complicated task learned by rote through long and hard practice. A good trick, but only a trick, was the conclusion. And so she developed her own approach, an approach that carried a large dose of carefully planned impression management. Not an ego trip, oh no, just the opposite. This was an approach that, whatever else, was calculated to make absolutely certain that her customers had to admit that she knew her stuff. For Lesley realized early on that she would never be "one of the boys," that it would be a mistake even to try. In the final analysis, the thing that really mattered was the customer's conviction that she could do the job. But, on occasion, the customer needed a little help in arriving at that conclusion.

Section Two

But Some Are More Equal Than Others
Socialization and Attribution

George Orwell's classic *Animal Farm* is an allegorical tale of social stratification, of the demise of an attempt to establish a classless society. The creatures of *Animal Farm*, having overthrown their masters, live by seven commandments, the last of which is simply, "All animals are equal." All comes to naught, however, when the deceitful and ambitious pigs establish themselves as the new ruling stratum and amend the final commandment to read:

BUT SOME ANIMALS ARE MORE EQUAL THAN OTHERS

Most of us working in organizations think of social stratification in organizations as an okay thing, a necessary thing. Achievement is rewarded by promotion, and there has to be a hierarchy of command. There have to be executives, managers, and workers. But we think it's okay mostly because *we'll* be up there in that hierarchy some day, after working hard to achieve that status and the re-wards that accompany it. In a similar manner, we understand that lower organizational participants are also there for reasons of merit —or lack of it. The net result in societies and organizations is a stratification into various ranks or statuses, arranged from top to bottom.

If you are well socialized into your organizational culture and are asked to account for the fact that a particular person holds a particular rank in the organizational hierarchy, chances are you will come up with answers that involve the *attribution* of traits and motives. Research in attribution theory tells us that, typically, when asked to account for some action they have taken, *actors* will explain their behavior as stemming from the *situation* in which they found themselves. *Observers*, on the other hand, usually invoke some explanation involving the personal *traits or motives* of the actor. And this is especially true when the situation is one of failure rather than success.[4] We thus attribute abilities and motives to upwardly mobile managers in accordance with the status they have achieved. These attributions enhance perceptions of the correctness of managerial decisions. And these perceptions, in turn, are self-fulfilling, for the soundness of the decision may ultimately rest on the willingness of subordinates to carry it through. "They must know what they're doing—they wouldn't be there if they didn't."

The myth, symbol, and ritual of organizational culture both signify and solidify attributions. Ritual imparts objective reality to myth and prescribes the behavior through which organizational participants enact the myth. Remember that myths are accounts of the origins of things, as well as unquestioned beliefs about the practical benefits of certain techniques and behaviors. I think it crucially important here to distinguish between the actual *practice* of those techniques and behaviors, and the *mythology* that supports that practice. It is entirely possible for a member of the organization to subscribe completely to the myth and still recognize that in *this* situation the practice supported by the myth is flawed. Take the myth of performance as an example. All corporate cultures hold to the myth that the only thing that counts toward promotion is performance. The myth further states that superiors have full knowledge of their subordinates' work and that this knowledge is carefully quantified in the performance appraisal (ritual). Ergo, the deserving and talented are promoted, others are not. But the fact that the performance appraisal ritual is supported by the myth in no way guarantees that it was carried out appropriately in a given case. The myth *encourages* that belief, but that is all. Put another way, it's possible that you may feel mad as hell that you got reviewed unfairly in this instance, but that only reveals your unquestioning acceptance of the myth of the ritual.

Symbols of rank also signify and solidify attributions—larger offices, better furniture, windows, rugs, and so on. And symbolic communication sometimes occurs in odd forms. I recall the day that Arthur K. "Dick" Watson brought a talking mynah bird to the executive floor of IBM World Headquarters—as it was then called. Although it is true that the bird was suitably attired in charcoal grey, this was still a most "unIBMmanagerlike" thing to do. It was, however, most symbolic of the fact that the Chairman of the Board's brother is above the usual corporate restraints on managerial behavior.

Up to now, we have been talking about earned statuses only, what sociologists term *achieved* statuses. But sociology tells us that there is yet another kind of status that accounts for social stratification—*ascribed* status. Thus, some members of society are assigned (ascribed) lower social statuses because of beliefs that society holds about them by reason of sex, race, religion, or ethnic background.

Examples? In 1960, many doubted that a Catholic, John F. Kennedy, could be elected President. Somewhat later, in the 1984 election, there was doubt whether Geraldine Ferraro could stand up to the heat of public debate against a man. (You may have heard about George Bush's "kicked butt" comment). Indeed, women were among the most doubtful, a significant point about culturally formed social expectations. Some people are accorded lower ascribed social statuses than others, and we don't elect low-status people to our most prestigious national office. It's going to be a while before you see an African-American or Chicana president of the U.S. of A., although the cabinet appointed by President Clinton does indeed more closely "resemble America" than any of its predecessors.

Let's look at ascribed status more carefully and see what it means for us in organizations. Not too many years ago you would have observed that most professionals, almost all middle managers, and all executives were white males. On the other hand, most clericals and almost all secretaries were females, mostly white. As a white male professional entering the organization, you might simply have taken this situation for granted. And if asked to explain the situation, you probably would have said, "That's just the way it is." If pressed further, chances are you would again come up with answers involving the attribution of traits and motives. In this case, though, your attribution of abilities, traits, and motives would not be to individuals, but to females or blacks *as a class*. These explanations would likely have something to do with motives and goals, based on the assumption that these people are where they are because that is what they want, or because they lack some of the qualities necessary for success. Thus, you would probably attribute the status—the organizational situation—of these people to personal characteristics like ability, motivation, values, and goals, rather than the situation in which they have been placed.

For example, during the infamous Clarence Thomas senate confirmation hearings, many people, including many women, found it difficult to understand why Anita Hill had put up with the alleged sexual harassment. They resorted to explanations such as Hill having been sexually attracted to Thomas, while Hill explained simply that in such a situation she was afraid of losing her job.

So pervasive are these explanations invoking personal characteristics that, when we witness a case to the contrary, we again resort to individual explanations to account for this departure from the general rule. She is an exceptional woman—"thinks like a man," someone will say by way of preserving the more general account. It used to be said of a successful black man that he was a "credit to his race." This again by way of preserving the general stereotype that blacks as a class are generally unwilling or unable to make the effort to succeed. As case in point, a baseball executive with the L.A. Dodgers lost his job when on TV he ascribed the dearth of black executives in the game to their not having "certain necessities."

Having established these explanations, the principles of perception outlined in the previous section help us see what we expect to see, and we interpret accordingly. Women are emotional, passive, and nurturing; blacks flamboyant, aggressive, and undependable. Perceptual distortion and "filling in" provide abundant support for our beliefs.

We thus begin to treat people as though the thing's we've assumed about them are actually true. We protect them from emotional upsets; we protect them from failure; we protect them from stressful responsibility and treat them differently in thousands of other little ways that we don't realize ourselves.

The final act of this ongoing organizational drama is the observation that people start behaving in *fact* the way we expect them to behave. How could our expectations have that much effect? Well, a number of research studies have been conducted on the effect of situational expectations on behavior. Two of these merit brief mention.

In the first, people were assigned at random to one of two experimental groups. These groups differed only in that one learned that their "jobs" were less important and less interesting than those assigned to the other group; furthermore, there was no hope of "upward" movement for them. The other group, given similar information about the nature of their "jobs," learned that "upward" movement was possible, depending on how well they performed. The results? The randomly selected group with no hope of movement spent considerably more time socializing among themselves and criticizing the actions of "management." Although the experimental situation was rigged so that the two groups were otherwise treated identically, the "not promotable" group started behaving just as we expect lower ascribed status employees to behave.[5]

In the second and more dramatic experiment, two groups of college students were randomly assigned the roles of prisoner and prison guard. They began behaving so realistically, so brutally, that the experiment had to be terminated a week early. The experimenter called off the experiment because of his horror upon this realization:

"I could easily have traded places with the most brutal guard or become the weakest prisoner . . . Individual behavior is largely under the control of social forces and environmental contingencies rather than personality traits . . . We thus underestimate the power and pervasiveness of situational controls over behavior because: a) they are often . . . subtle; b) we can often avoid entering situations where we might be so controlled; c) we label as "weak" or "deviant" people in those situations who do behave differently *from how we believe we would*" [italics added].[6]

What does all this have to do with people like you in The Company? Well, let's see how these principles apply to Stanley, Lesley, Claude, and the others as they make their careers in The Company.

Cat In The Hat

8

Stanley was sitting peacefully in Lesley's office waiting for her to return from an early afternoon meeting. He hadn't talked with her since she'd been moved to her new responsibility in Corporate Communications. The new position looked like a real opportunity to move ahead, so naturally Stanley wanted to find out how it was going.

Stanley and Lesley had been friends in The Company for quite a while now. Still, he wasn't quite prepared for what was about to happen. But wait, here comes Lesley now.

"You! You're probably just like the rest of 'em. Another sexist! Another male chauvinist!"

"Me?" was about all Stanley could reply weakly.

"Probably." Lesley's tone softened. "Oh, no. I don't really mean that. I know you're okay, Stan. It's just that . . . listen, *listen* to this. Here I am at this meeting. We're getting a project group together to cover Marsh's big research lab dedication next month. We're going to do a whole series for . . ." Lesley described her excited anticipation of the new job and of how the meeting had progressed.

They are waiting for the Corporate Director to arrive so that the meeting might get underway. And here she is, sitting at one side of the table, prepared as usual with her handful of sharp pencils and a fresh yellow pad. Being new, and knowing hardly anyone there, she's not saying much.

Okay, here's the Director. Let's get on with the job.

Now at this point, and according to Company ritual, the host manager takes orders for coffee; five black, two sugar only . . .

"Then he turns to me, *to me,* and says in this unctuous voice, 'Would you get these for us, honey. The machine's down the hall to the left.'

"Get these for us, honey?! Who the hell does he think he is? Why the hell should I get his lousy coffee? Just 'cause I'm the only 'lady' in the room? I don't even *drink* the damn stuff!" Lesley was greatly exercised.

Unfortunately, Stanley didn't help much, "Did you?" he asked. It was an innocent enough question, but Stanley just managed to dodge the phone book that sailed his way.

"Yes!" Lesley almost shrieked the answer.

"But why? . . ."

"I just didn't know what else to do. I . . ."

Hearing the commotion, Pat Jones (The Company's Director of Human Resources Research) poked her head in the door and caught the last of the conversation. "Sounds like you're having fun. Look, I apologize for listening in, but I really couldn't help hearing your story. Would you like some advice?"

Lesley nodded.

"I've worked with these guys for years now, and they're really not that bad a bunch. But you can see for yourself, it's like a men's club around here. Sure, there are women around, but almost all of us are clerks, secretaries, you know. I'm the odd ball. And whether or not you and I like it, those clerks and secretaries do little extra things for them like . . ."

"Like getting coffee!" Lesley cut in, "So that big jerk figured I was just another secretary! Why?"

"What did you expect? How would he know otherwise?" Then Pat added with a chuckle, "He's more to be pitied than censured, you know. He just assumed that you were there to take notes."

"But what do I do?" said Lesley, "I can't go around introducing myself and saying that I'm not a secretary."

"Oh," replied Pat, "You could. But it isn't necessary. Next time when you're with strangers, just make sure you wear a hat."

"A hat? I don't even *own* a hat."

"Then buy one," Pat countered.

"For heaven's sake why?" asked Lesley.

"Ever see a secretary at one of these meetings in a hat?" was Pat's simple answer.

"No, that would be absurd," said Lesley.

"Exactly. Important women wear hats at important events. The boys may not know who you are, but at least they'll understand you're not the one to get the coffee."

What's that you say? You think that's silly advice? Well, maybe so. I really didn't intend it as a serious suggestion, though indeed that was Pat Jones's advice. But the point is clear enough, isn't it? Old ways of doing things die hard, and male managers still expect female secretaries to get the coffee and to perform other petty non-work tasks. And, by and large, they expect secretaries to be females and vice versa. That's what they're used to. Consequently, as a pencil-wielding, yellow-pad-carrying female, they assume that Lesley

(a) is a secretary, (b) is ready and willing to get the coffee, (c) is waiting to be told what to do, and (d) has the primary job interest of pleasing male authority figures.

Lesley's problem is to short-circuit the process and avoid the accompanying discomfort for all involved by providing unmistakable cues that she is not a secretary or other lower participant. And though she probably would not wear a hat, other dress cues are also important. For example, carrying an expensive leather briefcase would be an unmistakable sign of professional status. Finally, in situations where she does not expect to be known, she might plan ahead, arrive early, and introduce herself by name and position to each new arrival. You know, that might not be a bad idea for all of us.

BOX 2

A THOROUGHLY MODERN MANAGER

Carol Bartz, 44 at this writing, is one of the new "baby boom" executives taking the helm as CEO of America's most important companies. After a recent stint at Sun Microsystems, Bartz was hired on at Autodesk to bring order to the increasing chaos at the hi-tech producer of computer automated design software. The culture of Autodesk was one that relied on decision by consensus among project programmers, carried on primarily over the medium of electronic mail. Unfortunately, good business decisions were becoming increasingly rare.

Bartz, by her own account, is a representative of the up-and-coming ranks of female executives, and in the hi-tech engineering environment of "Silicon Valley" where few women have gone before. Her experiences are probably typical of those encountered by many women, but possibly not her reactions.

- At one point, as a candidate for a corporate post with 3M, it was explained to her that women shouldn't expect to get that kind of job. Her response? Okay, I'll look elsewhere.

- In another situation, unhappily common for female managers, she was accused of sleeping with one of her fellow company conference goers, and fired. She immediately objected and shortly regained her job.

- Just after taking over at Autodesk, she learned she had breast cancer. After a radical mastectomy, she returned in one month rather than the usual two. A silly thing to do, she admits. But her motivation had to do with feeling a responsibility to forestall any possible criticism concerning whether or not a woman ought to be running a major organization. After all, she says, breast cancer is strictly a female malady.

This kind of reasoning stems from her conviction that women simply have to perform better than men to get the top corporate jobs. About her career thus far: she has unloaded two strategically unrelated businesses, acquired another, installed a new executive management, and had breast cancer—all in just six months. She figures that would have taken six years for GM to bring off.

Her personal life also seems to reflect the demands of executive living. Her first marriage ended in divorce, possibly due to the fact that she was outdistancing her husband's career. Her second marriage has given her a four year old daughter and apparently is doing well.

Source: *Wall Street Journal*, November 6, 1992, p. A1.

9

Cowboy

Time was when business used to bring me to Pawtucket now and again, and I would stop by to check on Stanley's progress. Thinking back on it, I suppose Stanley's first real career problem came as a result—of all things—of success. I recall one incident vividly.

Ben Franklyn and Ted Shelby were having one of their go-arounds, and this time the bone of contention was Stanley himself.

"No, you can't have him," said Ben. "He's the best damned management information specialist we've got."

"But this would mean a promotion for him," Ted pleaded.

"From manufacturing to Personnel? That's a promotion?! Listen, Stanley's doing great here. Any damnfool can push papers in Personnel. Listen, you oughta see what Stanley can do with that system. Besides, there's no way I can replace him. No. You can't have him, period!"

When the Manufacturing Information System (MIS) was first installed, Stanley was fascinated by it. He took a one-week company seminar, then wheedled a chance to play around on the Mill's mini-computer. He had a natural talent for programming, and the next thing he knew, he was handling the data for Ben Franklyn's unit. His reputation got around quickly, because in those days people were still impressed by someone who could make an information system actually do useful things. People in the plant got to know him as Ben Franklyn's "information systems guy."

Stanley still likes to work the system, but he's at the point where he'd really like to move on to something else. He isn't unhappy. He's not going to do anything rash, and as long as he's there, he's going to do the job in the only way he knows—as well as it can be done. Ben knows it, and he has managed to make Stanley the highest-paid MIS specialist in The Plant.

The problem is that Stanley may never be anything else. Ben has kept him there so long that most people think of Stanley and his computer as an inseparable team. Only rarely will someone like Ted Shelby think of some other kind of job for him. Usually, it's: "Oh yes, Stanley, our MIS guy. No, I was thinking of a different type." Or, "Well, there's no doubt that Stanley is capable. Still, he's never moved out of that MIS job. Maybe that tells us something, eh?" So it goes.

The lesson here is that indeed it is possible to be too good at something. Not that this is always a problem. The legendary "Duke," John Wayne, undoubtedly enjoyed his lifetime of cowboy parts (sometimes, of course, wearing an Army or Marine uniform, but always the same part). Yet most people enjoy doing something different every now and then; if a person fits his "type" too well, that's not going to happen.

Consider the prototypical John Wayne: What if he had been cast as a thug, or as a werewolf? Who would believe it? Who could watch the movie without saying, "Why is that cowboy sprouting hair and claws when the moon is high?" And there's always going to be a problem with a steady diet of Batman, Superman, or Rocky parts. What other role can Superman play? And Rocky has to be the Rocky we know, be it I, II, IV or . . .

So, "Ben's MIS guy" is stuck with his role unless there is some drastic change in the situation, or unless he manages to put his foot down before it's too late. Jean Stapelton came within a hair's breadth of being "Edith Bunker" forever, but she realized what was happening in time and escaped, being killed off to end the TV series neatly. Maybe Stanley will wake up in time and elbow his way out of being typed, but it isn't that easy. There is a guaranteed level of reward associated with the "type," and to try to break the mold throws a person into a very uncertain situation: what if he *can't* do anything else?

What I am talking about is the preordained failure of success. It comes from not knowing when to quit, from being too good at something that is a narrowly defined specialty. Then someone can label you with an easy phrase—"our man in Paducah," "MIS guy," "Cowboy." Even more to the point, being so specialized, being so valuable *in a highly specific setting* you are not easily replaced. And so under the time-honored management tradition, your boss may not give permission to the Shelby's who might like to talk to you about a different opportunity.

And it can also happen to departments or even entire organizations. The Company once hired a young operations research specialist to introduce new management techniques to all their plants. This young woman, in turn, hired herself a couple of cohorts, and they went to work. In the beginning, they had trouble; all the plant managers were skeptical about new procedures they didn't understand. Every now and then the team got acceptance from a department manager to install some sort of special system or other, but general acceptance was elusive.

In the early days, the "operations research (OR) team" would sit and dream of the time when they might get a shot at designing an entire plant. That was the only way to do it, after all. But in the meantime, they were building a substantial record of novel, effective applications.

Success eventually arrived. They got to design the entire system at the Portsmouth plant, and their system worked just great. No longer was plant management asking, "What is OR good for? What can these guys do?" Now every one in The Company knew; they wanted a system just like the one at Portsmouth. No, don't you guys change a blessed thing; give us one just like Portsmouth.

In fact, the whole endeavor was so successful that the operations research group persuaded The Company to come out with a Company Standard for Production and Inventory Control Systems —just like Portsmouth. And each plant hired its own Operations Research Specialist, reporting directly to the plant manager and responsible for maintenance of The Company standard system.

Now it wasn't long before the two young assistant operations research people departed in search of more "creative and challenging opportunities," and the creator wondered where she had gone wrong. For it was clear that the whole OR scene in The Company was suddenly very dead.

And where had she gone wrong? Well, her first mistake was in wanting success too badly, and then in defining success in the shape of an epic achievement. Her group succeeded, in the sense that she had defined, but in doing so they lost control of their achievement. Plant managers hired their own OR person, loyal to themselves, and at that point had all the OR they needed. Why send problems back to the staff OR group, when now you had your own OR person who *also* knew something about production (and who was sympathetic to the local management point of view)? What the plant manager had now was just fine—no new ideas, please. As it is, it will be years before we "get the bugs out" of this system.

And so the original Operations Research group lost control of the thing it created, by virtue of being too successful. That plant-wide system at Portsmouth has its equivalent in the cowboy part—just fine, no changes, please.

Prophet Without Honor

10

" . . . So what we find, managementwise, is that fully 80 percent of our management subordinates who, as we put it—start from SCRATCH—will, over a period of five years, be promoted more often and achieve higher levels of compensation than a comparable group not so selected."

Actually, Ted Shelby himself wasn't that enthusiastic about the Subordinate Readiness Program when he first came up with the notion. The idea came to him one day as he leafed through an article copied from the *Academy of Management Review*. The title of the article first caught his eye: "Managerial Subordinacy: A Neglected Aspect of Organization Hierarchies." "Every manager a subordinate," it began. Intrigued, Ted read on: ". . . a management course on 'Effective Subordination' might be difficult to sell," the article pointed out. "Yet the full implications . . . have been mostly overlooked in management thinking, research and education."[7]

Well, now, here was an *Opportunity*, no question. Although just a slight change in approach might be necessary. Hmm, let's see—yes! (1) All the programs we now have deal with *management* training; (2) management means getting people to do things you want them to do; (3) what about the people who have to do those things? (4) ergo, why not have a program for training *subordinates*?

But to return to our story—just what is Ted up to now? Well, he's pushing his latest variation on the subordinate readiness theme, "Subordinate Career Readiness Assessment and Training Centers—SCRATCH" (with the H added to form the acronym). Right now he's presenting his ideas to a group from engineering, production, and personnel including Ben, Kerry, Dr. Faust, and Pat Jones. Faust has been Ted's consultant on this one, whereas Pat is attending as the company's in-house expert on Human Resources programs. Lesley's there too. She's been working with Ted on the communications package. That "Start from Scratch" slogan is her invention. But here, let's listen to Ted. He's only just begun his pitch.

"The key to this approach," Ted continued, turning to his next flip chart, "is realism: realism in the situation, in testing, and in performance rating.

"First, it's a group situation. That's the *management* situation, isn't it? And then we use a number of different tests and procedures. But most of our tests aren't really tests at all. Mostly we're simulating the kind of situations that practicing managers find themselves in. Those are the tasks we rate our candidates on." Ted went on describing the group problems and the simulated manufacturing problem.

"It seems to me that what you're really doing here," Ben broke in, "is getting a bunch of staff psychologists to sit around and try to decide whether or not a guy knows how to manage from watching him work on a couple of dummied-up problems. Is that it? This is supposed to tell me *better* than watching my guys work on *real* problems what their *management potential* is? You want me to believe that?"

"Now just a minute, Ben," Ted shot back. "I knew you were going to say that. No. that's *not* what we do." Mustering up his best crisp/urgent tone, Ted added, "As a matter of fact, Ben, our raters—the people who are making these assessments—are a group of high-potential middle managers themselves. Don't you see, that's the beauty of it! These are the very people who are best qualified to make these kinds of assessments."

"Maybe so," replied Ben, "But I still think that this is a line responsibility. For the life of me I can't see why we always need so much help."

"Maybe I can help clarify the situation, Ben. I believe I have more direct experience with these assessment centers than Ted." The voice was that of Dr. Faust. "Pardon me if I'm wrong, but I think you are, ah—somewhat in error in the belief that these people are going to tell you whom to promote and whom not. No, this is intended strictly as a staff service. Ted's SCRATCH staff will provide you with a quantitative, objective appraisal of the management potential, of each candidate, together with an assessment of strengths and, ah—shall we say 'future developmental objectives.' How you use this, what you do with this information is entirely up to you."

"And no one from New York is going to be after Ben and me to see how well these high-potential characters are doing? Is that right?" Kerry sounded skeptical.

"Well, yes and no, Kerry," said Ted. "Naturally we'll want to follow the progress of those identified as high-potential future top managers. But no, as Dr. Faust has outlined, how you use the information we give you is strictly up to you.

"Still, there's another point I think we're overlooking," Ted continued, "and that's the truly *objective* nature of these ratings. With this program, all of our top managers will have a way of comparing their own subordinates' promotional readiness to those of similarly placed subordinates throughout the company." Ted grew almost lyrical in his description of the absolute fairness of the system, and how talent perhaps now buried by circumstance would be brought to light and justly rewarded through promotion and "increases in compensation."

Up to this point, Pat Jones, who probably knew more of these things than anyone else at the table, had been silent. Even so, Ted had been eyeing her uneasily, for she had a way of asking the most impossible questions. Well now, here it came.

"So as I understand this, Ted," Pat began, "what you are offering us is a way of increasing the validity of our managerial selection procedure for middle- and top-level management. Correct?"

Ted nodded.

"And by validity, I take it you mean the extent to which people who get higher marks in your procedure show higher levels of performance?"

"Well, er, yes. That's about it, Pat." Ted was hedging.

"About it?" Pat pressed on.

"Why, you know we've never had any really objective measures of managerial performance, Pat. You know that as well as I do. Heck, that's one of the main reasons we've developed the SCRATCH program—so we'll have some better idea, some more objective idea of who our top managerial subordinates are. Why, that's just the point of all this." Ted was afraid he could see where this line of discussion would lead.

"I know, I understand all that," Pat bore in, "But my question is, how do you know this is any better than the way we do it now? How *have* you validated your procedures, if not against direct and objective measures of performance?"

"I think that you will find that we have used the usual measures, Dr. Jones," Faust stepped in to rescue the floundering Shelby. "Number of promotions, number of merit salary increases, and supervisory ratings of future potential. We have achieved validity coefficients as high as point five zero with ratings of future potential, for example. I believe that you can see . . ."

"Hold it, Doc," Kerry interrupted, "you and I have known each other quite a while, right? And I usually think you make pretty good sense, right? So do I really understand? It seems to me that what we're doing is this: first you're asking Ben and me to tell you who's good and who isn't so good, so that you can figure out whether this

SCRATCH program of yours really works. And if it does, why then you'll be in a position to tell us who's good and who isn't good. What's more, you'll even tell us who has . . . what'd you call it—high potential—so that we'll know how to rate the future potential of our managers so that . . ." Kerry threw up his hands, lost for words.

"It's lifting yourself up by the bootstraps," chuckled Ben.

Pat, sensing that the situation was getting out of hand, that the systematic performance appraisal baby might be thrown out with the SCRATCH program bath water, decided to restore some sanity to the situation, "People—Ben, Kerry; I think we're in a little over our heads in the technical issues of this program. Remember that we do use testing procedures in limited ways right now to help us improve our managerial selection. They work. And we do use performance appraisals of all employees right now: executives, managers, subordinates, workers. Flawed as they may be, they are better than nothing. So that's not the issue here, as I see it."

Then turning to Ted in a surprisingly conciliatory tone, "What Ted, here, is trying to do is not something that hasn't been tried before. And, frankly, I think we ought to support this effort—on a *limited, experimental* basis. The value of these procedures is not that they produce something that we haven't had before, but rather that they can help us make systematic and objective the kinds of procedures that may now be haphazard and subjective.

"The risk is not that managers will ignore Ted's recommendations. Oh, no. The real risk is that they'll use it as a crutch to avoid the gut-wrenching responsibility for making those hard decisions. So, as Ben says, it becomes part of a bootstrap operation where 'subordinates' with high assessment ratings are given high performance ratings and, in turn, receive more merit increases and promotions. No, the risk is that the same kinds of impression management that may help candidates get higher ratings on the simulated exercise will also be mistaken as performance by their own management. So what you're left with is not prediction, but self-fulfilling prophecy."

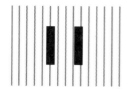

My Brothers' Keeper

Stanley's fist assignment in his new position working for Ted Shelby in Corporate Personnel was to "familiarize himself" with the assignments of others in the department. So it was this morning that he and Claude Gilliam were engaged in doing just that. Claude, it seems, had just been reassigned too, to the Technical Manpower Development Section. Claude's special project was to develop a plan for the recruitment of black professionals.

"I suppose you're going to find this hard to understand," Claude was saying, "but I'm not specially happy about this job. You know, it always seems that folks think I should really want to work helping out other black people. But hey, I just want to be thought of as another guy, and that's the guy I want to help get ahead. I've got enough problems with that, let alone everybody else."

"Then why . . .", Stanley began.

"Why did I take it? You've got to know the answer to that, Stan. You don't turn down anything here without having a pretty good reason. And 'I don't want to' isn't a very good reason in The Company."

That said, Claude's tone changed. "But hey, look here," he said, taking out a notebook with a breakdown of The Company's minority employees by category and location. "See, it's pretty interesting. We've got a goal of about 10 percent minority employment, and, if you look at these categories—blue collar, clerical—these kinds of jobs, why, we're doing pretty well. But look here, in the technical and professional categories. Why, we've hardly made a dent here."

"But wouldn't that have something to do with the availability of those people, Claude?" asked Stanley. "I mean, um, well . . . you know what I mean."

"I think you mean what Ted keeps telling me," Claude replied. And here Claude did a surprisingly good imitation of Ted given the short time he'd known him. "I think you'll find, Claude, that The

Company has pulled out all the stops in our minority recruiting. You see, it's just a question of numbers. Look, look here. These are the universities where we recruit our best technical people. And look, why there are only a handful of your people in each graduating class. Obviously, the competition for these individuals is enormous. So I'd have to say that we're doing extremely well in a difficult situation."

"But that's not an answer, is it Claude?" Stanley sympathized. "I mean, what the hell, how does that help when it's your job to improve the situation?"

"Right on. So I thought about it for a while and, you know, there's got to be lots of places other than The University and colleges like that. Now I know you probably haven't heard of many of them, but there are these places—they call themselves '*Negro colleges*'— lots of 'em in the South. So I asked, why not try there?"

"And what does Ted say?"

"He says, 'we have, but the students there just aren't getting the quality education we're looking for.' So I say, 'how's that?' 'Because,' he says, 'our experience shows that most all of them can't get an acceptable score on our standard recruiting tests.'"

Perhaps a word of explanation is needed here. The Company gave tests to all professional recruits interested in a career in "systems." Because not all colleges and universities, at least at the time, had a "systems" curriculum, The Company felt it had to do its own selection. Also, Company recruiters had learned that even people with backgrounds in such unrelated fields as English and history might have considerable aptitude for systems specialties. Hence, the battery of tests. But back to Stanley and Claude.

"Tests?" Stanley was surprised. "Why, I thought everyone knew that tests aren't valid for, um, minorities."

"Stan, don't be so sure about that. Look, the tests The Company gives are basically numerical reasoning, that's all. So if that's the kind of aptitude it takes to pass those tests, why, there doesn't seem to me to be any reason why black people shouldn't have it, too. And the last thing you want to do is to hold to different standards for black systems trainees. Listen, if I've learned one thing in this life, it's that when a white fails, well, that's just another person who doesn't have what it takes. But when a black trainee fails, that's something different, that's just another piece of evidence that *blacks* can't cut it."

"Okay, then, what are we going to do?" Stanley puzzled.

"I'm still not sure, but I think I've got an idea. Listen, I've got to go to lunch now, and then I'll be on the road for a while. Why don't you look me up when I get back?"

Stanley didn't get a chance to talk to Claude again for quite a while. Still, he did learn something of Claude's project by chance one day in The Company cafeteria. Ted and Kerry were sitting at the next table, Ted with his back to Stanley, conversing in a confidential/disturbed tone. ". . . so something doesn't smell right to me about this, Kerry. I'm not sure that it was a good idea to have, well, you know—to have someone with a personal interest giving these tests himself without some, er—independent check."

"Then you really think he's rigging? . . ."

"Well no, not really, I don't *really* think he's changing the scores. But coaching?" Stanley didn't learn much more that day. Still, he had pieced together the essentials. Claude had requested and been given permission to administer the tests himself, and not at the testing centers but at the home colleges of potential recruits. The results had been startling. Quite a few of the young people were now passing the tests, some even with top scores.

And what did Claude have to say about all this? Here's what he told Stan several months later. First of all, he pointed out, the testing took place at regional headquarters located in major metropolitan centers. These, especially in the South, were newer, imposing structures appointed in the decor favored by The Company: crisp and businesslike (also, some felt, cold and impersonal). So it was into this environment that The Company brought potential recruits from those small Negro colleges, putting them through several hours of rigorous testing. And by and large, they failed.

"You've got to understand, Stan, that this kind of situation is made for failure. These aren't sophisticated urban kids. And I think it is true that their education is lacking in some respects. But look, these tests are designed to get at *aptitude*, not education. Fact is, the tests don't seem to require much knowledge at all. Just a certain kind of ability."

"Then you're saying that you haven't, . . . you're saying that you didn't, um—modify the scores even a little?" Stanley still was dubious.

"I don't understand you dudes," Claude replied. "Can't you see how stupid that would be? If I do that, then I'm only setting these folks up for failure later on, and failure where it's going to hurt a lot more. And that's more unfair to them than it is to The Company."

"Then how *do* you explain it?" Stanley persisted.

"Look at it this way, Stan. Suppose you'd grown up black in the rural South. There are two things, at least, that you've got to fight. One thing is that you're sure the white folks in positions of power and influence aren't going to give you a fair shake. But the other—I think the other is even worse. A certain amount of what just about everybody believes about black folks is going to be buried in the back of your head; just maybe *some* of what they say is true. Maybe you really *can't* do it.

"Anyway, so now they say that The Company wants to hire you—maybe—if you have the stuff. First you say to yourself, to hell

with it. Why bother, just to be turned down again? But you go anyway, off to some place maybe you've never even seen before. And
there you sit in this cold, *un*human place, a knot in your stomach
and a lump in your throat. Just another scared black kid waiting to
be told once again that there is no place for you."

So that was Claude's diagnosis of the problem and the key to
his solution: Provide a familiar, warm, and supportive environment,
tested by an official representative of The Company who, by appearances as well as by word, believed in your ability and wanted you
to succeed.

You Can't Be Too Careful

But don't you *really* think he's over-doing it?" Lesley was saying. "I mean, people don't really think like that any more, do they? At least not educated people," The *he* in this case was television's lovable bigot, Archie Bunker. The overdoing was Archie's feisty commentary on the ways and overall worthiness of black people generally, occasioned by his discovery that in particular his new next door neighbor was black.

Lesley's remarks were directed at the group—Claude, Kerry, Ted, and Stanley. Kerry had invited the Technical Personnel and Communications Task Group out for a late afternoon celebration upon completion of their final report. As they sat at the table, there, big as life over the bar, was the umpteenth rerun of *All in the Family*.

As a self-appointed expert in most matters, Ted was the first to reply, "I think that's just the point of the show, Lesley, that's why Archie has to be so obviously . . . oh, so obviously working class. It's just because educated people don't think that way."

"Um, I don't think you've got that exactly straight, Ted," Claude said with a bit of hesitation. "I think what you mean is that educated people don't *talk* that way. And that's a big difference. 'Cause I wouldn't say that they don't *think* that way. Least from what I've seen."

Ted started to protest, but Kerry cut him off. "From what I've seen too, Claude. Let me give you an example. It's something that happened years ago, and I don't think it could happen the same way now—but I'm sure something a lot like it still could happen.

"I applied for a job as a teaching assistant in the engineering department of Another University in the Midwest. When the time for my personal interview came around, I was introduced to the head of The Department. He was also chairman of the committee on committees of the faculty organization, I recall. We talked for a bit, and then he asked me kind of hesitantly, 'Ah, is there some reason why you didn't attach your picture to your application?' I figured that I had done something wrong, and I really wanted that job, so I said, 'Well, sir, I suppose I should have, but I was in a real hurry and I didn't have a print handy, so I thought . . . anyway, it really isn't important, is it? Does it really matter what I look like?'

Now he got really serious. He moved up a little closer to me so he was speaking right in my face, and he said, 'Doesn't matter, you say? Let me tell you, young man, about a year ago we had another applicant just like you, another man who sent in his resume without a picture. From the material he submitted he looked first rate. Well qualified in all respects. The fact of the matter is we were ready to hire him.'

"With that he moved up even closer and told me in his most confidential tone, 'Then we had our personal interview with him. And guess what? We found out he was a Negro.'

"Funny, he didn't really have to tell me that. I guess he just assumed that it would help him make his point. But I've never forgotten that scene. It was all so unbelievable."

"To you, maybe," murmured Claude, "but I'll tell you, whenever I'm job hunting, I always get the same feeling. Maybe I'm paranoid, but I always feel they're looking at me as something special, looking for what's wrong with me. It's like a lot of people seem to think I really won't be able to do the job, so they'd better be extra careful in checking me out."

"Hey, Claude, I didn't know you were looking again," said Stanley, to break the tension.

But Ted just couldn't let it drop. He *knew* The Company didn't do those things, and he wanted that said. "Claude, I think maybe you *are* being paranoid," Ted began in his best informed/sincere tone, "The Company checks everyone out—carefully—whether they're black, white, or polka dot. We make no distinctions. And another thing, we couldn't discriminate even if we wanted to . . . which, of course, we don't," Ted quickly added for fear of being misunderstood. "We can't ask people about race, religion, or their mother's surname; we can't ask for a picture. There are all kinds of equal employment opportunity regulations. You just can't do it, that's all." Ted, now satisfied that he had put the matter to rest, settled back to enjoy the gathering. But it was not to be enjoyable.

"Now wait a minute, Ted," Lesley began. "I don't know how long it's been since *you* were on the job market, but I've got an idea that there are some things you don't know." Lesley wasn't going to let the matter drop so easily. "Stan, how about you, when was the last time you were asked about your 'family plans'?"

Stanley shrugged.

"And how about, 'would you be able to move to another location on a week's notice?' How about that one?"

"Right on, Les," Claude cheered.

"And how about . . . well, not me, but a friend of mine was asked whether or not she used 'the pill,' and even which *kind!*"

"Now, Les, you know I've never been asked that," Stanley laughed.

"Well? What business is it of theirs?" Lesley hadn't meant to get angry, but she was.

Poor Ted. He was on the spot, like it or not, so he took up the challenge in his best sincere/understanding tone. "I really can understand how you feel, Les, and, of course, those things have not happened to me. But still, those kinds of questions are illegal, you know. You could report those people. Have you?"

That was nasty, thought Les.

Ted continued, "Still, for the sake of argument, isn't it just possible that those people have a point? What if you're on the job for six months or a year, and then your husband moves? Your organization is just beginning to get some return on investment, beginning to depend on you, and bam! (Ted smashed fist into palm to emphasize the point) off you go. Doesn't your organization really have a right to know that may happen?"

Lesley started to protest, but Ted cut her off, "No, let me finish, Les. You've had your say. And it's the same thing with maternity leaves. How can you hold down a responsible position if you're going to be off four or five months every two years or so?"

"But that's discrimination, Ted," Lesley reminded him quietly but forcefully, "You said so yourself."

"That's what the law says, yes," Ted replied, "but damn it, it's also good business. Look, I don't even know why I'm arguing the point. When The Company says we're going to do it this way, why, that's good enough for me. That's the way we do it. But it just seems to me that nobody really appreciates what The Company's doing for them—what we're giving up to satisfy the law."

"Relax, Ted," said Kerry. He decided that this had gone far enough. "You're right. That's the law, and that's what we're going to do. And sooner or later that's what everybody is going to be doing. But here, let me ask Stan a question: How many jobs have you held since you graduated from The University?"

Uh oh, thought Stanley, he really didn't want to get dragged into this. "Um, three, I guess."

"In how many years?"

"Little less than five, I think. But look, I'm really happy here, Kerry, I don't see . . ."

"So let's seen then, how long were you on the first job?" Kerry continued, "About a year, I'll bet. And the next, maybe two years. And you've been with us about two years. Now tell me, what did those first two outfits get from you, Stan? Did they get a return on investment, as Ted says?"

"Why, er—I guess . . ."

"Naturally not. Nothing to be ashamed of. You were looking and they were looking. That's just part of the cost of doing business.

"And something else. Sometimes you're happy as hell when someone says they're leaving. That's when you shed those crocodile tears and breathe a sigh of relief. So, Ted, is it really so different? Come on, gang, let's forget this stuff and have another drink. Cheer up, Les." And then, as an afterthought, "Say, could you move to Pawtucket next week?"

The ensuing laughter broke what was left of the tension, and no one heard Ted mumbling to himself, "I *still* think it's different."

13 Scarlet Letter

Why these things happened only on Friday was a matter of some mystery. But there on The Company's bulletin board appeared a spate of new corporate announcements. Chief among these was that of the elevation of one Anne R. Wood. It read:

> M. M. Marsh today announced the promotion of Anne R. Wood to Corporate Director of Publicity and Communications. Making the announcement, Mr. Marsh said, "I feel that Ms. Wood will bring to this important post the energy, dedication, and intelligence that have been characteristic of her in every Company position she has held. As we enter today's new environment of telecommunications . . .

As Lesley read the announcement, her concentration was broken by some murmured comments from fellow readers of the corporate tea leaves. One said that the "boys in communications better batten down the hatches." But another, standing just behind Lesley, simply muttered to himself, "Boy, there's one tough broad."

Annoyed, Lesley turned and asked the speaker, "And just how do you know that?"

"Listen, kid," came the reply, "you can't have been around here very long if you don't know 'Red' Wood. Just ask around." With that he left.

Well now, maybe I'll do just that, thought Lesley. So she did ask around as discreetly as possible, soliciting opinions of the new Director. And what she found was a mixture of dislike, fear, and admiration. Wood was a tough lady, all right, in the opinion of both the women and men who knew her. Just about everyone had a story, too. One in particular seemed to have found its place in The Company's oral history.

It seems that a few years ago when Red Wood (incidentally, nobody ever addressed her that way) was in a less influential management position, there was a meeting between Corporate Communications and Corporate Personnel to "hammer out a policy" on the use of career vignettes of top Company technical people in Company institutional ads. Corporate Personnel didn't like this idea, largely because it wasn't theirs. So they threw up a smoke screen of objections as to why it wouldn't work.

"I just don't think you are looking ahead on this one, Anne," the staff man had said, "there are so many areas where we can get into deep trouble—compensation, invasion of privacy."

"No mind. We can handle that," replied Wood, brushing aside the objection.

Finally, after much pulling and hauling, the Manager of Corporate Personnel Planning came to the bottom line. "All right, okay, suppose we do go along with you on this one, shoulder the risk. What's in it for us? Give me one good reason why we ought to go along." Clearly a direct challenge from personnel.

Red Wood paused for a moment. Then turning slowly and fixing her steely grey-blue eyes on her antagonist, she replied slowly and simply, "My good will."

The message, of course, was, "Some day, Buster, I'm going to be your boss. So watch out."

But back to Lesley. Having garnered this intelligence, she was a little concerned. She wanted to talk to someone about it, and there was Stanley. "I mean, does it really have to be that way?" she was saying, "Why is it that to get ahead a woman always has to be so . . . so tough. Even the other girls I talked to didn't seem to like her."

"Um, I dunno. I've never really thought about it, Les. Maybe they do." Stanley was trying to be helpful but didn't know quite how.

"But people don't seem to say that about men when *they* move up, do they?" Les continued.

"I guess I never noticed if they did, Les," said Stan. "Look, I'd like to say something helpful, but . . ." Stanley stopped in midsentence, trying to think about what he thought. He really didn't know any women managers. He knew Ted, Ben—but Ben was special, and . . . oh, boy, Kerry! "Listen, Les, maybe you're on the wrong track. I don't know if you've ever run into Kerry Drake, but . . ." With that, Stanley related one of his earlier encounters with Kerry (recall *Sincerest Form of Flattery*) and how Kerry minced no words when he thought, no, when he *knew* it was warranted.

"But that's just it," Les observed. "It doesn't seem to bother anybody when a guy is 'crisp, hard-hitting, two-fisted,'" Les recited the lexicon of the media people.

But Stanley wasn't listening. His imagination was leaping ahead, "Hey, can you imagine what a female Ben Franklyn would be like, Les? Can you imagine?!" Chuckling to himself, he projected a mental image of this cigar-chomping, blasphemous harridan, careening across the mill floor, all the while booming obscenities at cowering subordinates. No, it wouldn't do. It just wouldn't do.

"I think I do see something, Les, but I don't really understand it. A woman just *couldn't* act like Ben Franklyn or Kerry. It . . . it would be out of character. Why, everybody would think she's nuts. So I guess it is true. There are lots of guys who act tougher than your Red Wood. But it just seems more, more natural. So then why? . . ."

"That's just what I'm getting at," Les interrupted, "so why the big deal about women managers being so tough?"

By now it was quite obvious that Stanley had contributed whatever he could to the matter, and Lesley decided to look up Pat Jones, the Company Director of Human Resources research. Pat listened quietly as Lesley explained her quandary, reflected a moment, and replied thoughtfully, "Maybe it is true that women use authority in different ways from men, Lesley. Maybe we're a little more, ah—covert about it because we're not used to using authority directly. Maybe so. But maybe not. I really don't know.

"But there are some things I *do* know that might make some sense to you. Take Anne Wood, for example. What else might she be besides a Company Manager?" Pat paused for a moment while Lesley looked puzzled. "She might be somebody's lady friend, of course, or somebody's wife. She might even be your mother—though she's not quite old enough for that.

"What's that go to do with it?" Pat anticipated Les's unspoken question. "Just this. Not only men, but women too, expect a wife or a mother to be a sympathetic, warm, understanding character. Someone who . . . let's face it, someone who will put your good above her own. At times, anyway.

"Now what happens when you step out of that role, when you project the Ms. Wood image? Well, you're not crisp, hard-hitting, and two-fisted (Pat knew the same media hype), I'll tell you that. Oh no, you're tough, cold, maybe even bitchy."

"But does it have to be that way?" Les was concerned. "I mean, can't Red, um . . . Ms. Wood sort of loosen up a little? Can't she be more um—human?"

"I think you're missing my point, Lesley," said Pat. "Actually, she is more human than you give her credit for. It's mostly that your expectations of her are different. And so, by comparison to the way you think she ought to act, why, she does seem a bit cold, a bit tough.

"But there's a second thing I know," Pat continued. "In some ways she can't loosen up, as you put it, because she can't do the same things people like Ben and Kerry do to make them seem more human. At least she can't do them in this day and age. She can't go out drinking with the boys. She's got to be careful whom she's traveling with, where, and how. I know it's unfair, but you know what the corporate gossips will say—especially when you're a handsome, young woman like Wood.

"Sleeping her way to the top, they'll say. They'll try to discredit her ability in every possible way. And that's bound to reduce her effectiveness as a manager. You've got to remember that one of the most important things you can have going for you as a manager is everyone's belief in your ability to get the job done; that maybe, just maybe, this guy or gal is going to be *your* boss some day."

"Let me see if I understand what you're saying, Pat," Lesley began, "because there are so few women in top management, why, everybody figures it's because we women don't really have what it takes to get there or stay there."

Pat nodded.

"When a women *does* make it to the top, then everybody— *including* a lot of other women—looks for some reason to explain it away. Then if they see that you've been going out with the boys, traveling with some other top manager, dating somebody from the office, whatever, why then they say, 'she's sleeping her way to the top.' And they say that to explain you away as being no exception to the general rule." Then, after some thought, "Listen, Pat, if a girl can sleep her way to the top, then from what I see around here we must have an epidemic of insomnia."

BOX 3

THE SOCIAL CONSTRUCTION OF
DONALD BURR

Where do popular images of corporate leaders come from, and to what extent is the business press responsible for the "social construction" of these images? Donald Burr and *People Express* airlines present an instructive case example.

The Airline Deregulation Act of 1978 allowed for complete freedom of ticket pricing by 1983, and thus presented new business opportunities for startup organizations. Thus it was that Burr founded *People Express*, which made its first flights in 1981. This was no ordinary airline. Burr literally preached the value of democratic management. Every employee was required to own stock, and was called an "owner-manager." There was no corporate hierarchy, and all were expected to pitch in, as necessary, to accomplish tasks that needed doing. Burr himself had no secretary, for example.

Initially, after the usual startup losses, business boomed as a result of unheard of low fares, and inexpensive, no-frills service. By 1983 *People Express* stock hit an all-time high, and *People* appeared in *100 Best Companies To Work For In America*. Burr himself was named "Man of the Year" by *Time* in 1985, even as clouds gathered on *People's* business horizon. Actually, 1984 and 1985 were years of mixed results. Stock prices fell from fifty dollars to as low as eight dollars, amid complaints of delays and overbooking. The name "People Distress" was coined. Finally, in 1986, following the disastrous acquisition of Frontier Airlines, *People* went belly up, and subsequently was sold to United Airlines. Burr resigned shortly thereafter.

How did the press deal with these events? First, the press presents leaders as extensions of the organizations they represent, whose personal qualities parallel, and shape, those of the organization. Thus, the construction of a leadership image is the process of matching leader qualities with organizational outcomes. But in the case of Burr, in the failure years the press has to deal with earlier images where leadership attributions are based on success. Consistency is crucial to continued press credibility. What we find, then, is that media themes of ability, people orientation, motivation, and innovation appear throughout (although ability is cited less often). But in the failure years we find new, yet consistent themes introduced. The earlier cited qualities are still good, but have been "overdone." Innovation is okay, but "ill-adapted" to a changed environment. Throughout, the press images maintain a consistent theme that emphasizes leadership efficacy in promoting performance outcomes, as opposed to a view that leadership is largely a symbolic function.

Source: Chen and Meindl, "The Construction of Leadership Images in the Popular Press: The Case of Donald Burr and People Express." *Administrative Science Quarterly*, (36) 1991: 521–551.

PART TWO

WHAT CAN'T BE CURED MUST BE OBSCURED

THE MYTH AND MYSTERY OF MOTIVATION AND DECISION MAKING

The most pervasive mythologies in our corporate culture have to do with the paramount importance of motivation and decision making. Curiously, I would have to say that I owe my understanding of the mythology of motivation to Ron Swoboda, right fielder for the world champion 1969 New York Mets. Though the incident is dated, his analysis serves still as a beacon of clear reasoning. During that season, the Pittsburgh Pirates contracted the services of a motivational consultant in an effort to improve the slumping team's standing. Learning of this, a local sportswriter asked Swoboda what he thought of that move. With hardly a moment's thought, Swoboda replied, "It's not their motivation—it's their batting averages."

Surely he was right, but hadn't he missed the point, I thought? No, he was right. No question. All ballplayers love to hit, and they just weren't hitting. So why the consultant?

Place yourself in the position of a midlevel manager of an organization. Things aren't going too well for you. Productivity is lagging. What could be the problem? Something *you* haven't done? Certainly not! No, it's those employees out there. They're just not motivated. So the answer is to start up a motivational program. That ought to do the trick. And look what you accomplish with this. First, the problem is acknowledged and officially identified as a problem of individuals, not of the management system. Next, you can pat yourself on the back for having taken corrective action. Crisp, hard-hitting decision making. You've gotten yourself a big name, "motivational consultant" (talk funny, make money) and you'll put a program in place. There, that should take care of it. And who knows? Maybe it will—given, of course, that it's *not* their batting averages. We do know, however, that sometimes just paying attention to people will improve their performance. But don't count on it in the long run.

Truth to tell, we know a good deal about human motivation. And most of what we know is probably correct. Then why the mystification of motivation? The answer is simply that we don't act on what we know. Frederick Winslow Taylor put his finger squarely on the problem at the turn of the century. Taylor said that if management would only show workers how to do the job better, and then share the returns of a better job with them, there would be no problem.[1] Still, he lamented, management will never do that, for fear of driving wages up. And, for the most part, he was right.

So it is that the most popular schemes for raising levels of motivation all promise you can get something for nothing, a kind of motivational perpetual motion. Stress the intrinsic motivators (these don't include money, naturally), enrich the job, allow participation in decisions. In short, do everything but what Taylor recommended.

I acknowledge that my viewpoint is something of a minority viewpoint, but that is what *The Ropes* is all about. Yet we do know a great deal about motivation. Let me illustrate with what I call the "dog yummy" model (it bears some resemblance to what is known as the operant model).

We start with "Shep," a very large and energetic German shepherd almost a year old. My first goal is to teach Shep how to "sit," that is, to do so when I ask. Because sitting is a natural position for a dog, I wait until Shep sits (actually, I can coax him into the position by pushing down on his butt) and immediately reward him from my ample supply of dog yummies. If I repeat this often enough with the command "sit," Shep will eventually consistently produce the desired behavior. He has come to associate the reward with the behavior. It's called *positive reinforcement* of behavior, and it's good for establishing new behavior, that is, for building behavior.

Because he is very big and very energetic and very affectionate, Shep does some things that I don't want him to do. For some reason he likes to jump up, smack his sledgehammer paws on my chest, and look me eyeball to eyeball—maybe to lick my face better. To get rid of this behavior, I deftly step on his rear paws when he does this. And this hurts. (In fact, though this is what I am supposed to do, I can't actually manage to do it.) Over time, Shep comes to associate the hurt with the jumping up and quits it. Its called *punishment*, and its good for getting rid of unwanted behavior. Note that the two strategies, reinforcement and punishment, are complementary and not substitutes for each other. You cannot build behavior with punishment, and you cannot get rid of behavior with reward, at least not directly. So one problem with punishment is that you may get rid of a behavior, but you can't be sure the behavior you want will take its place unless you also positively reinforce the new, desired behavior. Simple enough, what?

There is yet another commonly used technique that is more complicated to explain, and it's called *negative reinforcement*—not to be confused with punishment. Negative reinforcement involves the *removal* of something hurtful when the desired behavior occurs. It's another strategy for building behavior. Because it is more complicated, I will illustrate it later in this part.

The dog yummy model stresses the building of an unconscious association between a reward or punishment and a specific behavior. When applied to people, it must be modified. People do have conscious expectations, whether dogs do or not. And here is the link to decision making. When making choices, people may ask, "Am I better off doing A or B? Should I continue, or have I done enough?" But we shouldn't overemphasize the conscious rationality part because, as noted earlier, much of organizational behavior is rote; it follows those behavioral scripts without thinking very much about them. Nonetheless, almost everyone develops a formula for calculating the relative payoff when different courses of action are followed. On the one hand, you may be bored silly with your current project, but on the other, wouldn't the final product benefit from a few additional finishing touches?

So motivation and individual decision making are related. You try to anticipate what is likely to happen and figure out how much you care. What complicates individual motivation and decision making is that human beings find lots and lots of things rewarding. You would like to get on to a more interesting project, but you also get satisfaction from a job well done. And then there's that next promotion, and perhaps a fat bonus, and . . . Well, you get the picture.

Expectancy Theory is a most general model of motivated behavior that takes such factors into account. Expectancy theory is an explicitly cognitive theory based on workers' perceptions of the likelihood of obtaining desired outcomes contingent on higher levels of performance. The model can be summarized in terms of a series of four blocks of factors that mediate perceptions of the value or "valence" of increased performance.

Effort–performance expectancy.   First, workers must have the competence to perform at the desired level. They should know what they have to do and how to do it. They need to understand what constitutes the acceptable performance, and they must have the resources or equipment to do the job. In other words, workers must perceive that they have both the *capability* and the *opportunity* to perform.

Instrumentality of performance.   This is the question of which behaviors are perceived as leading to outcomes desired by workers. Many activities are potentially rewarding, but only those for which the organization has established the behavior-reward linkage will be perceived as *instrumental.*

Performance–reward expectancy.   Rewards need to be calibrated to specific levels of performance, and workers need to experience these rewards either directly or vicariously (by observation of others' rewards). Workers should know specifically what level of reward accrues to what level of performance.

Reward–cost balance.   This is termed the "valence" of net outcomes—is the outcome worth the effort? Theory predicts that performance levels will increase when the perceived value or valence of increased effort is positive.

We should note here that while this is a management oriented theory, stressing those things that an organization can do to control and improve performance, it is still a most general theory, one that easily can accommodate intangible rewards and costs in the crucial reward–cost balance. One other point deserves notice. Since it is an explicitly *cognitive* theory of performance, it is based on worker *perception* of the situation. Thus, even though activities may in fact *not* be instrumental to the attainment of desired outcomes, if they are perceived as such, then the theory would imply a positive link to performance. *The Ropes* has many examples of this principle.

Managerial decision making is another matter. The issue here is to arrive at the decision that is best for the *organization.* However, as we shall see, individual motivation is also involved. Let's first consider the case of managerial decision making under the assumption of technical rationality. The situation is as follows: the decision maker is confronted with a set of *uncontrollable events,* occurrences that affect the soundness of the decision, such as this year's demand for Expandrium. Then, the decision maker has an array of *decision alternatives* from which to choose. The *payoff* results from the pairing of a particular decision alternative with a particular uncontrollable event: for example, increasing Expandrium production 20 percent might be paired with a subsequent 10 percent decrease in demand. Probably a bad choice.

Technical rationality requires, among other things, that the decision maker have perfect knowledge of all decision alternatives and the present and future returns from each. Given this, three possible conditions are assumed for uncontrollable events: *certainty, risk,* and *uncertainty.* The difference among these is in the level of knowledge about which event will occur. Under *certainty,* the decision maker knows; it's just a question of pairing that event with the decision alternative that produces the maximum payoff. *Risk* means that only probabilities for all events are known. There is a simple strategy here, too. Find the pairing with the highest expected value for the payoff. Under *uncertainty,* there are a number of different strategies, like assuming that each of the possible events has equal probability. I'll illustrate others later on.

If it has occurred to you that the assumptions required by the technical rationality model depict an oversimplified world, you are absolutely right! Nobel laureate Herbert Simon made the same observation some years ago and offered an alternative—"bounded rationality." This model is much more akin to the way managers in The Company actually behave. It states that decision makers do not know what all the decision alternatives are, nor do they know all the present and future payoffs; they have limited motivation to search for additional decision alternatives. Basically, decision makers search until they find an alternative that meets their subjective standard of "good enough," and they select that one. Simon calls this behavior "satisficing"—satisfactory and sufficient—as opposed to optimizing.

Furthermore, it seems to me that all managerial decision making worth writing about occurs only under conditions approximating uncertainty. Decisions made under certainty or risk have rational solutions that can be programmed for a computer. They may be extremely complex, but they don't require mature managerial judgment or intuition. Real managerial judgment (or what passes for it) is necessary when we cannot estimate the likelihood that a given uncontrollable event will occur—and when, as just noted, we don't even know all the possible uncontrollable events. So this is where the link between motivation and managerial decision making comes in. Because some courses of action are less risky than others, a manager will ask not only what's best for the organization, but, "What's best for me?"

Actually, what's best for me and what's best for my organization are usually closely related, if "my organization" is interpreted to mean "that part of the organization for which I am directly responsible," or "my function." Under these circumstances, managerial decision makers are motivated to seek the rewards associated with advancing the interests of their own function and to avoid punishments resulting from failures in that function. This situation leads to some very interesting games that are played to insure that your successes will be attributed to you, while failures are lodged elsewhere. And this will be the topic of Section 4 in this part.

Let's turn now to a more detailed look at the topic of motivation and why motivational programs are felt to be necessary.

Section Three

Doin' What Comes Natcherly

Motivation and Reinforcement Theory

It is easy to overrationalize human behavior in organizations. You have to keep in mind that a lot of what we do is done simply because "that's the way we do it," with little or no forethought—those trustworthy recipes for thinking-as-usual. Only now and then do we come up against a situation different enough to make us resort to our motivational calculus to decide what to do.

Motivated behavior means behavior directed toward the achievement of a goal. This goal should satisfy both an organizational and an individual need. And that is the secret for management: to arrange things so that by achieving the organization's goals, people achieve their personal goals as well. Simple, no? Unfortunately, experience shows that this is easier said than done. This section of *The Ropes* is about just that: *why* it's easier said than done.

In the dog yummy model, positive reinforcement builds behavior. Shep is motivated to do his tricks because he has the incentive of a dog yummy. If he is given the yummy right after the behavior, he comes to associate the behavior with the reward. Punishment works in the same way, to get rid of behavior. What was not noted earlier, however, is the fact that if you stop providing the incentive (the dog yummy) Shep eventually stops the desired behavior. (In everyday life we usually substitute another reward, a pat on the head and or "good doggy, Shep"). Some form of reward has to continue to be associated with the behavior or the behavior is no longer motivated. Ditto punishment.

Finally—and this is important—Shep has to be able to figure out what the behavior is that is being rewarded or punished. If the reward or punishment comes before the act, or too long after it, Shep will just get confused. This is where the phrase "rubbing his nose in it" comes from, to make sure that Shep knows *exactly* what crime is being punished.

If we know all this, then why the motivational problem? The answer: because management doesn't, or won't, or can't apply what we know. That's why. Problems occur on both the incentive side and the performance side of the behavior/incentive link. To begin with, there are some problems inherent in the wage and salary system, the system intended to provide the incentive to perform. Perhaps the major problem is that, in most jobs, there is no link between goal-directed behavior and monetary incentives. There is a yearly raise, to be sure, but this is pretty much taken for granted and impossible to relate to day-to-day behavior. It's as though you sprinkled your yard with dog yummies and expected Shep to figure out somehow that they were a reward for "sit."

Under these conditions, beliefs amounting to superstition arise to explain differences in salary increases. Some years back I was doing a research study in an engineering organization, interviewing engineers in depth over a one-year period. When the raises and promotions were doled out that year, I found that the engineers in one department were comparing notes to try to discover the relationship between what they had said in their interviews with me and the size of their raises! Evidently, they could think of no other way to account for the size of the raise.

A second problem is that management frequently rewards one behavior in the belief that they are rewarding another; "Rewarding A while hoping for B," as my friend Steve Kerr put it.[2] An example? The management of a large corporate product development laboratory wanted to increase the number of patentable ideas coming from its engineers. So they instituted a program (Shelby at work again) that paid engineers a tidy sum for each patent disclosure they wrote up and submitted. These are not actual patent applications, just raw ideas. Well, for about six months, activity was brisk. The program seemed to be working. But then it quickly fell back to the previous level. What had happened is that the program had only motivated engineers to go back into their weekly logbooks (kept for legal purposes in case of patent disputes) and unearth all the ideas that they had previously considered not of sufficient merit to write up. These exhausted, once again it was business as usual. What was being rewarded, and what was being produced, was the behavior of writing up the patent disclosures, not the less concrete behavior of dreaming up patentable new ideas.

Another problem is that many monetary incentive systems are so rigidly constrained by corporate wage and salary administration guidelines, or by union or civil service regulations, that differential reward for performance is nearly impossible. Under these conditions, managers have no alternative but to resort to negative reinforcement. How? By rewarding the desired behavior through removal of an otherwise punishing situation: for example, freeing a person from paperwork, or exemption from some bothersome regulation, or perhaps awarding time off during working hours.

Then there is the misapplication of punishment in the attempt to build desired behavior by punishing some other, undesired behavior. People "not at their desks" are reprimanded in the belief that *being* at the desk is equivalent of *being productive* at the desk. Guess what? I don't know how many times I have witnessed a top manager complain that secretaries are not being kept busy. This is usually accompanied with a threat to reduce the secretarial force. The belief is that this threat of punishment will up secretarial productivity, right? Wrong. Now secretaries start paying attention to *looking* busy—typing personal letters to friends and peering intently at work which turns out to be a paperback novel concealed in a half-open desk drawer. But my favorite "looking busy" act was performed regularly by a respected program administrator. Most of the afternoon he could be seen intently reviewing notebooks labeled "Program Guidelines" and such. What a few of us knew, however, was that he had neatly concealed inside this official cover what I can best describe as a mildly pornographic magazine.

Ah, well. But let's return to Stan, Ted, and the good doctor, as they experience the motivational intricacies of The Company.

Fair Day's Work

"Excuse me ... uh, sorry ... ah, say is that seat taken? It is?" So began another hour of that test of flesh and spirit called commuting. Stanley now knew that assignment to New York was a mixed blessing. Among other things, cattle on the way to their final reward rode better than the average suburbanite headed for The City.

"Oh, hi, Ted. Say, mind if I take that seat?"

Ted was especially glad to see Stanley this morning because he was once again involved in a new program and wanted to talk about it.

"Well," he said, "the upshot of Dr. Faust's study—and you'll find this hard to accept, I know—is that we are operating at only 65 to 70 percent of industry standard.

"*Measurement* is the key. You know Mr. Marsh, Sr. always went on the assumption that Company people, because they *are* Company people, give you 100 percent." Ted went on to explain that there were some ways of giving 100 percent that were better than others. His new program was aimed at worker education, at helping them understand this. His *Procedures Improvement Program*—PIP—had for its slogan "Work Smarter, not Harder." Measurement was for feedback and individual improvement, not for policing, he emphasized.

"You see, the problem has always been one of determining what constitutes a fair day's work. We want to make sure we're getting a fair day's work for a fair day's pay. These scientific work measurement procedures will do that for us."

"Uh, how do you figure the fair day's pay?"

"*Well*, that's what we pay." Ted's look portrayed disbelief that such a question could arise in The Company, so Stanley let it drop and proceeded on a new tack.

"How do you think the guys in the mill are going to like this? I mean, my guess is that they're not going to see it the same way you do."

"We've thought of that, and that's why the educational aspect of this thing is so important. Remember, we're working on Procedures Improvement—Work Smarter, not Harder." Ted relished the words. "This is *their* program and *their* company."

A week or so later, Stanley was back in Pawtucket, digging out some data on the modified Expandrium line. Strange, although it had been some years, it seemed as though he had never left . . . without giving it a thought, he stopped by to see Ginny Szekely in the packing department. For eighteen years, Ginny had been doing the same thing—packing Expandrium fittings for shipment. She was so well practiced that she could do the job perfectly without paying the slightest attention. This, of course, left her free to socialize and observe the life of The Company around her.

Today, however, she was breaking in a new packer. "No, not that way. Look, honey, if you hold it that way, well, then you have to twist your arm when you pack this corner, see. This way it's easier."

"But that's the way Claude Gilliam (Methods Engineer) said we had to do it."

"Sure he did, honey. But he's never had to do it eight hours a day like I have. You just pay attention to what I say."

"But what if he comes around and says I should pack the other way?"

"Oh, that's easy. When he's here, you do it his way. Anyway, after a couple weeks you won't see him again. And slow down, you'll wear yourself out. No one's going to expect you to do eighty pieces a week anyway."

"But Mr. Gilliam said ninety."

"Sure he did. Let *him* do it. Look, here's how to pace yourself. It's the way I was taught, and it works. You know the *Battle Hymn of the Republic*? (Ginny hummed a few bars.) Well, just work to that, hum it to yourself, use the way I showed you, and you'll be doing eighty next week."

"But what if they make me do ninety?"

"They can't. Y'know, you start making mistakes when you go that fast. No, eighty is right. I always say, a fair day's work for a fair day's pay."

Player Piano

I won't do it! I *will not* do it—for you, Mr. Marsh, or anyone. Yes, that's final!" Ben almost knocked Stanley down as he bolted from the office. Then, without so much as a hello (Ben probably didn't know Stanley had been away from Pawtucket for over a year), "Can you believe it? *Can* you *believe* it? That dumb bastard (Ted) is going to try to come in here and hold his stopwatch on our guys." Stanley wished Ben would let go of his arm.

"His old man (Shelby III) would've had more sense. At least he knows what the inside of a mill looks like. These guys will crucify him—and *me* in the process."

Then, suddenly, "Say, how'ya doing, Stanley? Nice to see you back." And with that he was off down the hall.

Ben wasn't the only once concerned. As he talked to his old friends down on the mill floor, Stanley found that word of the new program was out.

"Seems like they don't trust us," Jimmie Szekely was saying. "But you know, we've always given The Company a fair shake. And for his part, Ben's been fair with us. We don't need nobody coming in here to hold a stopwatch on us. Look, you know, I've been working on this line for—oh hell—ten, twelve years. Well, I'd have to be pretty dumb not to know how to do the job wouldn't I?"

Ted's very thought, mused Stanley.

Jimmie continued, "Ben leaves things on the line pretty much up to us. Hey, here, see this piece. That's scrap. But look . . ." Jimmie went on to show Stanley a way he'd worked out to salvage those hundred-dollar Expandrium castings. "Takes a little longer, but you gotta figure The Company comes out ahead.

"Lemme tell you what we do if those pinheads come in here with the stopwatch." Jimmie opened the fusebox and yanked out a wire. The line stopped.

"Y'see, somehow, I don't know why, when we run these type A castings, that overloads the line and the breaker goes out. First time it happened I got the mill engineer over here and he don't know what to do, so I just jump the breaker. You're not supposed to, but this line will take it." And with a chuckle, "Uh, whatya think I'm going to do when the watchbird's watching me? You bet, down time. A free coffee break."

"But Jimmie," Stanley asked, "isn't that going to make it more difficult for you to make your quota?"

"Yeah, I know what you mean. That worried me too." Then, looking sideways at Stanley and pointing upstairs, "Say, you're not with them on this, are you?"

"C'mon, Jimmie, you know me better than that. I don't even know any of those time study guys."

"Well, I thought so but . . . Anyway, Joe over there came here from Another Company, and he says there's all kinds of ways to beat the system. Like if the line goes down from overload here. I can't help that, can I? So they, what'd he call it—they, uh, yeah, they 'adjust your base.' He says that means you still can get to 100 percent even when you're making less. Then there's scrap. You get your base adjusted if you got bad stock to work with. You get time to replace tools that burn out." And with a grin, "Y'know, if you try to run the line too fast, they just seem to burn out left and right."

They didn't, of course, thought Stanley. But setting those tools was an art known better to no one than Jimmie Szekely. And Jimmie never told, and never would tell, the Industrial Engineers what he knew about that line. Every now and then they would try out something new on the line. Usually, it didn't work—but Jimmie dutifully did what he was told, no more, no less. For their part, the IEs didn't care much about that line anyway. They got what they wanted from it, and it wasn't a very interesting process, so . . .

For his part, Jimmie had a firm idea of what was fair for The Company and what was fair for Jimmie; you might say it was his own unwritten contract with The Company.

"Uh, Jimmie, now don't get me wrong, but what if these stop-watch guys really do have a better way of running the line? Wouldn't you be better off?"

Once again, Jimmie gave Stanley a suspicious look. "How? They going to pay me more? They going to give me time off? Look, you know what really bugs me about this? It's these guys out there checkin' up on me. Makes it seem that I'm not doing my job, that you can't trust me. Fact is, I do more for them than they think. I don't have to save those pieces from scrap. But I figured out how to do that and, well, it puts some interest in the job and saves them money too. But they don't care about that. They just want to make sure you do it their way."

Later that day Stanley thought back to his talk with Jimmie. Was Jimmie right? Yes and no. It all depended on whose point of view you took. For Jimmie, it seemed to be a matter of pride and a struggle to keep from being turned into another machine. And from the engineer's point of view, it was a question of return on investment. Jimmie Szekely was being paid to run the line as effectively as possible. So if they came up with a better way, what was the problem?

The more Stanley thought about it, the less certain he was of his conclusion. But one point did seem clear: it was a mistake to idealize the motives of either Jimmie *or* The Company. And with that conclusion, Stanley decided to drop the whole matter.

But Ben Franklyn did not have such a direct solution open to him. Ben understood well the trouble that was brewing; that was one advantage of having come from the ranks. Any system that people can devise, people can beat. And here, Jimmie Szekely and the rest of the "lower participants" on the mill floor had the upper hand.

They understood Ted's slogan—"Work Smarter, not Harder"— far better than Ted. Hell, they invented it! Ben knew that if it came to a showdown, the mill hands would win, not the engineers. Oh, the staff guys would show numbers telling you that percentage of quota (adjusted) had gone form 70 to 80 to 90 plus. But what those numbers wouldn't reflect would be the real gains or losses in productivity that resulted and the strain (unadjusted) in the relationship between Ben and his mill hands.

So anyone within hearing distance (say a block or two) of the Pawtucket Plant Manager's office can tell you Ben's decision.

"I told you last week and I'm telling you again for the last time; *no*, I will *not* do it! Yes, I *am* prepared to tell Mr. Marsh that personally. Yes, you *will* have to fire me first!" And anyone who knew Ben knew as well that he meant it.

16

Back To The Drawing Board

There was a time when Kerry Drake was the Chief of Airframe Design, when The Company had a heavier investment in aircraft than it does now. Ted Shelby was on his staff, and one day Ted came in and exploded. "How does it happen? Every damned time we build a prototype structure, it comes out overweight! And this time it's serious! Would you believe that we are 15 tons overweight on this one?"

"Sure," said Kerry, "You guys in stress analysis see only part of the picture; you're only specialists, all wrapped up in your equations."

At this point Stanley came in. Ted turned to him and said, "Stanley, you worked on this latest model. It's 15 tons overweight. How did it happen?"

Stanley thought for a moment. "I don't really know," he said. "It seems as though those guys in design don't really care about the weight problem. But here, let me give you an example. I had seen a paper on some new techniques of stress analysis, and it had something on a new process for forming members that would have twice the strength of members formed the old way. So I go to the guy in charge of B Section—one of those old timers who's been here forever—and I say to him, 'How about trying this new technique?' He looks through the paper for a second or two, then looks me right in the eye and says, 'Can you guarantee it will work?'

"So I tell him, sure—here are the calculations. Look on page 1045—but I can tell he doesn't understand the first thing about it. So he says, 'I don't mean all those numbers. I mean, will it work when it's up there?' Well, Ted, you know what that section chief is turning out in there. It's the same as MOD 1, but about twice as big. So I say to the guy, 'Look, that component you're turning out there is about twice the allowable weight limit.' So he says, 'Well, what's five pounds? And I *know* this one will work.'

"So I tell him that the one I'm showing him will work too, and you know what he asks me? He wants to know if I would guarantee the structural analysis of the whole section if we use the new process! So I say, 'Wait a minute. That's not my job, it's yours. This design meets your specifications just fine, and beyond that it's not my responsibility.'"

"That's right!" Ted broke in. "Our job is to provide better components, not to guarantee his work! But you know they'll never use your new design anyhow. They don't have the technical know-how to evaluate your design, and they're afraid to try anything new. Kerry, you ought to get some new blood in that section."

Kerry held up his hands. "I've tried, I've tried. But putting airframes together is a pretty routine thing once you've done a few. Important but boring. And all the bright kids want to get into something where they can try all that stuff they learned in Aero E 467. My people can't keep up with them technically."

All true, yet the *real* problem here is not that the people in Kerry's group are getting technically senile. What we have, in fact, is a good example of *diffused responsibility*. Obviously, the object here is to make sure the part works. If it works, but is a little overweight, that isn't nearly the disaster for the airframe designer that would occur if the part fails. And because he already knows that parts made the old way work, he also knows that there is no real danger of failure if he keeps on doing it the old way.

But more to the point, if there is some sort of part failure, it can be traced directly back to the specific source—the designer. And what's five pounds? Not much in itself, although when you multiply it by 100 section chiefs and a couple dozen different parts each, you get an airframe design that is 15 tons overweight.

However, *that* malfeasance cannot be pinned on any individual. The responsibility for it is diffused over hundreds of people. Who's going to lose his job over 5 or 10 excess pounds?

* * *

Now let's take a look at a different case. Kerry was the chief of the reliability section, and Drew Bolt was the Project Director for the design and development of a new desktop computer. As project director, Drew made the decisions on the allocation of funding. Kerry wanted some money for designing a high level of product reliability into the new computer, but he was never able to get it. Drew simply wouldn't give him what he needed.

This seems to be irresponsible on Drew's part. After all, a designer should certainly want to ensure that his product is going to work for a good long time once it is in the field, and it is crucially important to The Company, especially in "today's business climate." Yes, in some ways it *is* irresponsible, but we also have to look at the situation from Drew's point of view.

In order to get Company funds allocated to a product development project, Drew, the project head usually has to promise a little more than he can deliver in terms of performance (what the product will do) and scheduling (how long it will take to develop a product that will do that). This is because others competing for project funds are also engaged in limited lying about their proposed projects. Inevitably, Drew comes down to the wire behind on those promises. If he is going to come out with his skin intact, he will have to take time and money from somewhere else to meet his commitments.

Scheduling can be checked against a calendar; if the product doesn't meet the performance specifications, punishment is swift and sure. But problems associated with reliability won't show up until the product has been out in the field for a year or so—and the product won't even hit the field until it's gone from design through manufacturing to production and distribution.

Oh, you say, but isn't a reliability test part of the final development phase . . . part of the Beta test? Well, yes it is, but somehow the results of those tests always seem inconclusive, with problems that will more or less take care of themselves "when we go into full-scale production."

And this is why Kerry Drake's product reliability section can never get support to do the job that was promised. Drew takes the time and money allocated to reliability engineering from his budget and uses it in a crash effort to meet his promises on schedule and performance. And this invariably happens, despite top-management policy statements and associated marketing campaigns emphasizing ideas like "Our product is so reliable we haven't yet found out how reliable it is."

What Drew Bolt knows is this: if his design doesn't meet the immediate specifications, he's had it, right here and right now. But in two or three years, even if there is a problem, he might have been promoted, gone to a different company, or otherwise managed to distance himself from the problem. And after that length of time, he can probably "selectively forget" how the problem developed. Or maybe they'll be so busy trying to solve the problem that they won't have time to look back into its history. More likely yet, it will be seen as just another operating problem.

This is an example of *deferred responsibility*. You put off facing the music as much as possible, under the assumption that you may never have to face it. This is a reasonably good assumption. In a large organization, the situation is so fluid that there is a good chance that everyone will be elsewhere by the time it is discovered. And problems, as often as not, are associated with the job, not with whomever was occupying it at some time in the past.

BOX 4

SAGA OF THE IBM PC—PART I

The year was 1980 when a group of twelve IBM systems engineers and engineering executives convinced the IBM Corporate Management Committee (CMC) that "Big Blue" ought to take a shot at developing its own personal computer. The CMC gave the group two weeks to develop a proposal for its approval, and that is how the fabulously successful IBM PC was born. When the time came to pick someone to lead the project, one of the twelve, Philip D. Estridge, volunteered and was given the position.

Don Estridge, a former engineer who has been described as something of a maverick in the IBM scheme of things, began doing the undoable. His fourteen-employee new Entry Systems Division (ESD) developed a PC prototype within three months and had a machine on the market in less than a year. Most of this was accomplished by working outside the usual IBM rules, such as by purchasing off-the-shelf components and assemblies from outside vendors. However, because IBM top corporate management saw the PC as a minor business venture at best, the Entry Systems group received scant management "attention" (read meddling).

And no one was more surprised than corporate management when in only four years the fourteen-person division had grown to almost ten thousand and accounted for $4.5 billion in new business. In fact, when IBM introduced its new AT machine in November, 1984, Esther Dyson, a respected industry analyst, felt that IBM had outdistanced the market and predicted that few clones of the AT would appear. Others hinted that this development might necessitate reopening the closed antitrust case against IBM.

But in 1985 clouds began gathering on the horizon. The ill fated PC jr., a machine with designed-in limitations and an incompetent keyboard, was clearly a flop and evidently a strategic error. And that new AT, IBM's much in demand top-of-the-line machine, was bogged down in production troubles.

IBM's sole source for hard disk drives was unable to meet its delivery commitments, and quality problems generally plagued the machine.

The PC business now very much had the attention of the IBM corporate management committee. (See Part II, p. 178.)

Rite of Passage

Looking back at it now, several factors had conspired to discomfort Stanley's first few days with The Company. For one thing, starting off in Ben Franklyn's section meant that his office was stuck back in the farthest reaches of the plant (a single building that sprawled over several blocks). For another thing, his parking lot was there too. This would have been convenient, except that Security Regulations required all employees to leave by the front door. Finally, Stanley had arrived in November, the start of the rainy season (which coincided with Stanley's first day on the job).

Stanley's routine was: arrive in the morning, park, walk all the way around the building in the rain, go in the front door, and walk all the way back through the plant to his office, which was about 50 feet from where his car was parked. At the end of the day, walk all the way to the front of the plant, walk all the way around the building (raining harder, usually) to his car, which was about 50 feet from his office.

After his third or fourth good soaking, Stanley noticed a door at the back of the building between his office and his car. It was a loading gate, attended by a Security Guard, who made sure that all employees left by the front door, at least the ones who tried to leave by his station.

But one day, Stanley could have sworn he saw one of his fellow workers coming in through that back door. So that night, just before quitting time, he stood by to confirm his suspicions. Sure enough, lots of people were going out that gate, and the guard was happy to let them do so.

Well, that's all right, thought Stanley as he hurried back to his office to get his briefcase. He strode to the door, happy to avoid the rain.

"Your name, please?" demanded the guard. Stanley recited his name. "Sorry, sir, you can't use this door." So saying, the guard stepped aside, nodding good-day as the guy from the office next to the candy machine went out through the door.

"But why not?" asked Stanley. "These other people are using it."

"Yeah, they're on the list."

"List?"

"Mr. Franklyn's list," said the guard. "He's got this list of people it's okay for to go through here."

"Oh, okay," said Stanley. "No problem. I'll get on the list and be back tomorrow."

So Stanley took his long walk, consoled by the thought that it was the last time. Only it wasn't. By now Stanley knew enough not to go directly to Ben Franklyn, but went instead to Bonnie, to find out about the list. He had reasoned correctly that Bonnie, being a secretary, would know everything about the office that was worth knowing. She told him: "Oh yes, Mr. Franklyn's list. Listen, nobody's supposed to use that door, not really, but Mr. Franklyn works it out with the guards so that some of his people—he has this list of them—can go through there."

"Well, how do I get on the list?" Stanley was becoming irritated. Having picked up a sore throat, he wanted to avoid pneumonia or influenza or whatever might result from a 4-block walk (2 coming and 2 going) in the rain every day.

"I'm afraid you don't, Stanley," said Bonnie. "When it's all right for people to go through that door, well . . . Mr. Franklyn just tells them, that's all. When it's okay, he'll tell you."

Thoughts that could never be uttered in front of Bonnie about Franklyn and the door and the list and Security Regulations race through Stanley's head. But he thinks them very loudly and for a long time, because he's really miffed. It's the most childish, the most bureaucratic, the most inconvenient, the most unfair, the most senseless situation he has ever encountered in his life, and who the hell does Franklyn think he is, and if there was ever a dumb regulation, and The Company, etc., etc., etc.

But, for the next several months, he takes the long walk twice a day (four times, if he goes out to lunch), and during those months he learns more about Ben Franklyn. Franklyn, a self-made man, has worked his way up through the ranks and is old-fashioned in a number of ways. His office is up a stairway in the loft of the mill. From strategically placed windows he can look down over his area like a feudal lord surveying his fief. Actually, he is a good guy to work for, but in that part of the plant, the world is divided in two— his people and other people. His people use that back door, other people don't.

Then, one morning, Bonnie came over and said, "Stanley, Mr. Franklyn wants to see you. I think it's time for your semiannual review."

This is just fine with Stanley. He is sure that he has been doing his work well. He's been getting along with everybody, and it was only last week that he drove in the winning run in the softball game with the traffic department. He strides up the metal stairway to Franklyn's office, only a little apprehensive. He thinks he deserves a raise, but he knows that Ben thinks of The Company's money as his own and doesn't like to part with it.

"Come on in. Have a seat," said Ben. "You know, every time we hire one of you high-priced college guys . . . I wonder if they're really worth it. But you're okay, you do good work, and you know how to get along with other folks. My mill guys say you're a pretty good centerfielder.

"You'll be getting a raise; next month you'll be making $2250."

Stanley is extremely grateful; Ben Franklyn has a way of making people grateful for things not only due, but overdue. They talk a little more, and then Stanley gets up to go.

"Oh yeah," says Ben, almost as an afterthought, "I've put your name on the list. Just tell the guard who you are."

Stanley hesitated a moment and thought . . . list? *The* list? The loading gate list? No, he hadn't forgotten. And wasn't it just like Ben to assume that everyone knew about the list, and the guard, though no one ever talked about it?

"Yes, sir," said Stanley, beaming. He bounced down the stairs back to his office, and in spite of himself spent the rest of the day looking forward to going home through the back door. At quitting time he strode to the door, gave his name in a confident tone, and was standing in the parking lot in a second. The rainy season was over, and the sun shone warmly down on Stanley as he walked the 25 feet to his car. All the way home he thought what a good day it had been.

Now, Stanley isn't the kind of person who likes to play The Company's game, and he's likely to tell anyone where to get off if they play "Mickey Mouse" with him. To this day, he still can't figure out why he didn't tell Franklyn to take the loading gate and shove it, that it was none of Franklyn's damn business who went where. Because, really, it wasn't.

But Stanley still remembers that his feelings that day had been quite the opposite—not irritated, or even indifferent, but genuinely pleased and grateful. That day he was part of the mill management. That day he knew he was one of Ben Franklyn's boys.

When you worked for Ben Franklyn, you did more than work; you became part of his family. Franklyn will never trust "the new approach." Instead, he finds ways of extending his own authority into areas not covered by the formal rules. Through his control of favors and sanctions, he maintains the personal loyalty of His People and broadens the range of his influence.

Franklyn, in handling his territory, is not too different from the medieval church. It granted indulgences to parishioners, who, in accepting the benefit, implicitly recognized the right of the church to bestow it. They thus bound themselves even more completely into the system.

18 Sunrise Service

I t was a trying time for everybody the year The Company built its Extruded Expandrium plant in Pocatello. The business office, the planning office, the architects, and Top Management finally got everything ready, and construction was begun. Ben Franklyn was to be Plant Construction Superintendent, and Ted Shelby and Stanley were his staff. Their task was to coordinate the efforts of the contractors, the mechanical engineers, the electrical engineers, and the operations people.

They soon found this was not easy, and about a month after the ground was broken, Ben called a staff meeting. "I don't like the way this project is going," he told Ted and Stanley.

"That's my take too, Ben," said Ted. "As I see it, there's a problem in getting everybody together on what's to be done."

"Yeah," added Stanley, "I can tell you *exactly* what's going on. One of the electrical engineers comes and says that his group needs another generator installed. So you go to the mechanical engineers to see about the structure to house it. They're busy working on the ventilating system, and anyhow, they can't do a thing about the generator structure until the contractor hires some ironworkers. So you go to the contractor. He's busy on the main building, and anyhow, he can't submit any plans until the operations people okay the specifications for the generator installation. So you go to the operations people. They're busy making modifications in the materials flow charts, and anyhow, they can't pass on the specifications until the electrical engineers explain to them why they want the extra generator in the first place. All those people have their own priorities and their own schedules, and none of them worries very much about the others."

"I know all that," growled Ben. "The question is, how do we fix it?"

"I'd say we all need to get together and talk it over. We need open communication," Ted suggested. Ted likes to have meetings.

"Meetings!" says Ben. "We've wasted enough goddamned time already!" Ben doesn't like to have meetings. But after a minute's thought, ". . . you know, Shelby, maybe that's not such a bad idea . . . no, not such a bad idea *at all*. Get together and get our signals straight . . . Yeah, each morning before work."

"But work starts at 7:30," says Stanley.

"Well, an hour should be enough," says Ben. "We'll start at 6:30." And almost absentmindedly, "Yeah, 6:30 ought to do it all right."

"Now just a minute, Ben," says Ted, who doesn't like meetings *that* much, "if we can't get those people together now, we certainly can't get them together when we're all half asleep."

"Never you mind," says Ben. "I know what I'm doing."

Ben schedules a series of meetings every morning at 6:30 A.M. for the supervisors and engineers from his various groups, and he notifies them that they are expected to be there. For two straight weeks they are there, and they are *not* happy. Still, they do manage to solve some of their problems.

The first meeting of the third week, Ben begins by saying, "I gotta tell you that I am real happy with the progress we've been making. In fact, if things go OK today, I don't know that we really need to meet tomorrow morning."

Things go just great that day, and Ben skips a day on the meeting. The next meeting ends with Ben saying, "It seems to me that we've got the next couple of days under control, so wha'dysay we skip the meeting until next week. You've all got your marching orders, so let's see how things go, and maybe we'll have a meeting next Monday morning."

As it turned out, everything kept going so smoothly, and next Monday's meeting was the last "sunrise service" that anybody had to attend for the duration of the project.

Why did such a tactic work? Could Ben Franklyn do anything but generate hatred by requiring his people to attend a meeting at 6:30 in the morning? Well, in the first place, he demonstrated that he meant business by showing up himself at all those meetings. In the second place, he made it quite apparent that all they had to do to quit having those meetings was to get together and coordinate their efforts.

The principle Ben used here we have termed *negative reinforcement*, that is, the removal of an aversive situation contingent upon the production of the desired behavior. Oh, Ben wouldn't have understood these words, that's psychologist's language. But he sure did understand the application of the principle.

Made To Measure

19

Ted Shelby, the Staff Director of Sales Management Development, is delivering the wrap-up pitch to new members of the sales staff group at corporate headquarters. Twenty bright, young trainees sat attentively.

"Let me say once again that this is your big chance," Ted began. "Each one of you has been sent here to sales division headquarters by your branch manager to learn how the game is played. Each one of you has been selected for your outstanding record. Each one of you in this room is a potential division manager. This is your opportunity to see the planning side of this business, and you've got to make the most of it."

Twenty heads nodded in unison. A pleased murmur filled the room. Ted continued: "As you know, the name of the game we're in is *competition*. We're the best, and that is what we're going to stay. If you've got no stomach for infighting, you don't belong in this league."

Twenty competitors nodded yes.

"It's not just a matter of doing the same outstanding job we've been doing. It's not enough to have a crisp and hard-hitting approach anymore. There are new management tools being developed to increase effectiveness and measurement, gentlemen and ladies— *measurement of results* is the name of the game now. It's not enough to do our best. We've got to know how good our best is."

With that profundity Ted wrapped up the final session. Stanley, whose assignment as Ted's assistant required that he sit in with the group and take notes, had scribbled tersely on his note pad, "measurement important." Another of Stanley's duties was to check on the progress of people who had received the ministrations of Ted's developmental programs (again, measurement). Consequently, following this session, Stanley was off to the Seattle sales office to interview Willa Diehl, now the Assistant Sales Manager under Kerry Drake.

Kerry was not happy on the occasion of that visit. (Not happy? Perhaps that is an understatement.)

"You," the word drilled straight through Stanley's chest, "and the rest of you at division, and *especially* that damn fool Shelby, are responsible for *this*!" Kerry now waved an 8½ by 11 floppy-covered notebook at Stanley's face.

"See this? It's my score card. Count 'em; 44 different monthly reports. Yesterday the division manager called me and said that I was two months behind in my 'Subordinate Readiness' report. *Subordinate readiness?* For Chrissakes, I've got so damn many reports to keep track of that I don't even know who all my subordinates are, let alone how 'ready' any of them is!" Stanley recoiled from Kerry's wrath.

"Let me tell you something. Now I've got forty-four of these (Kerry contemptuously shook the sheaf of reports in his hand), but just three years ago I only had four. That's how many—four! Net, percent of quota, deliveries, and accounts receivable. That's all I had then, and that's all we need now!

"I used to know where my business was. I even had time to get out there and do a little selling myself. But now it seems like almost every month I get another one of *these*. Here! This is the latest—Subordinate Readiness with Intermediate Milestones Program. How can I know where I stand on my Subordinate Readiness Program when I'm not even sure from month to month what it is? Now I've got to add someone to take care of it. I'll tell you one thing, I'd sure like to meet the damn fool who thought up this last wrinkle." You already have, Stanley thought. For that program was the brainchild of Will Diehl, as everyone called her.

Oddly enough, it turned out that Willa was just as concerned as Kerry. After assuring Stanley that things were going rather well for her and, in turn, getting Stanley's assurance that the author of the new program would remain anonymous, Will Diehl held forth at some length on the problem.

"Kerry's right, you know. But when I worked up the program it never occurred to me what I was doing until I got out here on the receiving end. Look at what you're doing at headquarters, even Ted. It all starts with Ted, you know. He wants some recognition just like the rest of us; he wants to get ahead too. So he points to something that I guess is necessary. He says that there is a lot of staff work that has to be done, so why not combine it with the management development function so that our sales people will get to see the thing from the headquarters perspective. Why not? So what we do is take the best salespeople from the field, bring them to headquarters, and get them involved in sales staff work.

"Now I don't know if you understand what that's like, Stanley, but let me tell you. In the field, you're in the thick of the action, doing what really counts; it's exciting. Then, just like that, you're in with a bunch of staff zombies from headquarters, up to your neck in paper and telephones. Nothing's ever finished, and it seems like nothing is ever accomplished either. One day is like the next. No offense, but Good Lord—would anyone be there if we could possibly avoid it? So finally, you've got one question: How the hell do I get out of here?!" Just the mention of it seemed to bring a note of anxiety into Willa's voice.

"The question is—what it really boils down to is—what do I have to do to get someone to say, okay, she's ready for the next assignment? I'll tell you what you do. You do what Ted and a bunch of other guys did. You dream up a program, get to talk to some of top management in the process, and pretty soon when the next chance comes up—well, they all know you and it's your turn."

Yes, thought Stanley, and along with Willa Diehl came the inevitable program. For she found out pretty quickly that the best way to do it was to develop a crisp, new, hard-hitting program to be responsive to The Company's new needs in the "changing business environment." And you needed to develop measures to go along with it . . . "it's not enough to do our best. We have to know how good our best is." Hence, Subordinate Readiness with Intermediate Milestones Program—SRIMP.

The point I am trying to make here is that the result of this arrangement is inevitable. Under the conditions I have described, programs designed to improve sales management effectiveness and accountability have just the opposite effect. Kerry will get his reports filled out one way or another—in this case, by the person who developed them. But the facts will be mostly "guesstimates" with an occasional sprinkling of lies. Consequently, it becomes more difficult than ever to find out how someone is really doing.

But why inevitable, you ask? Surely there are other ways of gaining attention. Yes, of course, that is true. And it is also true that not everyone uses the route of program development. But keep in mind that these are young people on the move. An extra year seems like a lifetime. Remember, too, that they are all sales people, and good ones. So what could be more natural than to sell—to sell a program and yourself with it. If modern management tools are the hot product today, well, that's what we're selling, isn't it? Finally, it is not until you get back into the field as Assistant Manager that you get to see the overall impact of the thing. After all, yours was just one little program, wasn't it?

And so this is where Kerry Drake is found, laboring under the burden of SRIMP and its near and distant relatives . . . a whole list of programs necessary to fit The Company to the changing business environment, and incidentally, to promote a number of desperate staff misfits away from division headquarters.

Spend It, Burn It

20

It was indeed a strange scene that Stanley happened upon: Ben pounding his fist on the desk and Kerry beside him, roaring with incredulous laughter.

"Uh, excuse me, I thought maybe Dr. Faust was here." But as Stanley turned to leave, Ben suddenly threw a thick triplicate form across his desk to him.

"Here, what the hell do you make of this thing? I'll be damned if I can figure out what's on these people's minds."

Stanley eyed the form for a minute and then, "Looks to me like it's a request for price quotation from The Agency."

"I think we have already figured out that much," put in Kerry. "We want to know what they want."

Stanley read it again. "They want . . . a tape, demolition, high-precision (a plus or minus 0.001 tolerance), stainless steel, nondestructible . . . Right?"

"See," said Kerry with a grin, prodding Ben on the arm. "You can read. That is what they want."

"Yeah, I can see your problem," interjected Stanley. "It beats me what they'd use something like that for."

"Oh, no," returned Kerry, "that's not our problem. I know exactly what they want to use it for, because I used to do the same thing myself with a piece of rope. You see, when I was an army engineer, one of our jobs was to blow up enemy bridges. All you needed was a piece of rope, some dynamite, and the ability to swim. The rope had a series of knots tied along its length, and you'd swim out in the dark, wrap the rope around the piling, and count the knots. For every knot you'd use a stick of dynamite. And that's what this tape they're talking about is supposed to do. The job of that piece of rope. But Jesus Christ—stainless steel, etched markings fully calibrated to hundredths of an inch—it'll cost them an arm and a leg and they won't even be able to use it at night. What's more, it says they want a thousand *prototypes* for field trial!"

"Wait a second." The light of revelation was shining in Stanley's eyes. "That RPQ is from The Agency, and this is the end of the fiscal year."

"What the hell are you talking about?" Ben had had his fill of nonsense for the afternoon. "I'm trying to find out about this idiotic request for price quotation, not about the time of year."

"All I mean is, well, maybe you're looking at it the wrong way. See, we used to do this kind of thing all the time when I was at The Agency. They had me working in Purchasing. Everybody called it 'spring madness,' because that was when it happened. The main thing was to get rid of it any way you could. I'm surprised that people didn't just put it in a trunk and sink it in the Potomac. That would have been a lot cheaper and easier than what we ended up doing. But I guess you really have to have a receipt to show what you did with it . . ."

"Hold on," Ben interrupted. "What's this 'it' you're talking about? You mean . . ."

"Money," Stanley completed the sentence.

"But it just doesn't make sense." Ben was now more puzzled than annoyed. "You say these people are *trying* to spend a lot of money on something they don't need? And they want to do it *now*, and they wouldn't want me to show them how to get the same job done for one-tenth the cost?"

"Oh, I don't think they'd care," answered Stanley, "but you wouldn't get their order. They'd have Another Company do the work. But why do you say it doesn't make sense?"

"But that's no goddamned way to run a business," Ben exploded. "What possible sense could it make to throw money away?"

Faust, who had arrived a minute earlier, saw that Stanley was becoming intimidated and came to the rescue. "Perhaps I can supply a little, ah—perspective, Ben. We at The University work under a very similar system, though the amounts are far smaller. What you must understand, Ben, is that we, and they, are *not* running a business. We are, shall we say, providing a service. But just as you do, we work on a yearly budget. And so does The Agency. Now if it's an important agency—and certainly The Agency is—the justification of this budget will be laced with statements about how very important, how crucial it is for The Agency to have these funds. Now let us suppose that at the end of the year—June 30th—The Agency has not spent the funds so urgently needed for such important work. What happens when they submit the next budget, once again supported by the same arguments justifying the need for that much money?"

Stanley did not answer, for this was obviously one occasion when Faust's Socratic exercise was meant for another. Kerry, for whom the whole thing had been a joke from the beginning, was chuckling at the new revelations. So it was left for Ben to answer. "I can see what happens all right, even though I don't think it makes any sense. The head of The Agency is in trouble. Someone's going to say 'you must not be doing your job if you didn't spend all your money.' Or they might even say, 'looks to me like you never needed that money in the first place. Now the boys at Another Agency ran out last year, so . . .'"

"Precisely," Dr. Faust was pleased that the lesson had taken so well. "So you see that running The Agency is quite *unlike* running a business. One cannot grow unless one overspends. It is most necessary to show that one needs more money each ensuing year, for there is no profit and loss statement to show how well one is doing his job."

With that, Kerry, shaking his head and still smiling, turned to Ben, "Let's see that RPQ again . . . Hmmm, stainless, high-precision, nondestructible, M1-A1 . . . all righty." And then, putting his arm around Ben's shoulder, "Ben, know something? They've come to the right outfit."

BOX 5

THE 1980S: SOMEBODY'S GOT TO SPEND CAP'S MONEY

One day in January of 1985 a senator from Delaware learned that the Pentagon was paying $640 apiece for fifty-four "toilet cover assemblies" for use in aircraft. The senator learned of this through a disgruntled small manufacturer who was having difficulty gaining entry to the bidding process.

The contractor, Lockheed-California, after being questioned about the cost, performed a company review and determined that the actual unit price should have been 550 some dollars rather than 640. They offered to refund the difference.

On further inquiry from the senator, who presumably was still not satisfied, Lockheed offered a "policy price" of $200, with a refund of the remainder.

After still further dickering, Lockheed, in order to terminate the matter, settled on what it termed a "token price" of $100 each for the seats. Still, even at the token price of $100, many small manufacturers would more than likely be happy to produce as many of the plastic toilet seats as the Pentagon wanted.

Of themselves, the seats are unimportant, but they're symptomatic of problems in the military procurement system as a whole. At least part of the problem has been the enormous increase in the Pentagon budget for weapons procurement during the early decade of the 1980s. One result of this is that, far from being discouraged, high costs are rewarded. Obviously, the contractor benefits, but bureaucrats who raise additional money from Congress are rewarded as well. Critics assert that the basic problem is that there simply is too much money available.

The net result is that the Pentagon is hard pressed to allocate appropriate funds to programs and manage the programs efficiently.

Still, there's more to the story than this. There is evidence to suggest that the Pentagon indeed encourages contractors to overspend, and discourages those who reveal it.

A Pentagon civil servant who testified on several occasions before Congress that the Pentagon consistently underestimated the final cost of weapons systems ran into trouble with his superiors. Defense Secretary Weinberger and an assistant who heads the Program Analysis office disputed the civil servant's testimony. But apparently they did more than that. For years the employee had been given job ratings of "outstanding," the top civil service rating. Yet after his testimony, he was reduced first to "exceptional," and then to "fully satisfactory." The remaining rating would be "minimally satisfactory," a rating that could lead to dismissal. While political appointees are not allowed to interfere in the rating process, the employee had been told by his immediate superior that the agency head (like Weinberger, a political appointee) initially had insisted on the terminal rating of minimally satisfactory.

Finally, the employee had been reassigned from work on military budget matters and may no longer have access to such data.

In 1982 a Pentagon audit agency manager reported to his superiors that a government contractor in Florida was charging excessive amounts for travel and entertainment and was paying excessive salaries. He called for a nationwide investigation.

The result? Not only did top officials in the Pentagon's audit agency ignore the complaints, they gave the agency manager a reduced performance rating, and threatened him with a transfer. The employee claims he was pressured into retiring in 1983.

However, in this case the employee was ultimately vindicated by the Merit System Protection Board who ordered the firing of the head of the Pentagon's auditing agency for harassing the manager. However, while pleased to have been vindicated, the former manager noted that the waste and abuse continue, and that the Pentagon has not changed its approach to procurement.

Source: *New York Times*, February 6, 1985, p. E-15; *New York Times*, January 27, 1985, p. 1-F; *New York Times*, August 20, 1984, p. B-12; *Wall Street Journal*, June 14, 1985, p. 33.

Section Four

To Be Or Not To Be

Managerial Decision Making and Motivation

Shakespeare's tale of the Prince of Denmark exemplifies the plight of the indecisive decision maker. In sure knowledge that his father's brother has slain his father and married his mother, and charged by his father's ghost to revenge his death, Hamlet cannot act decisively. And in his indecision, he makes an awful mess of things.

Look, he's got complete information. He knows all the decision alternatives, and he knows the payoffs, so to speak. In short, this is a decision under conditions of certainty, a pushover. But his basic problem seems to be that he keeps wondering if he can't do just a bit better. In IBM, we used to call that "overthinking the situation."

Here he is, alone with his villainous uncle. He's got his sword, and his would-be victim is kneeling, back turned. Now Hamlet! Do it!

Then Hamlet starts thinking again. Why, this fellow is praying. I would actually be doing him a favor by dispatching him in the moment of cleansing his soul. No, better to wait. Catch him in a more damning circumstances—drunk, or best, in the "incestuous pleasure of his bed."

The upshot of all this indecision is that Hamlet goes on in short order to kill his beloved's father accidentally. He becomes directly or indirectly responsible for the expiration of just about everyone at court, including himself. Nice going, H!

Hamlet's folly illustrates a paramount rule of crisp decision making. Once you know all you're going to know, act. By the way, the decision to do nothing at all is a legitimate decision as well. Some problems take care of themselves, and some are too risky to handle. Notice that even Hamlet considered this alternative . . . "to be or not to be." The main thing is to avoid confusing a decision not to act with not being able to decide to act.

We'll be considering two main types of decision-making contexts. In the first, we will play a game with fate, with those uncontrollable events. "Outrageous fortune" as the melancholy prince called it. In the second situation, we will play a game against an adversary. To analyze these situations, some additional terms must be defined. The *payoff* is a one-shot outcome, the result of the pairing of an event with a decision alternative. An *Expected Value* (EV) is a long-run concept. EV involves consideration of the probabilities of the uncontrollable events together with the payoff from the event/decision pairing. The EV is the payoff of this pairing weighted by the probability of the event. Even though the potential payoff may be very large, the EV is small if the probability of the event is small. The EV of a given decision alternative is the sum of the EV's overall possible events when paired with that particular decision alternative. EV is a long-run idea because it is the value of the average payoff you can expect if a situation were repeated over and over.

Never mind if the details escape you. Just try to keep in mind the distinction between the single short-term payoff and the long-run idea of EV.

But what if the probabilities are not known? Then there are several other decision rules to guide the managerial decision maker: the minimax, the choice of the alternative that minimizes maximum possible loss; the maximax, the alternative that maximizes maximum gain; the minimax regret, the choice that minimizes maximum "regret"; and so on. From my own experience I would have to say that the minimax rule is the most widely employed. It is the strategy that is used universally in the peacetime army, civil service, and by petty functionaries throughout the world. The minimax is immortalized in the slogan, "You can't do anything wrong if you don't do anything," or, if you prefer, "going by the book."

The theory of managerial decision making is framed in terms of payoff to the *organization.* But there is another set of payoffs that comes into play, payoffs to the *individual,* and these don't necessarily agree with each other. To illustrate, I'll use a decision situation I'll call "uncertain risk." It means the decision maker has some idea of the probabilities, but not enough knowledge to put much confidence in the expected values. To simplify, say that Ted is looking at alternatives A, B, and C. Alternative A is essentially "do nothing," let it pass. Alternatives B and C call for action, and their overall EV's are superior to A's. Only one hitch—B and C each contain at least one instance of a low-probability, but highly negative payoff. From The Company's point of view, it has been here before and will be here again. It is best off with the alternative with maximum EV. But Ted is in a different position. He and many other managerial decision makers want to look carefully at those payoffs. Just suppose that low-probability disaster *does* occur. In that case, it's a full-blown disaster, low probability or not. Or what if that disaster is more probable than he thought? This is why the motivation for Ted's decision and many other managerial decisions is based on personal payoffs. Remember the minimax! Choose A.

Now let's look at the second situation referred to earlier, the managerial game. It is formally called *game theory,* and it pits managerial protagonists against one another in the corporate arena. These corporate games come in two basic varieties: *zero sum* and *nonzero sum.* The term zero sum is used to indicate that what one player wins the other loses. The sum of A's winnings equal B's losses, hence the sum is zero. A two-person poker game or a debate are examples. However, in this discussion, I will call it zero sum if, when one wins, the other must lose.

The term nonzero sum is applied to games in which both players may win or lose. To illustrate, let me use an example that appeared in *Scientific American* some years ago. It uses the characters in Puccini's opera *Tosca* to make the point.[3] The venal Baron Scarpia (also Rome's Chief of Police) covets the womanly charms of Floria Tosca. Recognizing his limited appeal, and being a straightforward sort of scoundrel, Scarpia announces to Tosca that he has her lover, Cavaradossi, in jail and will have him shot unless Tosca agrees to entertain Scarpia that night. Scarpia will order blanks placed in the firing squad's rifles if Tosca consents.

Tosca is no fool. In the quaint manner of times past, she places some value on her virtue and has availed herself of a stiletto with which to dispatch the Baron to his final reward. Thus, the payoff matrix for each appears as follows. Each can either keep (yes) or fail to keep (no) his part of the bargain.

Tosca's Payoff			**Scarpia's Payoff**		
S T	S yes	S no	S T	S yes	S no
T yes	+5	−10	T yes	+5	+10
T no	+10	−5	T no	−10	−5

What happens, of course, is predictable from the fact that both Scarpia and Tosca are minimaxers. Failing to see that theirs is not a zero sum game, and that a coalition solution would produce positive payoffs for both, Tosca stabs Scarpia as the firing squad (no blanks) is heard in the background. Goodbye, Cavaradossi. The problem is that the coalition solution requires that one trust the other, yet the maximum loss occurs to the trusting player. Because neither Tosca nor Scarpia trust each other (with good cause), the outcome is the unsatisfactory minimax.

How are we to identify favorable and unfavorable decision situations? From time to time you will be aware of a situation that seems to cry out for action, yet no one seems to be stepping forward to seize the opportunity. Watch out; this is the first warning sign. Next, find out what you can about the reputations of the people who usually wind up handling this kind of . . . ah . . . opportunity. None of them highly regarded? Thought of as not having the stuff to handle real responsibility? That aces it. Don't go near this one. You don't see the point? You think this sort of situation should be a good thing, not too difficult to do a better job than has been done?

This is a typical mistake made by amateurs. Most of the people who fail in a management job do so not because they are incompetent, but because the job is impossible. Sooner or later the job will be changed, but don't count on it happening sooner. A far better strategy is to seek a position where the incumbent is generally regarded as a brilliant success (though not too brilliant). Chances are that no one has realized the position is a lead pipe cinch. And if you play it right, they won't find out during *your* tenure, either. So it goes.

Then there is the case of the "heroic decision maker." The folklore of every company contains accounts of heroic decision makers, stalwarts who made crucial decisions under conditions of great uncertainty and were right. And they did this time and time again.

Yes, such people exist, but to accept them literally is one of the most persistent human delusions. Admiring such heroic decision makers makes about as much sense as admiring the heroic pennies that come up heads in each of the twenty tries of the usual introductory probability theory example.[4] No, you wouldn't do that. But people feel they must impute special abilities to The Company's human pennies who have comparable achievement records. The fact is, the chances of having a given decision at least *look* correct are probably better than 50–50. Over the years there have been thousands of decision makers. Inevitably, by chance alone, at least a few will turn out to have been right at every turn! And human decision makers have the added advantage of contriving to make a decision look good after the fact, by working like the devil to make it come out right.

But enough! Now let's apply these lessons to The Company.

Excess Inventory

Thwak!! Stanley's tee shot on the 3rd flew like a bullet from his driver and climbed straight up the fairway—for a bit. Then it wandered right in a lazy, but pronounced arc that even the considerable body english Stanley was applying failed to correct.

Faust and his protegee were engaged in a "business meeting" that afternoon, presumably discussing progress at the Portland construction site. It was an interesting match. Stanley was an adherent of "power golf," or, as Faust more aptly put it, "gorilla golf." Faust, as usual, was an advocate of finesse—drive for show, putt for dough. Stanley, however, preferred to describe the good doctor's game as "power scoring"—on the scorecard, that is.

"Well hit, my friend," Faust observed dryly, "two hundred fifty yards, I'd wager. Two hundred out and fifty over."

"Don't forget, you're OB Doc. That's a stroke and a penalty. I hope you remember you're lying 3."

As they headed up the fairway, Faust noted Stanley's new and quite expensive clubs. "I take it you've had a pay increase recently," said Faust tapping Stanley's golf bag.

"Er . . . they're really nice, aren't they? But actually, they didn't cost me anything. They were, um, kind of *given* to me."

"Kind of given? And how might that differ from just *given*?"

"Well, because Woody Sawyer just, he just passed them on to me." Stanley faltered a bit.

"Oh, they're not new then?"

"No, they're new alright. Lemme hit, and I'll tell you the whole story."

The story was this. Woody Sawyer (site foreman for the general contractor) had walked into Stanley's office late one afternoon with this beautiful, complete set of clubs. He said he'd heard that Stan was becoming "quite a golfer," and he'd like to do something to help out. Stanley replied that he'd sure love to have those clubs, but there was a Company policy against accepting gifts from contractors. Woody then explained that these weren't a gift, that the contractor owned a sporting goods store in Pawtucket, and that these were "excess inventory," an overstocked item. She didn't want to just toss them away, so she gave them to Woody. But Woody doesn't play golf and so . . .

Stanley finished his account as they approached the green. Faust, sensing the distinctly defensive tone of Stanley's account, didn't help much. "I see. Then of course these clubs are not a gift?"

"Well, jeez, doc . . . you make it sound like, I mean, it's not as though Woody flew me to Hawaii or something!" Thok!! Stanley skulled his 8 iron on the line into the sand trap.

After putting out, (with Faust just 1 over?!) they decided to sit for a minute or two and finish their discussion.

"I can see that my attempt at humor didn't much amuse you. I apologize. And I see that you are indeed quite sensitive to the ethical implications of your situation.

"But why do you think that Mr. Sawyer . . . ah . . . arranged to have those clubs sent to you? Surely he could have disposed of them more easily back in Pawtucket."

Stanley mumbled a bit, then, "But it's like I said doc, Woody told me that he couldn't use them, so . . ."

"No, I don't want to hear what Woody said," Faust replied gently, "I believe you. What I want to hear is what *you* really think."

"Okay, so he wanted to do me a favor," Stanley acknowledged sullenly.

"And . . . ," Faust prompted.

"And I guess *that* means that he expects me to return the favor when the time comes. But look, how big a favor can he expect for a set of golf clubs? It's not as though I'm driving his Porshe, or . . ."

"Of course not," Faust agreed, "but a favor nonetheless. And I would hazard that your Mr. Sawyer himself expects nothing in particular in return. Let us simply say that all he expects is to engender some friendly feeling toward himself and his contractor.

"They all do it, you know," Faust continued. "Every contractor, every lobbyist, everyone who depends on the good will of some representative of a client organization."

And every consultant? Stanley mused.

"Consider it in this light," Faust tapped his putter for attention. "Large organizations have many . . . ah . . . lower-level professionals, who, while not empowered to make large-scale decisions, *collectively* make decisions of enormous importance to our hypothetical contractors or lobbyists. Consequently . . ."

"Sure," Stanley interrupted, "I can see that. For each contractor the *overall* benefit can really be a big deal. But for each guy like me, why it's really not that much. Golf clubs? Big deal! Still, when

Woody comes to me and says, 'Hey kid, it looks like our fittings in B Building are a little off spec, and I'll tear them out if you tell me to. But that spec *really* wasn't meant to apply to . . .'

"And I know that too. Still, a spec's a spec, so what do I do? Well, I guess I say to myself, 'Woody's really a good guy, and no harm's done anyway, so why cause him grief? And who's to know but me.'

"But is this really ethics, Doc? I haven't done anything really wrong, have I. And I'm sure not thinking about those golf clubs when I say, 'Sure Woody, forget it.'"

Dr. Faust realizes, of course, that Stanley's soliloquy is just that. Still, some instructional comment is in order.

"Yours is not a question that I, nor anyone else, can answer for you, Stanley. As in all matters of human judgement, there is no firm line of demarcation, one side of which is unambiguously right, and the other wrong.

"And this is why The Company has its uncompromising, if rigid, rule. No gifts, period! Even if those gifts are . . . ah . . . 'excess inventory' that needs to be disposed of."

22

Like It Is

It is a fundamental irony of human existence that chance sometimes provides the opportunity for which otherwise we have sought in vain. I can think of no purer instance than Stanley's first two weeks with The Company. Strange, it seems like only yesterday. Stanley was right here in the study with me, narrating this ghastly experience as though it were happening at the time.

"Our second session this P.M. will be given over to familiarizing you with the accounting and inventory system we use here in The Plant. You will be given a capsulized view right from the expert, the Chief Accountant of our plant, Erno Orne. I hope you will all appreciate how good it is of Ernie to join us this afternoon; he's a very busy man, and we're lucky to be able to get this much time from him. I know I'll be listening. Ernie . . ."

Meeting rooms in mill buildings are not designed for hosting sixteen bright new college graduates for eight-hour training sessions in the middle of July. But for lack of alternative, here they were. Orne, a small, round, balding man, stepped to the front of the room. He placed what must have been at least 1000 charts on the easel and started to talk in the purest monotone that Stanley had ever heard. What followed is difficult to put in words, but easy to describe in feelings.

"There are several basic systems we could use—LIFO, FIFO, possibly FILO, under the right conditions. So let me describe these concepts to begin with." Orne, though obviously relishing the opportunity, betrays no hint of emotion in the tone or pattern of his delivery. Time passes. Eternity passes. The great exhaust fan whirring in the rear of the incredibly stuffy room hums away in a hypnotic, undulating pattern. Orne also drones on.

"There. Now we are ready to go step-by-step through plant operations. Let's start here with Receiving. Notice that . . ."

Christ! thinks Stanley, '*Receiving*'! How long will it take to get to Packing and Shipping? The hypnotic beat of the exhaust fan and the heat create a new problem. Anxiety mounts on boredom. I'm falling asleep. That won't do. Not in my first week with The Company, in front of their top management.

More Erno Orne, fan, and heat. Stan digs his nails into his palms. Pain ought to keep him awake.

Stan thinks he hears the words Packing and Shipping but can't be sure of anything in his current state.

Orne, like most accountants, seldom gets the chance to make management presentations. So he's making the most of this opportunity. Every beautiful detail of the impregnable accounting fortress that protects the fortunes of The Company should, and *will*, be relished.

"Oh, I see I'm running a bit over. It's 5:05. Well, I can cut it off here, or, with about twenty minutes more I can wrap it all up. What do you think, Ted?"

"Oh, by all means finish up. It's fascinating. And that's what we're here for—to learn—right, everybody?"

A murmur of "right, right."

Ted's look belies his words, thinks Stanley, but at least he's suffering, too.

Finally, mercifully, it's over.

"Any questions?"

Inevitably, there will be two or three questions. Some people always want to show their interest and their understanding of the material. But now it's really over—for today at any rate. Only two more days to go.

And now the orientation week is over. Ted, who has been responsible for planning and organizing the sessions is out seeking feedback.

"Well, Stan, I'd like to get your thoughts on our orientation program. You know, things you'd like to see changed or added, general impressions, that sort of thing."

Stanley has a few warm-up comments, more to show that he knows what has gone on than for anything else. But, finally, he cannot restrain himself.

"Frankly, Mr. Shelby, I thought it was pretty awful. Too long, too boring, too superficial in some ways, but too detailed in others. What I mean is . . ."

Stan gave some examples of what he was trying to convey to Ted. He wasn't doing a particularly good job, but he was honestly trying to help.

"I find that hard to believe," said Ted. (Apparently, he really did find it hard to believe.) "You know, I've talked to most of the others, and every one of them thinks the program was great."

Now it was Stanley's turn. "Well, I find *that* hard to believe. I talked to every one of those people in the hall during break, every day, and there wasn't one of them that didn't feel pretty much the way I do. I wouldn't say they're lying, but they sure aren't telling you what they really think."

"Well, then," said Ted, regaining his composure, "what would you suggest? From what you say, this hasn't been of much value to you. How would you like to do it?"

Oh-oh, thought Stan. Put your money where your mouth is, in other words.

In truth, Stanley would just as soon have let the matter drop, but Ted wasn't going to let that happen. Training programs are necessary and good, and this man Stanley will have his!

Stanley suggested that perhaps something more personal, more individual, more in depth (those are Ted's words, not Stanley's) would be valuable, so it was arranged. Stanley spent about a week in every major department of The Plant doing some of the work and gaining, as Ted put it "an in-depth, hands-on understanding of the departmental mission." Even though there was an ineluctable aura of punishment involved, Stanley got to know every major department head in The Plant. (Being centerfielder on The Plant softball team didn't hurt either.)

Hardly six months had passed when Stan found himself summoned for the second time to Ben Franklyn's aerie overlooking the mill floor.

"Well, son, I've got a proposition for you. Seems that the people in New York are now getting The Program off the ground. They've sent word around to all The Plant locations asking for bright young people to work in The Program. We'll be sending someone from here. And yes, everyone seems to think you're the man."

Ben went on to lay out the details of the new assignment, saying how they'd be sorry to lose him here, but that this was too good an opportunity to turn down. It was agreed that Stanley would go.

As the meeting ended, Ben felt the need to give some fatherly advice to Stanley, who, heaven knows, needed it.

"Son, you've got to remember that the people in New York are the best The Company has. That's why they're there. This is a real chance for you to learn about The Company and how it does business. So listen to them and learn."

And then as a parting word, the summation of a lifetime's wisdom.

"Remember, keep your eyes open and your mouth shut!"

Good God, thought Stanley, I'm doomed!

And so, all's well that end's well. But what is the moral of this story? Tell it like it is? Honesty is the best policy? No, not at all. Sooner or later, absolute honesty will be fatal. Well then, what?

Go back over the sequence of events and see. First, Stanley *did* tell the truth, but he assumed that the others did too. So the net effect was to single himself out. Next, the particular form of experience/punishment selected for him made his name the only one of his recruiting generation known in every department of The Plant.

Now, follow this sequence carefully, for it is important. New York goes out to The Plant locations to recruit people for The Program. One from each plant, and only the best, of course. Naturally, each plant thinks it *has* only the best, so the decision is based on other criteria. And the first of these is—don't laugh—whom can we spare? Well, those who can be spared are generally the new recruits who have not yet earned themselves a spot in the "starting lineup." (You can also send an older failure, but there is some danger in that.) Then how do you make a plantwide decision about which of these young unknowns to select? Of course. Plant management says, "Yes, that young Stanley fellow. Yes, I know him. Bright enough certainly. Yes, he'd be a good man. Fact is, everyone seems to know him."

And so it goes.

The important thing to remember is that the organization has a vast, lumpenproletariat whose identities are mostly unknown to management; for them, the game is to become known. And it doesn't have to be for good works, either. Most of the time the name sticks after the event has been long forgotten. No, the first step up, and by far the most difficult, is to get a dozen people in middle management to know your name. "I don't care what you say about me as long as you spell my name right," is a slightly exaggerated way of putting it—but only slightly.

23 Hold That Line

"**B**en, *Ben,*" Ted implored, "You've got this thing all wrong. We most certainly have *no* intention of demoting your first-line managers." Ted himself was indignant just uttering the thought. "Our SUREFIRE program (SUbordinate REadiness by Frequent Interval Role Exchange) is only a training device. A dynamite training device, to be sure, but only that. As it says, it's a sure-fire way to build superior/subordinate empathy relationships on the job."

"Now you listen to me, Shelby," Ben replied in a low growl. "It's a wonder to me that The Company is still in business with all the damn fool programs Corporate keeps dreaming up for us. Production is the backbone of this company, not some . . . some . . ." Ben was at a loss for words.

"And might I remind you, Ben, that there won't be any production at all if the union makes good on their strike threat. I don't agree with you that there would be any slowdown at all with SURE-FIRE, but what if there were? What are a few hours compared with weeks of possible shutdown?"

"Seems to me there's a big assumption you're making here, Ted, that this, this *program* of yours," Ben drew out the word to express his distaste, "will make one goddamned iota of difference to these guys. The real problem is that 'PIP of a program' you staffers wished on me last year. Oh yeah, 'Work Smarter, not Harder' you said. I didn't want that one either. But Mr. Marsh wanted it, so I got it.

"So to fix *that* up, you've got this damn fool SUREFIRE. Only this time *you've* got it. Not me. You can take you're damned program and . . ."

"Now just wait a minute, Ben," said Ted, having taken enough abuse, "perhaps you've forgotten that our vice president for personnel has said that we *are* going to have these SUREFIRE sessions.

"No, you wait a minute, Ted," said Ben pointing a blunt finger at Ted's chest. "It's you at Corporate that have forgotten the difference between staff and line. It's line management that makes the decisions on what goes on here at the plant locations. And that's me and Marshall Mason (Vice President for Production of the Expandrium Division) not the bleeding hearts at Corporate Personnel."

On that note, Ted Shelby stalked out of the office. And was that the end of the matter? Guess again. A few days later, the following memo appeared on Ben's desk, marked "confidential."

To: Ben Franklyn, Mill Superintendent, Pawtucket
From: Edward W. Shelby, IV, Office of the Vice President for Personnel
Re: SUREFIRE Employee Relations Program

It is the opinion of this office that the SUREFIRE program will be a strong step in building positive employer–employee relations in this corporation, and as such will be a vital step in preventing labor unrest. My recent discussions with our top corporate management indicates full concurrence in this view.

In our recent discussion you indicated to me your total unwillingness to participate in this program. This office sees your position as most regrettable in view of the wholehearted endorsement SUREFIRE has received from plant management generally. However, as you indicated to me at the time of our last meeting, the decision to mount such a program is yours. I must therefore assume that you understand that you alone are fully accountable for employee relations developments in consequence of this decision.

cc: Mr. Marsh
    Marshall Mason

After several exchanges of this sort, documented by appropriate memoranda, Ted Shelby now finds himself giving a kick-off speech to a conference room filled with Ben Franklyn's first-line supervisors. How did it happen? First, we need to take a look at the possible payoffs for Ben and Ted. I'll spare the details. You just remember that there are four possibilities that result from the combination of the uncontrollable event—the union calling a strike or not, and the decision alternatives—to have SUREFIRE or not.

The managerial goal here is to prevent the strike. But the difficulty is a common one: Ben and Ted disagree completely on how to do so. Ben's right, of course; personnel has no authority to order him to institute SUREFIRE. So let's take it first from Ted's point of view.

For Ted, the best outcome is that Ben okays the program, and there's no subsequent strike. He gets what he wants, and he can claim that SUREFIRE worked. But if there *is* a strike, Ted still hasn't lost all that much. He did what he could, and it *is* ultimately Ben's responsibility. And what if Ben doesn't okay the program? If there is no strike, well, there will always be future opportunities. How about that memo, you say? Two things. Because everyone is happy with the outcome, no one is going to dig up that memo. This is because "not happening" is not an event like "happening." Because it doesn't actually take place, it doesn't require an explanation. So for Ted it's only a lost opportunity. A loss, but again a minor one. If there is a strike, Ted actually stands to benefit (careerwisely speaking, of course). Subordinate Readiness-IV will not be resisted so easily!

The outcomes for Ben are different. If there is no strike, he gains a little if he resisted SUREFIRE, because now he has a better argument against the inevitable SR-IV. If he goes with SUREFIRE, well, in that case he can start preparing for Subordinate Readiness-IV.

But if there is a strike, Ben's outcomes are markedly different from Ted's. This is because he *is* responsible for the management situation at The Plant. Program or not, he's going to lose in the event of a strike. Oh, from the viewpoint of the TED/BEN game it might be argued that Ben will actually gain if both program and strike occur. At least he would have a good future reason for saying no to Ted and the inevitable descendants of SUREFIRE. But what Ted, his memos, and his cc's have arranged is that Ben's maximum loss comes if he refuses the program and the strike occurs. He will have refused to heed the warning and take what, in retrospect, will seem like a necessary corrective action. A big loss, no doubt about it.

So what has Ted done here? Just this. He's set it up so that Ben's maximum loss will be as big as possible—Ben has ignored expert advice that could have avoided trouble. Ben's obvious minimax is to go with the program. But Ted's maximum loss isn't nearly as big. And, Ted's maximax—program, no strike—coincides exactly with Ben's minimax!

Now, you probably have noticed that it does not look like Ted and Ben are trying to reach the best *managerial* decision. Indeed, it looks as if they are working with—how should I say it?—a personal decision dressed up as a managerial one. You might mull that over for a while. And how about all those present and future outcomes that are supposed to be considered? For example, Ted is certainly looking ahead to more and better programs—SR-IV, V. . . . That's his thing. And different outcomes have different implications for those programs.

Finally, the moral concerning staff authority: it is true enough that, in most cases, staff has no *direct* authority. This doesn't mean, however, that staff has no way of exerting its will. Ted has done just this by carefully structuring the situation so that Ben's minimax just happens to coincide with his own maximax.

24

The Rating Game

Ben Franklyn's gravelly voice carried conviction. ". . . so it seems to me that we are all in pretty clear agreement that Drew Bolt is our man for spot number 52. He's not been with us long, but those of us who know him can already see the kind of job he's capable of, and . . ."

Stanley is observing the annual merit ranking session at the Pawtucket plant. The task at hand is no less than the rank ordering of 238 Level Two production engineers. What is rank ordering, you say? Well, the job of the assembled management group is to take those 238 engineers and assign a number from 1 to 238 to each of them. Number 1 stands for the very best Level Two engineer in the plant, number 2 for the next best, and so on down to the anchor, number 238 (the worst . . . or, ah, that is, "least best").

But, why would The Company indulge in a questionable exercise like this, you ask? Because it has to give promotions and salary increases, and it would like to give them to the people who deserve them, and not give them to the people who don't. If you are one of those engineers, and you are ranked number 1 or 2, you'll get a promotion and a fat raise. But if you're number 237 or 238, forget it; it's been a bad year, and you've had your warning.

Oh, that's not what you mean? You want to know why it is necessary to go through a procedure that, at first glance, strikes you as impossible? Then the best thing for you to do is to hear what Ted Shelby has to say about it. In fact, right this minute he's talking to Management Development Session 6, Level 1: New Managers. Come on, let's go have a listen.

"As all of you know, The Company believes strongly in rewarding superior performance. We want to have our top people where top people belong—in the management of The Company.

"Now, none of us is infallible. Don't get me wrong—we're as good as they come in this business. But we're human, and we do make mistakes. But when it comes to judging performance, we can't afford to make mistakes. We want our best horses in the lead team. Of course, the work of technical professionals is hard to put numbers on; our own judgements are inclined to be subjective. And because most of us like to give someone the benefit of the doubt, our individual ratings tend to be a bit high. When we found 20 percent of our people rated 'superior,' 50 percent 'above average,' 25 percent 'average', and only 5 percent 'below average,' we knew something had to be changed. Seventy percent 'above average' and only 5 percent 'below average'?

"We found our way around these problems with our MERIT system—MErit Ranking in Teams—and I'm pleased to say that I had a small part in developing MERIT.

"What are the advantages? First, by ranking, we know exactly where each one fits. Oh, I know, there won't be much difference between, say, 43 and 44, but at least we do know that our best thinking indicates that number 43 is a better performer than number 44. Furthermore, the team aspect means that all our managers who have worked with the individual have had a chance to input their knowledge. In summation, we now have a sound, scientific procedure here, instead of the old 'seat-of-the-pants' game that we used to play."

What Ted meant in his reference to "the team aspect" is the fact that all sixty or so first-, second-, and third-line plant supervisors participate in the final ranking sessions. It is a *group* effort, to be sure, but to a person witnessing the spectacle, there is some reason to be skeptical of its description as a *team* effort.

And Stanley was witnessing the spectacle. Part of his role in the CATCHUP program is to "familiarize and orientate" himself with Company procedures. Specifically, he happened to be on hand to "familiarize and orientate" himself with the procedure by which Drew A. Bolt arrived at spot 52 out of 238.

"I think we've made some real good choices in our top twenty spots," said Ben Franklyn, as he began his nominating speech, "and I've got a guy here who belongs right up with that group—Drew Bolt. No, he's not a 5 or 10, but I think he's our choice for number 21. He's worked for me for six years now, and I know he's done a job, . . . etc., etc. Here's a letter from . . . etc., etc. If you look at his record, you'll see that . . . etc., etc. Who'll second my nomination?"

"I'll second it!" says one of Ben's old cronies.

"Any discussion?" asks the chairman.

There is plenty of discussion, the gist of which being that Ben Franklyn must be crazy. There are plenty of better people for that spot. In fact, one of them is nominated and voted in. "Okay," says Ben, "I respect your judgment, but I still think you're making a mistake."

Now they are down to position number 35, and Ben pops up: 'Okay, I've paid attention to your arguments; and while I'm not happy about it, I'll be willing to accept position number 35 for Drew Bolt. Any seconds?" Another buddy of his seconds the nomination. "Well, we've already gone over this pretty thoroughly, and I guess there won't be any need for discussion this time," says Ben. "Certainly there's no question now about his qualifications for a spot as low as 35." But there is discussion, culminating in No Deal. Ben looks stricken.

Ben gets up again, at position number 50, and Stanley is worried. He's never seen Ben like this, Ben is a beaten man, and that's not the Ben Franklyn that Stanley knows. "Listen, folks," says Ben. "It seems that I've done something terrible to Drew Bolt here today. I can yield on your judgement that he's not our number 21 man, and I guess you're all convinced that he isn't number 35, although I don't agree. But 50? Number 50 spot for Bolt? Yes, I've hurt this man's career. I can see that now."

My God, thinks Stanley, I never thought I'd see the day when they took all the fight out of Ben Franklyn. This is tragic. Can't these guys see that they've really screwed him?

Ben went on: "I guess I just haven't been able to present his case for him, haven't been able to show you the job he'd done for us. Maybe by matching him up against our top ten guys I put him in the wrong light. Okay, okay—maybe he's not our very best, but he's still a top man. Look, we're down to spot number 50! Come on. If we've got any sense of justice we'll . . . etc., etc." Stanley, in spite of himself, gave a quiet little cheer when Drew wound up a number 52. Poor Ben, he thought. Well, he won't make this kind of mistake again.

At the end of the day the meeting adjourns until tomorrow, when MERIT is to pick up again, at position number 162. As Stanley is going back to his office, he overhears Ben Franklyn talking and joking with his buddies. "Yes sir, we did all right," Ben is saying. "All in all, a good session. What about Bolt, hey? Now tomorrow, we've got young . . ." What is this? wonders Stanley. Has the strain been too much for Ben?

What this is, is this:

Rule 1: If you don't take care of your own people, nobody else will.

Rule 2: Take care of your own people, and they'll take care of you.

Rule 3: Any successful manager is a good actor, and the less he looks it the better an actor he is.

The fact of the matter was that Ben figured Drew Bolt for a solid 70, and anything better than that was pure gravy. The problem

Drew had was that he had worked for Ben for so long that nobody else knew him very well. So Ben went into his act. First, he brought up Bolt often enough to associate him with the top candidates. Then he acted terribly disappointed that he had to settle for spot number 52—not the number 21 he'd "expected" for Drew. This tactic is to mollify the pack of jackals who are sure that everyone is cheating (which they usually are).

The managers who learn to beat System A will have little trouble in figuring out how to beat Systems B, C, and D. After all, systems are only systems—that is, something that a shrewd person can figure out how to beat. In this case, the system was beaten by Ben's manipulating the expectations and definitions relating to "his people." On pencil-and-paper rating systems, Ben would routinely rate his average people as "better-than-average" and his better-than-average people as "superior." If Ted Shelby tries to make the system more "scientific" by having everybody rated as to separate attributes—"creativity," "initiative," "personal appearance," and the like—Ben will simply rate his people as excellent on those attributes that really count ("performance," "initiative," "responsibility"), while rating them as average on those that don't count for much ("personal appearance," "punctuality," and so forth). That way, it looks like he is being "objective"—who would believe him if he rated his people as "excellent" straight across the board?

BOX 6

INNOVATION IN APPRAISALS.
SOUND FAMILIAR?

In December of 1991, browsing through the *Wall Street Journal,* a piece on a new personnel rating system caught my eye. As I read on, suddenly it didn't seem so new after all.

The "new" scheme, it seems, is IBM's response to the perceived need at the time to reduce its workforce by 20,000 employees (now 40,000 and gaining). The new "rating and ranking" approach would work this way:

- Each employee is first assigned a rating ranging from one, "superior", to four, "needs improvement."

- Workers are now classified into groups of people who have like job classifications. For example, all Senior Technical Sales Representatives for a common product group in a given region might be grouped together.

- Everyone in this group would now be rank ordered from most to least productive. If the group had fifty-five employees, ranks one to fifty-five would be assigned, for eighty employees, one to eighty, and so on depending on the size of the group. Clearly, *someone* will be at the bottom.

- Presumably the lowest ranked employees would be selected for implementing the required rightsizing effort, although officially IBM says only that the intention is to give Big Blue (Little Blue?) a better idea who is contributing most to its business success.

The reaction of outsiders? Well, a professor from the Harvard Business School is reported as saying that he believes other corporations will soon pick up on the innovation, since IBM has always taken a leading approach in human resources policies.

Others are not so sure. One business consultant, noting that the approach had earlier been tried in the former Bell System, observes that it didn't work too well there. The problem is that managers have great difficulty in making such fine grain judgements when large numbers of people are involved.

Perhaps IBM should have called in Dr. Faust before making the leap!

Source: *Wall Street Journal*, December 13, 1991, p. B1.

Watchdogs

On the staff of every well-run business you will find watchdogs, and some businesses have quite a few. As a general rule, it seems the larger the enterprise, the greater the proportion of watchdogs to productive people. The Company, being a large enterprise, is no exception.

The term *watchdog* is used figuratively, but these people's behavior is very much like that of their canine counterparts. If you violate the rules, take care! Watchdog will get you. No questions asked. Don't bother with appeals to kindness, reason, or good fellowship, because these won't get you anywhere. The watchdog's behavior is a perfect example of what we illustrated earlier in the Tosca game. Watchdog plays zero sum only; he has no use for coalition strategy.

Let's look at two examples of Company watchdogs in action.

EXAMPLE 1

Kerry Drake and Ted Shelby are sitting in Kerry's office having a heated discussion, and Stanley is taking it all in. Kerry says, "The trouble with The Company these days is that they've got too many of these staff wiseguys right out of management schools in the Vice President's office. They look at the title on their door, and they get power-crazy. They like to tell you what to do, but they just don't understand the problems we have out here."

Ted answers, "They're only doing what the Vice President for Finance wants them to do, Kerry. Listen, they are very bright people. You think they'd be in those jobs if they weren't?"

"Sure they are," says Kerry. "That's why they do things like what happened this morning. My project is going over the budget a little bit, so this kid tells me I've got to cut back. Cut back? Why, I'm funded for next year at 25 percent more than this year. This project is taking off, and the only reason I'm over budget is that we ran into a few problems that we couldn't have figured on anyway. But, other than that, we're right on target. So this staff kid comes and tells me that I've got to transfer twenty people to another project!"

"Transfer?" says Stanley. "Can't you find the money somewhere else?"

"Oh, certainly," replies Kerry with an edge of irony in his voice, "I suppose I could lease some of our equipment to Another Company." Then, more seriously, "Listen, you guys know what a product development project is all about. Ninety percent of my budget is personnel, so the only choice I have is to cut personnel costs. And that means *permanent* transfers out of this project. You know Company policy on transfers. No phony paperwork transfers just to make budget. So I can't hide 'em and I can't hire 'em back in four months (the next budget year). I've got to transfer productive people off the project permanently! It's crazy! So next year I bring in twenty brand new people and lose at least six months while they learn the job . . . *plus* the new people I'm budgeted for anyway!

"Go ahead, go ahead. Tell me *that* makes sense!"

Ted says, "I guess you shouldn't have gotten into budget trouble in the first place."

"Thanks for the advice," says Kerry.

Later, Stanley asks Ted Shelby why something, which is obviously as wasteful to The Company as Kerry's having to transfer his people, is allowed to happen.

"I take it you're aware," says Ted, "that I've been on that financial staff side myself. Here's what happens.

"You've seen Kerry's problem, but you've seen it only from *his* viewpoint, the viewpoint of the individual program manager. But every Program Director in The Company is just the same. They all have something they want to do very badly. They all figure that stretching their budget a little won't hurt anything. And they all have the same story: 'You'll kill me,' they say. 'I'm on the verge of the biggest breakthrough in twenty years, and all I'm asking for is a lousy 500 K.'

"There are *hundreds* of these people out there, but there's only one of you."

"Well, okay, I see what you're saying, Ted," says Stanley. "But we both know what's going on with Kerry. He's got a good case."

"Sure," says Ted, "some of them *are* right, and you *do* have a few dollars to play with for overtaxed budgets. But when you're working out of the Vice President's office, it just isn't possible to know the details of every project. And as Kerry likes to say, you just don't have the time to separate the unfortunate from the incompetent. Every one of those bandits is *very* convincing, and what's more, just like Kerry, they all genuinely believe they're right.

"But me, I'm working for the Vice President for Finance, my job is finance—the Budget. Only one thing is expected of me: make the Budget! Now if I don't, and if that gets *my* boss in trouble with Mr. Marsh . . ."

Ted didn't finish. It didn't seem necessary.

EXAMPLE 2

"Just finished my paper on the reliability problem," said Stanley. "I'm going to send it off to *The Journal* this afternoon."

"That's great," said Lesley. "communications okayed it with no trouble, eh?"

"Who?" Stanley asked.

"Communications," Les explained, "is the department responsible for The Company's media image. Before anything goes out from Company employees, they have to approve."

"But there's nothing proprietary in my paper," said Stanley.

"Well, then you've got nothing to worry about, but you still must have it approved."

Later in the week, Lesley saw Stanley shaking his head in disbelief. She asked him what was wrong.

"It's incredible," he said. "They won't let me send this out. One of those idiots in communications said that it wouldn't look good for The Company to admit that it has a reliability problem with The Model M Machine."

"I don't blame them," she said. "Why did you put something like that in your paper?"

"But I *didn't*," said Stanley. "I didn't say anything like that. Here, see for yourself."

He handed Les the paper. It's title was about as long as the text: "A Note on Reliability Analysis for Certain Machines of the Model M Class with Relaxed Restrictions on the Allowable Distribution of Parameters."

"Must be exciting," Les remarked.

"So this guy says, 'I don't think we should say that, because it seems to me that this implies that we have reliability problems with our Model M—and that certainly won't do The Company's image any good.' Well, it was clear to me that he didn't know the first thing about any of this, so I told him, 'Look, The Company wants us to publish papers like this, and it's good for our reputation, not bad.'"

"What did he say to that, Stan?"

"He said, 'That's for *me* to judge, not you. And I can't see how saying that our products are unreliable is going to help anything. But I'm not trying to be difficult, and by the way, I *am* on the Committee to Encourage Technical Publications. Tell you what; you rewrite this and take out all the references to reliability, and I guarantee that we'll put it through.'"

To understand the watchdog and his behavior, think of a sentry standing guard in a war zone. As far as the sentry is concerned, there are only two types of people—friends and foes. He hears a suspicious noise and shouts, "Halt! who goes there?" The noise is still there, but there is no response. The sentry can either shoot at it or not shoot at it. If he shoots, and it is a foe—good. If it is a drunk from Company C—too bad, but the guy should have known better than to be out there like that. If he doesn't shoot, and it is a friend—thank goodness. But if he doesn't shoot, and it's a raiding party . . . well, that's the ball game. The moral is: Don't play games with sentries, because if they're doing their job, you'll get shot at.

The situation is similar with regard to Company watchdogs. Take the communications example; the first thing to realize is that the watchdog isn't playing against Stanley. All Stanley has done is create a situation for the watchdog in which there is an unknown but foreseeable antagonist who will come forward waving a copy of The Journal, opened to Stanley's article, and saying, "This could hurt The Company's business. Who let this out?" This is the uncontrollable event.

Stanley himself is safe. His perfectly predictable reply will be: "Watchdog okayed it." So, from watchdog's viewpoint, the situation looks like this.

If watchdog okays a suitable article, or nixes an unsuitable one (suitable and unsuitable refer to after-the-fact problems, or lack of them, engendered by the article), he gets the usual reward for doing one's job and not getting into trouble—nobody notices. If he rejects an article, which really ought to have been okayed, he'll take some flack from Stanley, or from someone else who might accuse him of being overzealous. Still, it's a judgment call. But, if he lets an article out, which later causes trouble, the corporate 'witchhunt' is on. This is what watchdog fears, and the only thing he fears, really. You and I (and watchdog, too) already know what Stanley will say. So you've guessed it. Minimax is the order of the day.

Wait a minute, you say, it looks to me like poor watchdog has no positive outcomes. Just so. At the very best, he has nothing to gain by saying yes, but plenty to lose.

What annoys Stanley is that the expected values—The Company's stake in this situation—are quite different. Watchdog can't possibly know the probabilities of a major SNAFU and tends to exaggerate them in any case. So all watchdog can see is the possibility of that unacceptable loss. It's a single outcome decision.

But The Company is in it over the long haul. Its outcomes are weighted by true (though unknown) probabilities: let us say, 1 in 10 that a problem will occur, and 9 in 10 that it won't. Also, The Company will get a positive payoff from the publication of Stanley's article, but nothing if watchdog says no. I leave it as an 'exercise for the reader' to derive the best strategy for The Company based on expected values.

The financial watchdog is in a different situation. Again, he is not playing against Kerry Drake, but what sociologists like to call a "generalized other." Kerry takes it personally, and he is wrong to do so. Minimaxer watchdog knows only one thing: exceed the Company budget and he's dead. No expected values, just a one-time payoff. And if he says yes to everybody, this is a certainty. Add to this, a) watchdog doesn't have much time for each individual case, but each individual manager does, b) watchdog's got to get most of his 'facts' from that manager, and c) all Project Managers are convinced that lying to a watchdog is inherently a morally redeeming act.

So the only objective decision is to say no every time. And if the Project Manager really has a good case, let him take it up the line. Funny how seldom *that* happens.

But, you say, it looks again like the watchdog has only negative outcomes. Why would anyone want such a job? Why? Because they want to be decision makers, and because they fail to understand the nature of the situation at the outset—something that shouldn't happen to you.

Top Secret

"**N**eed *to know*?!" bellowed Ben Franklyn. "For chrissakes, we only 'need to know' because we can't meet *their own* goddamned specifications if we don't know what they are! You get back on the phone and tell 'em that I'm going to backcharge them $1000 a day—starting this very goddamned minute—for every day I've got those guys sitting around on their tails waiting to find out what to do next!" Ben was never one to take obstacles to progress lightly, especially obstacles like security regulations, when they seemed to be irrelevant to the task at hand. He stabbed his finger accusingly at Stanley. "You go and tell that guy that in this business . . ."

But by that time, Stanley was out of Ben's office and halfway down the hall to his own. There was no sense talking to the engineering officer at The Agency again, he figured, so he dialed the security officer this time. He was not optimistic, however, because during his brief military career he'd been cleared for "Top Secret" at Another Agency; he knew a little about the security business. He knew, for instance, that security officers lived in the completely ordered world of security regulations—and liked it.

And so his phone call to the security officer at The Agency held no surprises for him.

"Yes sir, that project is classified as Top Secret."

"No sir, it isn't *my* responsibility to say whether or not a project should be classified. That judgment is left to the engineering officer."

"Yes sir, it says here in two-five-six-dash-c that such information is available to those who establish a reasonable 'need to know' as described in S. R. two-eight-zero-prvn-five-sec-three." (Good grief, thought Stanley, he even pronounced the abbreviations!)

"No sir, it isn't my responsibility to say who has a reasonable need to know; that judgment is left to the engineering officer."

"Yes sir, glad to be of assistance."

Well, what else could you expect? mused Stanley. Wait till Ben hears this. But by that time, Ben had simmered down. When Stanley entered his office, Ben was talking with Ted Shelby. "Sorry, Ben, no luck," said Stanley.

"Oh, it's okay, Stanley," said Ben. "I was just trying to save ourselves some trouble. Actually, we can figure it out from the other specs. It'll take a few days, but we can do it. But we could sure do a better job if I knew what they were going to use it for—what kinds of conditions, how far from basic supply sources, how much continuous operation, and so forth. And you know, I'll bet that anybody who really wanted to find out that stuff could do it. You can bet that our enemies know everything about it that's worth knowing. Sometimes I get the feeling that the main point of all this security stuff is to keep our *own* side in the dark."

At that remark, Ted Shelby spoke up. "No, Ben," he said in a concerned tone, "I think you've missed the overall systems strategy here. When I was in the intelligence corps, it was stressed in the officer training program (Ted never failed to let information like that drop in his conversations) that, yes, The Enemy probably could get any single item of information they wanted, if they wanted it badly enough. But Security kept them from getting enough pieces to fit the Big Picture together. That's why every piece, no matter how trivial it might seem, has to be guarded in the same manner."

This was too much for Stanley. "Well, Ted," he said, "that may be what they told you, but I had some experience on guard duty in a secret military equipment depot. From what I saw there, I'd say that Ben is closer to the truth.

"During the war, I was a corporal assigned to engineer corps liaison at Another Agency—not very exciting, but better than getting shot at. Like all soldiers, I had to pull guard duty. But unlike most, I had security clearance because of my other work. So here's this depot full of stuff dreamed up by Another Agency's technical-warfare specialists, and all classified 'Secret.' You wouldn't *believe* some of the things they had parked in there.

"Hey, how's this strike you?," Stanley started chuckling. "Here's this tall frame scaffold sitting on top of an earth-moving rig. There's this 3- or 4-ton weight that's supposed to be hoisted up to the top of this frame, about 20 feet in the air. The weight has a pointed rod underneath it, and the whole idea of the thing is to punch holes in enemy roads to plant charges. You hoist the weight, let it go, and zonk! It punches the rod through the pavement. Then the demolition guys run up, stick the charge in, and it's done.

"Just one thing wrong with that gadget. Most roads are banked a little, and more often than not, about the time that 4-ton weight gets to the top of that 20-foot scaffold, the whole business falls over on its side. No wonder it was never used in combat. That thing would have spent most of the war like a beetle on its back. Come to think of it, I don't even know for what war they were built, or how long they'd been there.

"There were lot's of other things in that secret depot just like that. In fact, if there had been some way to get the enemy to put those 'secrets' to use, the war would have been over a lot sooner. I finally figured out that those machines were classified because Another Agency didn't want our side knowing what they'd been up to."

Ben Franklyn looked at Stanley with new respect. "You mean the security the project director at The Agency has in mind is his own job security? Har, har! That's pretty good. Come to think of it, there's a few things around here that I'd like to have gotten 'classified' myself."

At this point it was Ted Shelby who could stand it no longer. "Now just a minute," he said, excitedly. "The kind of thing you're talking about may have happened in a few isolated instances, but as a general rule . . ."

But nobody was listening. Ted spends a lot of his time trying to explain why it is necessary and proper for things to be the way they are; but meanwhile, Stanley (and Ben Franklyn) pursues the more profitable course of trying to learn why things are the way they are. Ted, finding it necessary to fit everything into the framework of what he already believes, has a difficult time learning from experience. But Stanley, in this case, has observed and understood a fundamental fact—that all organizations have counterparts of security and intelligence. Companies are aware that competitors would like to possess their proprietary information, and it must therefore be restricted to responsible people only.

And who decides what information should be kept secret and who should be allowed access to it? Why, just about everybody with people below them. Yes, you begin to see. By using the unquestionable reasons of "security" (Company or national), management has a useful and flexible device for hiding its gaffes and/or controlling the behavior of subordinates. Well, if you keep your eye on the tube or read the newspapers you know all this. And you must have noticed that classified information does The Enemy very little good, although it makes some people on our side look pretty bad.

27 As I Recall

“**I** still say drawing a straight flush is impossible. Only an idiot would expect . . .”

“Better watch your language, Kerry,” Ted cut in. “Maybe the Doc's recommendations will include a new head of Automation Engineering.”

Typically, the premeeting banter centered on last night's poker game, its winners and losers. Dr. Faust (winner) felt little need to justify his game to Kerry Drake (big loser). And, in truth, in his role as consultant, the good doctor tries to avoid liberating too much of his companions' loose cash. For he is well aware that the big game lies elsewhere.

Ted finally brought the meeting to order. “As you know, we have been extremely fortunate in having Dr. Faust's full-time services with us in our first phase of the CATCHUP program. I know of no one better suited by experience and training to carry out this important mission.”

The meeting had been called to deliver the results of CATCHUP —Phase I. Kerry, Ted, Ben Franklyn, some staff people from New York, and several top-management people from Manufacturing were present. The importance of the project was underscored by the presence of one of Mr. Marsh's “handlers.” And Stanley was there, too, having spent the past year putting together a detailed development program.

“I am sure you are aware of our charge here,” Ted continued. And now he read from a document. “The CATCHUP task force is charged with the responsibility of examining *all* phases of our Company manufacturing activities with the end in view of devising a comprehensive master plan to bring The Company abreast of recent explosive changes in the manufacturing environment.” The words, of course, were Ted's own.

As Chairman of the Task Force, Ted would report on the results today, as would Faust. Dr. Faust, as Chairman of The Department at The University, had been accorded responsibility for developing a detailed master plan for both the technical and "people" components of the program, and for developing the data to back it up. Accepting this challenge had required a year's leave from The University (for which The Company had shown its appreciation in a most tangible way).

"Before we get to the results, let me bring you all up to date on what we have been doing. Dr. Faust and I have visited every one of The Company's manufacturing locations this year and personally interviewed both top management and groups of our top technical people." (People are known by the company they keep, thought Stanley.) "In addition . . ."

Stanley's attention wanders. He's heard this all before, many, many times. It is embellished each time, naturally, but the outline is the same. The fact remains, however, that just about *all* Faust has done during the past year has been to visit and talk. And it calls for a great deal more than that. Certainly, a year's effort ought to produce something tangible, something concrete. But if it has, I haven't seen it, Stanley is thinking.

"So that's about it to date," Ted has finished his recapitulation. "Now let's take a look at some of our findings. Dr. Faust?"

"Ahem, yes. I know that you people have a great deal to think about, so I will not bore you with the details of our findings. These will be in a later report. (Always a later report, thought Stanley.) So let me go over the highlights, the key findings of this phase of CATCHUP.

"Number One. We have a clear and pressing problem of obsolescence, both in equipment *and* in people. As our Plant Manager at Portland put it . . ."

Nice one, thinks Stanley, can't lose on that. And best of all, nobody's fault in particular, so no one is going to fight you on that. Nice one. As Faust went on, Stanley had a growing sense of déjà vu. Sure enough, there were those surveys of Other Companies (a consultant's role is to bring in the bigger picture). Sure, all those points—the "Findings"—are right from Dr. Faust's original proposal. What do you know—The Company *did* have these problems after all.

As Dr. Faust went along ticking off the "focal issues for action" and documenting them with highlights from the data, Stanley had the distinct and uneasy feeling that CATCHUP—Phase I was about where it had started one year ago, at least for Faust's part. As for Stanley's own involvement, it is now clear to him that his detailed plan for the Subordinate Readiness Program stands by itself as perhaps the one real accomplishment of Phase I.

"Thank you, Dr. Faust. So much for our data base." Ted went on his crisp/confident tone. "I think you can see that we have been exceptionally fortunate to have Dr. Faust involved in the mission of this task force. Certainly his credentials are unique, and he's proven himself once again to be the hard-hitting, no-nonsense type of person you want when the chips are down." Beaming, "Nice work, Doc."

Stanley notes at this juncture that, although polite approval is being expressed about the table, enthusiasm is lacking. But not for long.

"Now, where do we go from here? As I recall . . ." Ted began by recounting the goals of Phase I. *The* major goal had been to define the goals of the program, for only then could satisfactory solutions be found.

Oh? thinks Stanley, that's new.

"We have been acutely aware of the manufacturing challenges in today's marketplace—methodswise and peoplewise. There are the modern management methodologies: information systems, cybernation, just-in-time inventory. And there are the contributions of the behavioral people. As we saw it a year ago, I recall . . ."

Ted went on setting forth, point by point, the goals of Phase I. And as he did so, he neatly reconstructed the original purposes to bring them into line with what Dr. Faust had delivered, including credit for the conceptual development of Stanley's Subordinate Readiness Program. Bewildered and increasingly angry, Stanley wonders what in the world is going on. Why is Ted doing this? Can't he see that Faust produced little that entire year, except perhaps a hole in the budget? Why doesn't Ted show him in his real light, as having dropped the ball? True, the Phase I position paper was a bit vague in outlining specific goals, yet Ted had spelled out a strategy in the early meeting that was quite different from what he said today. Why was Ted (to put it charitably) "rewriting history" here today?

Why indeed? Had Stanley been around a bit longer, he would have seen the truth immediately. As it is, it will dawn on him pretty soon.

Why was Dr. Faust there at all? *Answer:* Because Ted Shelby brought him in.

And why was that? *Answer:* Because Dr. Faust was the best answer to the question, "What are we doing to push ahead on CATCHUP? (We've got the best there is on it—Faust from The University, full time. He took a leave from The Department just to do this.")

But still, why pretend that Faust has accomplished things that he hasn't . . . and closer to home, why give him credit for doing things that Stanley did?

Perhaps you already have the answer yourself. Ted Shelby is defining the situation and rearranging the credits because *he* is responsible for Faust and what he achieves. In cases like this, The Company is not judging Faust, but Ted Shelby. Thus it well behooves Ted to make Faust look good. Ted *is* short-changing Stanley, that's true; but he's not hurting him, because no one outside of the Task Force knows or cares about Stanley. He has little to gain from his contribution and is losing little by not being properly credited. He is still just another face in the corporate crowd.

Ted, on the other hand, stands to lose plenty if Faust comes off as a highly visible, and expensive, flop. So Ted borrows a little against the future. For all Ted knows, he'll be out of this position in six months or a year (and in fact he was).

So this is his strategy: reconstruct the goals of the past and borrow from the future; announce to all involved that you've had a smashing success achieving your goals (which does indeed seem to be true) and hope for the best.

For the Stanleys of the world, the message is: be patient and learn. You will get your turn.

And as for Faust—he's trading on his reputation, and the time is near when Another Company will need that experience. He's come out looking good as far as The Company is concerned, because somebody had a strong vested interest in precisely that outcome.

But you say, what of Ted and his relationship with Dr. Faust? Once burned, twice shy, eh? No more business there.

Sorry, wrong again. Give Ted some credit. He knew quite well what he was and was not getting. Faust is no worse, and perhaps a bit better, than other consultants. (An expert, as Ben used to say, is just an ordinary guy 50 miles from home.) But Dr. Faust gives Ted what Ted needs most, expert legitimacy in the eyes of his superiors and, hence, the authority to say what must be done. True, Ted had to do some quick reshuffling at the end. But after all, that's all in the management game.

28

Figures Don't Lie . . . ?

Often, when I'm called upon to make a point with an illustration, I relate Stanley's experience in the construction business. The examples seem to be particularly vivid. I suppose this is because Stanley was new to The Company then, and everything seemed larger than life to him. Take the matter of cost estimation, for example. Because he was so new to it, Stanley accurately perceived some things to which most of us would have paid no attention.

". . . And the machine base will be set true and level to ±⅛ inch and dry packed with sand–cement grout not to exceed ½ inch in thickness."

Stanley has just finished the construction specifications for the new addition to Ben Franklyn's Expandrium mill building. Ben had told him that these specifications were extremely important, because they would be the basis for contract bidding.

"You can't trust these bastards," growled Ben (presumably referring to the antecedents of *all* contractors). "If you haven't got 'em pinned down right to the letter they always call it 'extra work', and you pay through the nose for it."

Before Stanley could ask the obvious question—if it's so important why am I doing it?—Ben handed him three older sets of specs and told him simply to copy the appropriate paragraphs and make the necessary substitutions for place and date. As in so many other instances, Stanley had learned that no job is ever done from scratch. What appear to outsiders to be monumental efforts are usually nothing but the most recent exercise in accretion and substitution on the part of some organizational nonentity.

As usual, Ted Shelby had been assigned from the corporate staff to coordinate the construction work. Not that Ted knew a great deal about construction (that was not required). Rather, it was an "opportunity," Ted's chance to be exposed to yet another phase of

The Company's operations. And again as usual, Ted never let lack of knowledge stand in the way of his managerial efforts.

After the bids came in, Stanley was going over them with Ted. He skimmed through several, then observed, "Doesn't it strike you as kind of funny, Ted, that these bids are so different from one another? I mean, look, here's one for seven hundred fifty thou, and then here's another for a million five! You get the idea that these people are really shooting from the hip on these bids, that they really haven't got any idea of what this job will cost."

"No, you're wrong there, Stanley. These people have precise methods of estimation. When I was an officer in the Corps of Engineers . . ."

Not again, thought Stanley. Ted had spent six months active duty in the reserves, and you'd think he was another, well . . .

". . . we had *precise* methods of estimating cost and time factors for all elements of the work. No, I'm afraid you're wrong, Stanley. You should see the records these contractors keep—what every job costs, broken down by manpower, machine time, you name it. No, I think you'll find the variation comes from two sources: efficiency and motivation. Some, naturally, are better businesspeople than others; their costs are lower. But mainly, some want the job more than others do. Your high bidder there, the one with double the costs, he just doesn't want this job; so he makes sure that he doesn't get it with that high bid. They always bid, of course, because they may want the next job."

"Okay, maybe that does make some sense, and it does look like that's what some of them have done. But look at this." Stanley waved his hand at the cost breakdowns for the various subsections of the work. Even among the low bidders, different contractors were obviously in wild disagreement with one another. "How do you account for that?"

"Oh, those differences . . . they just reflect different accounting procedures. Listen, I've got to get down to see Ben. I'll give you the full rundown when there's more time."

Sure you will, thought Stan. Skate fast when you're on thin ice. Ted always had an answer, even when he didn't know what the hell he was talking about.

As the mill job got underway, Stanley learned quite a lot about the cost estimation business. The first thing he learned was that he was pretty good at it. He had a simple formula. First, he would make an educated guess about the number of hours he thought it should take to do the job; then he would multiply it by two. Worked pretty well. And in the process of doing this, he also learned something else; he learned that, although the hours were recorded *correctly*, they were *not* recorded *accurately*.

You don't understand? Well, maybe we should let Woodrow Sawyer, the construction foreman, explain it as he did to Stanley. He and Stan had become pretty good friends. Late one afternoon, while involved in his cost estimation exercise, Stanley asked Woody if he could see the day's time sheet.

"Checkin' up on us again are you?" asked Sawyer with mock suspicion.

"Oh, you know I'm not, Woody, I wouldn't know what to check if I was . . . Now let's see, the way I figure it . . . ah, 6 workers times 18 hours, then multiply by 2 and . . . hey, wait a minute, this isn't right! You've got three guys over by Bay Twelve all day and you know nothing's even *started* over there. I mean, don't get me wrong. I'm really *not* checking on you, you know that's not my job, but . . . but I mean, how come?"

Stanley was a little flustered, as though he'd found something he wasn't supposed to know. But Sawyer put his big bear paw around Stanley's shoulder in a comforting way.

"Don't worry, no problem. Just a little internal accounting. We're an honest outfit; you know that, and I know that, else you'd never have seen that time sheet. Those workers put in those hours today, didn't they?"

Stanley nodded yes.

"It's just that they didn't put 'em in like it says here, right?"

Again, yes.

"Well, you see, I got this problem. The people in the office who bid this job think that the work in Bay Twelve should cost about twice what this here will. But I happen to know that it's more likely to be just the other way around. So-o I make it come out right. No problem. Don't worry, kid."

And with that, Woody was gone, cursing out a crane operator who had just nearly dismembered one of his workers.

Next day in the office Stanley was debating the wisdom of confronting Ted with his new insights on cost estimation, when Dr. Faust dropped by to inquire after his sometime protégé. Stan quickly rattled off his new discovery and asked the master's opinion.

"Yes, it does seem that you have observed a modest instance of a ubiquitous fact." Faust paused to light his pipe, a sure signal that an instructional dialogue was at hand. "Let us suppose that you, Stanley, were the one commissioned to work up the bid price. How do you think you would go about it?"

Remembering his experience with the specifications, Stanley replied without hesitation. "I suppose I'd look up our records on how much jobs like that had cost in the past, and I'd make the bid about the same. Maybe a little higher than average just to be safe."

"But what if you couldn't find another job like it? What if this were the first of its kind?"

"In that case I suppose I'd ask . . . or maybe I'd use some kind of factors . . . or I suppose I'd just have to make some kind of educated guess. Wouldn't I?"

"No matter;" said Dr. Faust, "you have grasped the main point. The most reliable way to make a bid appears to be on the basis of past experience. Where that is lacking, there is much guesswork involved."

"Excuse me, Dr. Faust, but it seems that we're off the track. What I was getting to is that this 'past experience' is phony. And you're trying to tell me that it's the best way."

"You," commanded Faust with the stem of his pipe, "*must* learn to listen. I did not say *best* nor did I say *is*. I did say *most reliable* and *appears to be*."

"Sorry," murmured Stanley contritely.

"Think a bit. Since this past experience is, ah . . . as you say 'phony' (Faust pronounced the word as if it were a bit unclean) why then do we find that, (a) foremen do nothing to correct it, and (b) management never uncovers it?"

"Oh, the second part I can understand all right. How could management find out? I suppose if we were talking about some real small job they could. But these big contractors don't bother with the small stuff. And out here (Stanley gave a sweep of his arm) where workers are moving from job to job all day, why, who can tell?"

"Precisely. Then you can understand Management's problem, but you cannot fathom why the *foremen* act in this way. Yes, I suppose it is difficult to comprehend. We shall need several principles. The first is our old friend, the minimax, and the second is what I shall call coincidence versus accuracy. Now, you do understand that each contractor has a historical record of estimated and actual costs for the type of job; that is, their bids and their actual costs. As the job progresses, the foreman sees that bids and costs do not agree. So he has a choice. He can opt for accuracy or for coincidence. If he chooses the former . . ."

"He's got some explaining to do, no matter what," interjected Stanley. "But if he goes for coincidence, for agreement with the estimates right down the line, well, he's a good manager. Sure I can see that, but that's no big deal. And where does your minimax come in?"

"Yes indeed, where? You are making an assumption, Stanley, the assumption that the contractor will be satisfied with the job done by his foreman. But what if the contractor is not? What if costs seem excessive, if the job is unprofitable. Then what do the strategies imply?"

"Okay. I do see. If the foreman goes for accuracy then a lot of his numbers don't look anything like the estimates. Obviously bad management, right? And since over the years estimates and costs agree pretty good . . ."

"Pretty *well*," supplied Faust.

"Since they agree, why he's going to have a hard time convincing management that in the past the cost figures have always been phonied up. So the foreman's maximum loss is where he records his costs accurately and later comes out on the short side on profit, which is bound to happen sometimes."

"Of course."

"But if he's pretty much in line with experience, well, it's not good . . . but it happens to anyone now and again."

"Precisely," added Dr. Faust.

"And uncertainty is the important element here. One cannot know the final outcome until it is too late to change the cost allocation, so why take a chance? And perhaps it *would* be possible to convince Management, but perhaps not. Again, why take the chance? It is simply a question of good career management."

"One last question. Don't any of the guys who are doing these things get into management? And if they do, why don't they put a stop to it?"

"Why, yes, they do; and they do try to stop it, or they try to for a while. But you know what it is like to verify those records, it is next to impossible. And in the final analysis, the system works; with human nature being what it is . . ."

What Dr. Faust left unsaid is that it is Management's greatest folly to believe that organizational members, when called upon to supply information that can affect their own organizational well-being, can be neutral with regard to that information. And in spheres of endeavor as diverse as the military, the church, government, charities, industry, managers pore over pages of statistics that are tributes to little else than human creativity.

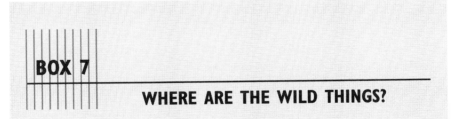

BOX 7

WHERE ARE THE WILD THINGS?

Things happen. When, as a part of her U.S. Forest Service management training program, a trainee surveyed her fellow employees she found:

- About one-quarter reported preparing sites for reforestation when in fact the work had not been done.
- Almost one-third reported planting more seedlings than they had, or reported plantings that had not been made at all.
- Over 40 percent reported having done work at the wrong time or under inappropriate circumstances.

Quite understandably, the Forest Service management ordered an inspection of the surveyed area and one of its neighbors. The results of *this* study, however, showed nothing to be grossly amiss, and management concluded that if any problem exists, it is confined to the earlier surveyed area.

Yet skeptics abound. They point to the lack of confidentiality in the follow-up study and the obvious motivation of the Service to dismiss the earlier findings. So what's going on here?

Over 80 percent of the surveyed group reported extreme pressure to meet the productivity targets set by management and said that they felt that reporting the lack of reality of their assigned targets would affect their performance ratings. Even the head of the affected region is willing to admit that there may be inordinate pressure on employees to meet unrealistic targets. He talks about "numbers" being passed down from level to level, and by the time they come to rest at the working level, possibly being unrealizable on the ground.

Creativity is the order of the day. Foresters with targeted responsibilities but no funds borrow from one source to pay for another. One reported using funds allocated for killing gophers for the purpose of preparing timber acreage for sale. In fact, he did kill of a few, then reported the job done, and then misapplied the remaining 90 percent of the funds to the more immediately visible work.

What are we to make of this? Several things. During the early 1980s there had been a constriction of *non*defense government spending. Lacking realistic feedback, and under pressure to increase productivity, upper and middle managers created a system of unrealistic targets. Finally, foresters fear that reporting actual productivity figures will not change the system, but only bring negative consequences to the reporter.

Source: *Wall Street Journal*, November 12, 1985, p. 29.

PART THREE

WHATSOEVER YE SOWETH THAT SHALL YE ALSO REAP

THE ROMANCE OF LEADERSHIP AND THE FORMS OF COMMUNICATION

The images still live: Churchill promising blood, sweat, and tears; Martin Luther King promising that we shall overcome. And most of you have probably seen TV footage of Adolf Hitler haranguing the frenzied masses from his flag-draped balcony. More recently we saw Boris Yeltsin clamber atop a Soviet tank and exhort the crowd to resist the "coup plotters," a move which surely solidified his bid for leadership. (The frailty of leadership is illustrated by what might have happened had he been shot in this exercise). Finally, George Bush's contretemps in the 1992 election is laid to his lack of leadership—the failure of his "vision thing."

Over the centuries, scholars have been fascinated and puzzled by the phenomenon of leadership. What makes these people so special? And what could people as different as Mahatma Gandhi, Adolf Hitler, and Ronald Reagan possibly have in common, or Eva Peron, Indira Gandhi and Margaret Thatcher? There must be more to leadership than personal traits such as intelligence, honesty, forcefulness, craftiness and yes, even the "vision thing."

There is another line of thinking that says "the times make the man," or that each age deserves the leadership it gets. Political scientists have even asserted that individual leaders make no difference in world events! They reason that if we had not been cursed with Adolf Hitler, for example, someone else would have filled his role with similar results. The sweeping forces of history are not to be denied. Unfortunately for knowledge (but fortunately for humanity) we cannot rerun history experimentally to find the answer. The upshot of all this is that, although there is plenty of speculation about the nature and consequences of leadership, we know little more about leadership on a grand scale today than we did a few centuries ago.

What does the term leadership mean, anyway? For one thing, the existence of leadership is inferred from the behavior it presumably causes, as is the case with motivation. Where followers are found—people who accept and follow the wishes of another—then that other is said to possess "leadership qualities." You don't find this satisfactory? Well, neither do I. But keep in mind that this is basically the way we define people as great leaders. The good or evil of their works is another matter.

I'll come right out and say it: leadership is one of humanity's most cherished myths. Historical recountings of leadership are embellished and purified in our mythologies. I'm certain that George Washington was not all that his myth portrays. The Soviet Union was not alone in rewriting history!

Everything just said applies to organizations, and perhaps doubly so. The *Wall Street Journal* and the *New York Times* business sections powerfully portray the myth of leadership. Larger-than-life leaders are single-handedly responsible for the prosperity, resurrection, or demise of great enterprises. In these pages the personalities, passions, and problems of these leaders are skillfully correlated with their organizations' achievements. There is little doubt that there is a causal connection between leadership actions and organizational results.

To put it differently, the leadership myth is "enacted" within the culture of the organization by all participants. That is, participants perceive and interpret events selectively to support the myth of *management efficacy.* Note that the term efficacy is defined as "the capacity to produce results." Attributing efficacy to leaders includes both the good and the bad. Leaders share in this process of enactment by following the rules of leadership behavior, by paying attention to symbol and ritual.

If there is some truth to this description, are we then to take it that leaders count for nothing? Not at all! Remember that *The Ropes* is examining organizational behavior from primarily a cultural/interpretive perspective, that "other side of the coin." Consequently, it is still entirely proper to claim from the technical/ rational, or scientific, perspective that we do have evidence of leadership effectiveness.

And what do we know *scientifically* about leadership? On the one hand, a great deal; on the other, not that much. Scientific studies of leadership come primarily from the tradition of group dynamics. Most of what we "know" is based on contrived studies of the leader and the work group, often experimentally isolated. The problem is that observation of leaders in natural organizational settings shows us that most of the leader's time is spent relating to superiors and peers, not to immediate subordinates; we don't know nearly as much about this situation.

Another issue is that these scientific studies, as do media presentations, define effective leadership in terms of performance, not simply in terms of followers. This seems reasonable, except for the fact that performance is easier said than measured. For example, let's say that company A has had three outstandingly profitable years, and that its president has been written about on numerous occasions in the *Journal* and the *Times*. She's certainly willing to take credit for the achievements (as you and I would be). But is credit due? It could be the economy, it could be . . . well, it could be almost anything!

The problem of measuring the performance of first-line leaders is analogous, perhaps even more difficult. A given department is embedded in an entire system of organizational inputs and outputs and enmeshed in a web of superior/subordinate authority relationships. Much of what transpires that is organizationally significant, both good and bad, is beyond the direct control of that first-line manager. This is not the way it is perceived by subordinates, of course, who see their manager as very much in control of their own destinies—for better or worse. After all, who would rather feel that their direct superior is powerless to look after their interests?

From such a viewpoint, the dramaturgy of the leadership training program can serve much the same purpose as does the motivational program. Corporate-wide problems can be framed in terms of the "lack of leadership" in the lower level ranks. For example, in 1988 the *Wall Street Journal* reported that General Motors was investing $3 million in a program called "Leadership Now." Hindsight from 1993 would suggest: a) it may have prolonged Roger Smith's tenure a bit and b) it didn't help GM a whit. (*Manager's Journal,* October 3, 1988, p. A-16).

So again we look to corporate culture, myth, perception, and attribution for explanations. Superiors are likely to identify high performers as those with "obvious" managerial attributes like energy and crispness of action. If the person's department has performed middling well, then myth, perception, and attribution processes take the reins, and our budding executive is on the way.

Which brings us to the second theme of this part and why leadership is paired with communication rather than with decision making. What we know about leadership in real organizational settings persuades me that communication is crucial, decision making only incidental. Leadership requires convincing people—superiors, peers, and subordinates—to follow courses of action that are required to make the decision work once it is made. That is the essence of successful communication: to bring about a tangible result. But at least a part of this convincing is the result of communication that comes not from the leader, but from the *idea* of leadership. Members of the organization, through symbolic and other forms of communication, come to share a common stock of knowledge that presupposes the efficacy of leadership actions.

What makes for successful communication? If I knew the answer to that, I'd be rich and famous (which I'd like). One aspect of effective communication is that the receiver's conclusion is his or her own and is seen as a self-evidently true and natural consequence of this situation. To put it another way, the conclusion drawn is a first-hand product of the receiver's own powers of observation and reasoning and not a second-hand product conveyed directly by the message. The conclusion should also be in accord with the myth, symbol, and ritual meanings of the organizational culture. Being in accord with "what everybody knows," with the stock of knowledge of those "things taken for granted," leads directly to the assumption of truth and naturalness. Perhaps an example or two will help.

How about that performance appraisal ritual? A belief central to our organizational mythology is that performance is rewarded in direct proportion to merit and effort. Who would have it otherwise? As a consequence of these beliefs, organizations arrange a yearly ritual meeting between superior and subordinate. Two things are communicated by such meetings. First, performance is the thing that counts, and second, we can measure it (and yours) on a scale of one to seven. There is usually another element, too: an enumeration of the things you can do to improve your performance, for no one must be left with the belief that they cannot improve.

What Kerry Drake will tell you is that the plain and unvarnished truth of the matter is that most of these performance appraisal ratings are notoriously unreliable—they aren't very accurate. Most managers hate to do them, largely because they harbor the gnawing suspicion that they are making judgments based on very little hard data. Yet the ritual itself is the very best way to communicate a message that is vital to the maintenance of the culture of the organization, a message with which most managers agree. After all, weren't they promoted within that system?

Just one other brief example. In the wake of the revelations concerning the Iran/Contra dealings—arms sold to Iran with the proceeds secretly (and illegally) sent to the contra-Sandinista forces —serious questions arose as to the role played by President Reagan. I recall one cartoon posing the political dilemma, "Knew It and Blew It," *vs* "Should've Known But Didn't." But the White House "spin doctors" *did* know how to cure it. "Leadership style" they pronounced, the president's hands-off leadership style is what led to the problem. Appoint the best people you can find for the job, and leave them unfettered to do the best job they can. This neatly solves two problems. First, the president isn't a snoozing septuagenarian who misses most of what goes on in cabinet meetings. No, he's a take charge, but hands-off guy. Secondly, if it's leadership *style* that's the problem, well, we all know that style, unlike personality, can be changed. So have no fear.

The point is that by framing the problem as one of style, no more need be said. The rest of the interpretive context is self-supplied and evidently true.

The organization as a cultural context provides an interpretive framework for actions. When Ted Shelby stays after working hours each day, he is saying something that his superiors understand within this framework. Ditto for that performance appraisal and the three-piece suit. Communication is based on the pairing or juxtaposition of situations, symbols, or actions in such a way as to make the conclusion self-evident to the observer. It is not just the suit, it is the meaning of that suit as a symbol in the interview context. And it is not just hanging around the office; it is staying late as symbolic of effort in the work context. Remember the company picnic? That flowered shirt communicates something in the picnic context that is completely different from what it would communicate in an office context.

One final point. At one time or another, usually upon the discovery of a major SNAFU, you may have heard that there was "a failure to communicate," or "a communication problem." These phrases can be quite misleading, for they usually do not mean that information failed to pass from A to B as had been expected. Rather, the phrases signify that information was indeed passed from A to B, but was rejected by B as false, irrelevant, or unimportant. Of course, A would like to have observers of the scene believe that B just didn't get the point. But in most instances, B probably did get the point, and only too well!

Section Five

SKATE FAST OVER THIN ICE
The Myth of Leadership Perception and Attribution

As Stanley moved through the ranks of The Company, he became aware of Ted Shelby's distinctive qualities. Ted wasn't one to admit he didn't have the answer to a critical question, nor was he one to let a lack of convincing reasons dissuade him from taking positions he felt were advantageous. Sometimes he would skim over major points on his way to his final conclusion. On these occasions, Stanley would say to himself: "That's right, Ted—when you're skating on thin ice, you'd better skate fast. Because if you stay in one spot too long, you're going to fall through."

As stated earlier, we do know a great deal about leadership. There has probably been more research and theory building devoted to leadership than to any other single topic in management. But *The Ropes* is devoted to different questions and is aimed at a different level of organization. For example, the ability to skate lightly is the kind of leadership attribute that will appear more than once in the tales that follow. How do leaders act strategically within their organizations? How and why do they choose subordinates? How do leaders manage power, and how do they curry favor with superiors? In a phrase, how do leaders work within the culture of the organization? Here we are interested in a different sort of organizational effectiveness than the technical/rational kind and in a different set of relationships than the manager/work group kind.

Perhaps you were less than enthusiastic about some of the things said about leadership in the introduction to this part. That may be because you were hoping to pick up some tips on how to become better leaders yourselves. Although the approach taken here may be unorthodox, I still believe you can learn some important things about being a leader in your organization.

Here are two guiding principles for our further investigation of the leadership phenomenon.

- Unquestionably, such a thing as leadership does exist. We shouldn't be dismayed if a good measure of it consists in getting out in front of the crowd and heading wherever they happen to be going.

- Leaders do make a difference in the success of organizations. On the other hand, good fortune bears an uncanny resemblance to good judgment.

In recent years, the people who study organizations have been asking a new set of questions concerning the beliefs we all hold about leadership. And they have been getting some thought-provoking answers. Although still a minority viewpoint, these ideas are well illustrated in the results of two studies.

In the first, participants were given a very brief description of an organization, its activities, a manager, some subordinates, and the results of the first year's business.[1] However, different groups of participants were given different results, varying from poor to excellent. Participants were then asked to record, among other things, how much these results differed from what might be reasonably expected, and to what the results might be attributed. The outcome? When the results were better or much worse than expected, they were attributed to the manager far more often than to other alternatives like market conditions. Only when the results were slightly worse than expected were other alternatives cited more frequently than leadership.

It seems that the socialization provided by our organizational culture leads to a taken-for-granted belief in the efficacy of leadership. So when there is something that calls for an explanation, like results much better or worse than expected, participants once again fall back on those "trustworthy recipes for thinking-as-usual." Actually, nothing good or bad was said about the leader in this experiment. The perceptual processes of filling in and distortion were at work once again.

Finally, there is the presence of a "perceptual set." Once people see a situation or problem in a particular way, they settle into a rut and find it difficult to see that situation or problem in any other way. So now we have all the ingredients for the attribution of leadership efficacy: the motivation to explain a situation, perceptual distortion and filling in, and, a preexisting perceptual set, derived from socialization, for the attribution of results to leadership.

Now the second study.[2] Suppose we created an organization so that participants were randomly assigned to the positions of superior or subordinate. This mock organization will perform tasks labeled specifically as "managerial" or "clerical" in much the same way as in real organizations. After a few hours of operation, participants are asked to rate the group of managers and the group of clerks, as groups, on such traits as leadership and assertiveness, and on the likelihood of *future* outcomes, such as whether or not they would be successful in later careers or would make good executives.

The startling result is that both managers and clerks rate the managers, as a group, significantly more favorably than the clerks as a group. And this is true despite the fact that (1) these ratings were of *future outcomes* and (2) virtually 100 percent of the participants, clerks and managers alike, acknowledged on the rating form that they realized that the positions of clerk or manager had been *randomly assigned* to individual participants!

The very fact that this seems a bit difficult to believe illustrates the point that I have been trying to make. Let's look at some of the dynamics of the last experiment that might lead to such an outcome.

First, the hierarchical organization of work tasks distorts the information that workers have about each other. Subordinates are expected to act deferentially and work in the way their superiors expect. For this reason, they must frequently ask the superior's advice to ascertain whether or not what they are doing is what the superior wants. And this must be done despite the fact that subordinates may be perfectly capable of proceeding on their own. Thus, observers can see for themselves that managers are dominant and resourceful, whereas subordinates are quite the opposite. In addition, managers control the timing and frequency of the inspection of work. Subordinates are expected to present work for criticism at any point; managers can time the presentation of their own work to their best advantage.

Similarly, subordinates are often assigned tasks that give little opportunity to demonstrate superior abilities, unlike managers. Observers make inferences on the basis of what they see, seldom on the basis of what they *do not* see. Thus, what both the "managers" and "clerks" actually observe going on in the experiment is, as we know from attribution theory, derived from the *situational* context yet attributed to the actors' *personal* traits. Not so strange after all.

In real organizations, in addition to these factors, there are other arrangements that support the attribution of leadership qualities to superiors. Some of these are: access to privileged information, reinforcing the appearance of superior knowledge; the power to bestow rewards and punishments, reinforcing the appearance of leadership efficacy; and, not in the least, the subordinates' active desire to believe in their leader's superior qualities. Who would have it otherwise?

At this point something said earlier needs to be reemphasized. None of the foregoing should be taken to mean that leadership skills make no difference. As my buddy Stu Klein pointed out to me, I've had the experience of working for both good and bad leaders in my own career, and it didn't take much thought to figure out who was which and why! So there is every reason to believe that on occasion, and under certain conditions, leaders *do* make a difference. If this is the case, then it probably is important for both leaders and subordinates to hold an exaggerated belief in the efficacy of leadership. For without this belief, it might prove exceedingly difficult to energize the organization to action when needed (the "rain dance effect" referred to in the introduction to Part I).

By now you may be wondering, well, all right, you've half convinced me, but what am I to do with all of this, anyway? Two things, perhaps.

First, what is presented here is a *perspective for understanding* leadership as it actually takes place in organizations. From this perspective you will be able to deal intelligently with some events that would otherwise be most puzzling.

Second, you should be able to spot, and perhaps to use, some of those organizational supports that lead to the favorable attribution of leadership effectiveness. And that, after all, is no mean thing in itself.

29 The Men's Hut

I suppose I should not have dropped by on a Saturday morning, but I was curious to find out how it had gone. That meeting with the Task Force had been a continuing source of anxiety for Stanley for the last five or six weeks.

"And how did your Task Force meeting go?" The Task Force, I should explain, was the final "contribution" of a Vice President on the verge of retirement who wanted a lasting monument to his name left to The Company. He put together a Task Force, mostly composed of people at the plant manager level—or above—whose purpose was to "ensure The Company's continued leadership in product excellence."

"I don't know," said Stanley, "sort of a letdown, I guess. I came away from there feeling that somehow I just hadn't scored. And you know how I'd been waiting for this."

"Waiting" was quite an understatement. About a year ago Stanley had first started trying to persuade Ted Shelby to let him present his own report to the Task Force. At that time Ted had pointed out that only recently had he himself been able to attend any meetings of the Task Force, and Stanley knew he was telling the truth. Prior to that, Stanley had spent afternoons loading Ted up with all he knew. Then Ted would spend the following mornings briefing his boss so that he could report it. This struck Stanley as terribly roundabout, because in this case he was the person most familiar with what was going on.

But Ted, as usual, had a perfectly logical explanation for it. "Those people on the Task Force," he reasoned, "are important, very busy. They don't have time to listen to every project report. By the time it gets to them, it has to be down to the bare essentials— crisp and hard-hitting. You know what I mean. If everyone working on a project went to those meetings, things would get out of hand."

But, Stanley remembered, Ted had distinctly told him that he would eventually meet with this important group.

Now, a year later, Stanley had just had his crack at the Task Force. For weeks he'd worked on his presentation, complete with rehearsals—five dry runs on his series of flip charts. Ted had cautioned him that he would be up in front of the sharpest people in The Company, that they don't hesitate to ask pointed, even embarrassing questions. Stanley would have to anticipate the questions, know all the answers, have his talk down cold. Above all, he should not drag out his presentation. Those people have no sympathy for time wasters.

"Well, what happened?"

"I'm not sure that anything *happened*." Stanley looked downcast. "Here's how it went: first of all, you know where they hold those Task Force meetings—far away from everything—no distractions at all. This one was at an off-season ski resort in the Poconos. So I arrive at about eleven in the morning, and the place is still pretty well deserted. They've got this suite of rooms on the second floor, so up I go. The room they use for the meetings is really messy, and a couple of guys I recognize—Plant Managers—are having coffee at a table. In comes the Paducah Plant Manager.

"He looks a little sick. Something he ate, maybe. One of the guys at the table gives him the elbow and says "Hey, Kenny! What'd Bill take you for last night anyway? He's some player, huh? I figure that's another pair of galoshes on your expense account after that one!" The Plant Manager, Kenny they call him, goes over and makes a crack about this cocktail waitress. I didn't hear much, but he's really laying it on this other guy.

"Well, what the hell, it's the third day of the meeting, and my report is about the last thing on the agenda. Why *shouldn't* they play some poker? They've been working hard. They've got to blow off some steam. I'm scheduled to make my pitch that afternoon, then the meeting is going to break up. If they're going to relax a bit, I suppose this is the time for it. They've probably gotten most of the important work done already.

"The meeting starts a little late; they can't find a couple of Task Force members. But I finally start my talk. About every fifteen minutes somebody says, "Let's break for a minute or two," and then they disappear for a half hour. One guy keeps going out to the telephone—turns out that he runs his plant single-handed and the place falls apart in his absence.

"But I keep plugging away and finally finish my report, flip charts and all. By now two guys are almost asleep and Kenny from Paducah is still looking a little shaky. Even so, I don't think he looks a whole lot worse than the rest of them. So I ask for questions. Okay, the guy from Portland doesn't understand one of my charts.

I explain it to him, and when I finish, it turns out I've confused another guy, who thought he understood it the first time around, but isn't sure now.

"Then this guy from Plant Operations staff asks why I haven't taken account of the five-year forecasts New York sent around earlier this year. But my whole point is what those forecasts mean for what the Task Force is doing! This guy hasn't listened to the first thing I've said—not that he's the only one. Keep cool, Stan, I say to myself. So I try my best to go back diplomatically and rehash what I'd said earlier. And now the plant operations guy breaks in and says, 'Son, you'd better do your homework. Those forecasts say a lot about what we're doing here. If you can't talk about *them*, why'd you bother to come up here in the first place?'

"And then Ted pipes up, 'I'm afraid Bill's got a point, Stanley!' Jesus! Ted knows what I'm doing all along, and he knows damn well that I've answered Bill's question and a few more besides. And here he is putting me on the spot.

"Then, just as I'm about to try again to make my point clear, there's another coffee break and everybody runs off to the bathroom or the phone or the bar. Half an hour later most of them come back. Then the meeting's adjourned; or, at least, they send me home.

"So what I want to know is: with people like that running The Company, how come we're still in business?"

How come? Well, at least one reason is that the people running The Company are no different from the people who run organizations throughout the nation. Stanley's observation is that the members of the Task Force are not extraordinary. But neither are they ordinary, for after all, it takes talent and acumen to reach top management. It's just that Stanley's expectations of them are over-inflated.

The difficulty is that Stanley has gained admission to the Men's Hut too soon, in the wrong context, and before he has had sufficient preparation. Had Stanley been with The Company longer he would have seen some things more clearly; he would have had a more realistic idea of how things actually work. And, most important, he would have had a greater investment in the system—an investment that would help him see things in a different light. By the time he is admitted he would have paid his dues and would be committed to the system and its continuation. Consequently, he would find that the other members of the Men's Hut are people not much different from him. Obviously, they are there on the basis of merit, just as he is.

And so the procedure of subordinates briefing superiors, who, in turn, brief their own superiors, who only then carry the message to executive councils, is not so foolish as it seems in the eyes of youth. "The Management" of The Company is symbolic as much as it is real. The social order of an organization depends at least in some degree on the imputation of special and extraordinary abilities to those in charge. This myth provides an unassailable answer to the question continually asked by Stanleys throughout The Company, "Why should we do it this way?"

The Task Force is in large part another ritual of the Men's Hut. Their project is important, but things in The Company are so arranged that nothing and no one is really indispensable. The work involved could be done by fewer, more junior people, and the people who are working on it certainly had better things to do with their time. But again, the Task Force is symbolic. It requires the prestige of people in high office, and for the participants it is partly duty, partly a reward. It is right that Stanley should have taken his own part in it seriously—for that is his proper place in such things. Yet had he been in the system longer, he would have had a truer appreciation of the meaning of the event. To put it another way, don't be overanxious to take your place in the Men's Hut. Each thing in its season.

30

Better The Devil You Know . . .

"Howyadoin', how's Bette and the kids?"

"Not too bad, I suppose, How's y'self? Still trying to break 80?"

The initial meeting of the Portsmouth Plant manufacturing staff group was being convened in New York—a group selected from various company locations that was getting together for the first time. As *The Company Clarion* put it in a recent feature story:

> The manufacturing staff team put together for the Portsmouth effort represents the very best of The Company in this area. New York wanted the top people regardless of current responsibilities, so the new staff team represents many of our plants and facilities—a Company team.

The story went on to describe the team members and their previous responsibilities, with special emphasis on the expertise and representativeness of the individuals selected.

The Company is a big company and a growing one, which means, of course, that it is also a successful one. Growth comes from expansion of existing plants and facilities and the construction of new ones. Growth also means the expansion of management opportunities for people within the Company, for, quite typically, the policy is to promote from within. Finally, growth means that every two to three years you will be moved on to a new management opportunity at least several hundred miles away.

Stanley knows all this. Consequently, he is surprised to find that of the roughly dozen or so people here, most of them (a) know one another pretty well ("How's Bette and the kids"/"still trying to break 80") and (b) don't *really* seem to represent the "best thinking of The Company in the area." This last observation is based on Stanley's estimate of his own abilities and his opinion of Ted.

As the meeting continues, the initial impression is strengthened and other anomalies appear.

"I think you're right, Kerry," Ted was saying, "the way we handled it at Paducah is the right idea, with a little more sophistication systemwise."

"Leave the systems aspect to Sheila, will you, Ted? That was the one angle we had whipped in Pawtucket. We need *you* in training."

Kerry, it turns out, is on his fifth or sixth assignment for The Corporate Director heading the team. He's worked for other people, but sure enough, every other year or so the current Corporate Director moves up; so does Kerry. And the same with Sheila, and now Ted.

For his part, Dr. Faust had Kerry in his Middle Management Advanced Study Course at The University for four months. And Stanley, of course, has been Faust's graduate assistant.

On the operating side things aren't much different. Ben Franklyn, the new Plant Manager, has worked with Robbie, his manufacturing manager, at four locations, and Bill, Robbie's Chief of Expandrium Operations, has been with Robbie off and on since he was recruited from Another University ten years ago.

Among the anomalies are the fact that Bill probably wouldn't know an Expandrium pellet if he had it for lunch (he had been plucked from maintenance engineering at Portland) and that Kerry really didn't seem to think all that much of Ted's ability.

Mulling over the situation and its apparent contradictions with both the story in *The Company Clarion* and the genuine importance accorded the project by executive management, Stanley approached Dr. Faust cautiously.

"Uh, it strikes me as kind of funny that most of these people know each other so well. You know what I mean?" Faust's expression answered that he saw nothing untoward here.

"I mean, if this group has been selected *individually* to get our best people from all the plants—uh—isn't it kind of funny how they all know each other so well? And isn't it kind of funny that some of them—uh—well, they really don't seem to know very much about the new Expandrium process, either?"

Faust puffed on his pipe noncommittally. "I think that you will find the group assembled here to be entirely adequate to do the job," he intoned.

Swell, thought Stanley. And then, throwing caution (which God knows he has little enough of) to the wind, "C'mon, Doc, you know what I mean. I really think these guys picked each other as sort of a personal favor, not because they were the best for the job."

Faust thought a moment and then decided that no harm would be done by answering Stanley's question. As usual, Stanley seemed to have the facts but to have missed the point.

"Hmmm, yes, you are right. But no, you are wrong. You are right that all these people have worked for one another on numerous occasions, and that it is not by chance that they are here as a group today. In fact, *you* (pipe stem pointed accusingly) are not here by chance today.

"But you are wrong in thinking that, because of this, these people are not the best for the job. True, some know very little about Expandrium processing, but they know a great deal about each other.

Stanley's expression posed the obvious question.

"Why is that so important? I will tell you. These people have to work together as a team on a new and risky venture. This means that, occasionally, one must, ah, subordinate one's own interests or ideas for the good of the project. Now I *absolutely* guarantee you that the group made up of the top Expandrium processing experts in The Company will be incapable of doing this. Some simply will not fit in, will not be able to get along with the others. But more to the point, it will take months, possibly years, before they develop sufficient knowledge of one another, and hence trust, to be able to work together effectively. And that is just too long."

Dr. Faust paused to relight his pipe, then continued.

"I think it would be impossible for you to overestimate the importance of past relationships in helping these people work together. Kerry has been with our Corporate Director in a number of situations. Kerry knows that he will be, ah, taken care of later no matter how things look *now*. And the Director knows that Kerry understands this and is intelligent enough to be counted on to do the right thing at the right time. And now it is the same with Kerry and Ted.

"And, yes, I see that you have concluded that Kerry does not place a high estimate on Ted's technical capacity. Quite right. But that is not what Kerry it looking for from Ted."

Now is was Stanley's turn.

"I see your point, all right. But still, it seems to me that this is a little too cozy. I mean, wouldn't it be better to bring in *some* outside talent. Isn't this a little incestuous?"

Faust actually smiled. "Well, yes. I suppose it *is*. But one must consider the alternatives. Suppose one does bring in a stranger to a key position. First, one never knows whom one is going to get. There is a tendency to unload problem people on this kind of venture—especially bright problem people. One rationalizes that this sort of person will work out better in a new setting. Possibly yes—but mostly no, unfortunately. And one simply cannot tell much about a new person in a day or two, much less an interview situation.

"The second point is one that I have already made. Over the years these people have built a bond of reinforcement. Ted knows that Kerry will be able to move him ahead in the future. Ted, for his part, will do what is necessary—and Kerry knows this. And yes, Kerry also knows that there may be better men than Ted for the job—in a technical sense. But he also knows that Ted will never get him in trouble by doing something organizationally naive, stupid, or self-serving."

With this, Faust got up abruptly and walked off.

"Better the devil you know than the one you don't," thought Stanley.

Yes, that's the principle here. But typically, Stanley did not grasp the entire principle, for Faust necessarily had left some things unsaid. For example, one thing that Kerry had learned at Dr. Faust's Advanced Management Training Course was that Faust understood well the role of the consultant—to help Management get the job done. Faust wasn't the kind to embarrass you with untimely facts. For his part, Dr. Faust saw that Kerry was properly appreciative of an effective consultant. He knew that Kerry would see to it that his consultants received proper credit within Management (and, as a consequence, additional opportunities).

Faust also left unsaid anything of Stanley's relationship to the project. And that was unfortunate, for Stanley is the type who has to learn the ropes himself. Faust had expected Stanley to understand the nature of their mutual obligation. But in his naïveté, Stanley was going on the assumption that, in fact, he actually was the best man for the job, and Faust had been lucky to find him. I'll finish the story for you later. But if you can't wait, you might turn ahead to a tale in Part 4, *Your Job, My Reputation.*

Success Story

Stanley looked at the front page of *The Company Clarion* with wide-eyed amazement: "Mill Hand to Vice Chairman of Board in Ten Years." Incredible!, thought Stanley. With increasing interest, Stanley read the story beneath the headline.

> Beginning his career with The Company as an operator of an Expandrium extruder in the Pawtucket plant, Mr. C. Marsh Bell was, after three months on the job, made foreman. Three months later he was promoted to assistant mill supervisor at the plant in Pawtucket. During his six-month sojourn, the mill achieved a rate of production that stands as a Company record. He was then selected as marketing manager for Expandrium products in District 7 of the Southwest Region, where he set a sales record that has never been equaled. His next promotion, after one year, was . . .

It was a fascinating article, and Stanley could see why Mr. Bell had risen so far, so fast. Obviously a man of talent. Up and up and up he had gone, each time with longer tenure—Assistant Marketing Director for the Western Region, Assistant to the Plant Manager at Punxatawney, Corporate Director of Personnel, Assistant Vice President in Charge of Systems and Components, then to Vice President in Charge of Personnel, before finally being made Vice Chairman of the Board.

Fantastic!, thought Stanley. How lucky we were to land a guy like that! What if he'd hired into Another Company? Then Stanley noticed another story on the front page, a biographical sketch of the new Vice Chairman of the Board.

> . . . son of Mr. and Mrs. Coolidge M. Bell (the former Miss Belle C. Marsh of Scarsdale, N.Y.) . . . Best School for Boys Choate

. . . degree from Dartmouth . . . traveled extensively in Europe before joining The Company . . . family well known to employees, dating back to the merger of Bell Products and Marsh Industries into the present corporation, The Company . . .

Stanley suddenly felt that he understood a few things that had puzzled him scant moments ago. But still, Mr. Bell had done the job—set records in all of his assignments, as a matter of fact. He may have had a few advantages in getting his foot in the door, but clearly, given the chance, he had shown that he could perform. But there was a lingering doubt in Stanley's mind, borne of his observation over years with The Company that not many things happened by accident.

Then he heard Ben Franklyn ambling down the hall, muttering to himself: "Well, well, well—little Cooley Bell finally made it . . . records at Pawtucket—har, har . . ." Ben obviously was enjoying himself. Then he looked up and noticed Stanley.

"Look here," he said, waving his copy of *The Company Clarion,* "did you read this? Just goes to show you, stick with old Ben and you'll get places fast—har, har. See, little Cooley Bell was my assistant supervisor at Pawtucket . . . and look where he is now!"

Little? Cooley? What is this?, thought Stanley. Ben doesn't usually speak of top Company management so irreverently. "Sorry, Mr. Franklyn," he said, "but I don't think I get the point."

"Sure you do. C. Marsh Bell . . ." Ben exaggerated each syllable, "was the most successful Assistant Mill Superintendent I ever had. And did I work my backside off to make sure that happened! Listen, the Old Man himself . . ." (here he was referring to Marsh, Sr.) ". . . brought little Cooley into my office. He said, 'Ben, you and I have been business associates for years (those were his very words, 'business associates'), and I believe that you know more about mill operations than anyone else in The Company. I want you to take young Coolidge here and teach him all you know about the business. Don't spare him. He's a bright lad, and he's got a future in The Company.'"

"Well," said Ben, "you don't have to be a rocket scientist to get the idea. The Old Man was telling me that Cooley was going to make it big, no ifs, ands, or buts."

Something still wasn't right. "Mr. Franklyn," said Stanley, "tell me—the way you call Mr. Bell 'Cooley,' it sounds to me like you don't like him."

"I like him fine," said Ben. "He turned out to be a swell kid. But you know, I don't think there was one day in his life that he had to work hard. I don't think he knew how then, and he probably still doesn't. But I'll give him credit; he never acted like he felt he was better than the rest of us, and the men liked him. He could take a joke, and he could play one, too. Still, I was glad as hell when he left. Some time when you get down to the Southwest Region, ask old Kerry Drake about those sales records that Cooley set. Betcha Kerry slept for a month after his star assistant got promoted—har." With that, Ben wandered off.

It was tough for Stanley to figure. Ben didn't seem to resent Mr. C. Marsh Bell, even seemed to like him; but he obviously didn't *respect* him. And that probably accounted for his strange attitude, for his calling him "Cooley" instead of "Mr. Bell." Ben knew why C. Marsh Bell was where he was; and he was honest enough not to pretend. Stanley knew that Ted Shelby would have no trouble at all mouthing the appropriate, "Mr. Bell."

Why does The Company go through a charade like this, if it causes a fair amount of trouble for everybody concerned? Well, for one thing, The Company would like to have everybody believe that hard work and talent (in that order) are what it takes to succeed. And as a general rule this is true. What *do* you do with the C. Marsh Bells? Left to the vagaries of Company life, there is a chance they wouldn't make it on their own. Furthermore, it is impossible for an ordinary Company Manager to have a normal relationship with a subordinate who is the President's nephew and the Chairman of the Board's son. So you can't stick him somewhere in The Company and let him work his own way up. And because there is a deep family involvement and a well-founded loyalty to The Company, you wouldn't want to have Cooley working for Another Company; that wouldn't be right either. How about taking up law or medicine, you ask? Well, that's not everybody's cup of tea. So The Company has to make it look as though C. Marsh Bell has made it on merit . . . or at least, even it he's made it because of who he is, he *could* have made it on merit if he hadn't been who he was. Hence, the job experience and the records. And The Company is smart to do it this way, for even though there will be cynical interpretations, very few people will really know for sure that it happened that way.

But no harm is done, really. Cooley will be charming and well connected as a member of the Board. He can carry his share of the corporate load by making speeches to Kiwanis, Rotary Club, and various other civic groups—duties that must be performed by some top Company officer. He will be loyal, and he'll represent The Company well. Of course, he'll never be President, Comptroller, or hold any other key position where he might botch up something important—that is, unless it strangely turns out that he really *does* have what it takes.

BOX 8

A MODEL CORPORATE CAREER

In April of 1984 the *New York Times* ran a brief column noting the retirement of Alfred M. Hunt as Vice President and Secretary of the Aluminum Company of America.

Just a century ago Captain Alfred E. Hunt and several others had formed the Pittsburgh Reduction Company, which later became Alcoa. Their aim was to exploit commercially a newly developed process for the reduction of aluminum ore into metal. The continuing association of the Hunt family, together with the Mellon and Davis families, other major Alcoa stockholders, is chronicled thus in the article.

Alfred Hunt, the founder, was succeeded by his son, Roy A., who served as President from 1928 to 1951.

A.V. Davis, who was Chairman in 1928, appointed his brother Edward as President of Alcan in that year. Alcan at the time was a wholly owned subsidiary of Alcoa, though in 1945 an antitrust agreement forced its divestiture.

Alfred M. Hunt, the subject of the article, joined Alcoa in 1942 following his graduation from Yale. In 1952, just ten years later, after having held "operating positions" in New York, Ohio, Pennsylvania, and Tennessee, young Hunt was elected Corporate Secretary, responsible for Alcoa's corporate affairs and real estate and insurance divisions. And that was the year (although naturally the article doesn't mention it) that a newly graduated Alcoa engineer, fresh on the Pittsburgh corporate scene (let's call him Stanley, shall we) picked up the Alcoa corporate newspaper and marveled at the meteoric progress of Alfred M. Hunt.

Hunt subsequently was made Vice President in 1963, and served in that capacity until his retirement in 1984. Prominent among Mr. Hunt's accomplishments reported in the article is that he was named Man of the Year in 1977 by the National Steeplechase Hunt Association. Horses, that is.

Source: *New York Times*, April 13, 1984, p. D2.

Stitch In Time

When the devil are they going to finish that thing? It seems to me that they have been putting up that new building forever. Not that I care, understand. But the incessant clanking, hammering, and honking is not suitable accompaniment for my work.

Still, the sight of new construction brings back some interesting recollections. This incident goes back many years now. Stanley had been with The Company not more than one year at the time.

It was his first really big assignment with The Company, working on the construction of the Portland plant. Not only was he given some major responsibility as Kerry Drake's assistant (Kerry was Construction Superintendent), but it was a brand new plant, on a site about 3000 miles from New York. All in all, it was an exciting occasion for Stanley.

But there were some problems at Portland, and Stanley was discussing them with Kerry.

"Now, how're we doing over at B Building, Stanley?" asked Kerry. "Still having problems?"

"I'm afraid so, Mr. Drake," said Stanley. "In fact, construction hasn't even started. The contractor says he has to finish up in A Area before he can move his workers."

"Listen, we can't take that kind of answer from him," said Kerry. "Did you point out to him that he's already behind on B Building? The construction schedule calls for that to be finished by the end of the week!"

"Well, yes, I did," said Stanley, "But then he said that he would have finished with A Area except for our own screw-up. He told me that he could get to work on B if that was what we wanted, but that it would cost us some overtime."

"Great, just what we need," muttered Kerry. "Listen, I want you to . . ." Just then the phone rang, Kerry answered it. Marshall Mason (corporate staff watchdog) from New York was on the line.

"Mase? Fine. How's the weather back there? Oh? Is that right? . . . Oh, Mr. Marsh? . . . plant schedule, eh? Urgent? . . . you've got a list you say? Most important buildings? . . . okay, fire away . . . B Building . . . ?"

Stanley blanched. They were in for it, sure as hell. When Mason found out that the ground hadn't even been broken, Marsh's watchdogs would be all over the place in a couple of days, fouling everything up and generally making life miserable.

"No problems there," said Kerry, "I'd estimate B Building at about 80 to 85 percent completed. Oh, say 80 percent, just to be conservative . . . yeah, things are going very well. We've been getting in some good licks the past couple of weeks."

Stanley couldn't believe his ears. Had Kerry Drake gone crazy?

"Yeah, we've been pushing it hard since your last visit, Mase . . . well, I'm sure glad that Mr. Marsh will be pleased . . . Say, one other thing, we've been pushing this so hard that we got a little ahead of our construction plans in A Area and . . ."

Stanley listened in awe as Kerry neatly wrote off their goof, came up with some extra money, and got a pat on the back besides. When Kerry hung up, Stanley said, "Kerry, uh—don't get me wrong, but I couldn't help overhearing your conversation, and . . . you *do* know that we haven't even started on B Building, don't you—I mean, like we were just talking about? I mean, 80 percent complete? What if someone from Corporate comes out to check?"

Kerry guffawed. "Look at it like this, there's no way I can be worse off than to tell them exactly what's going on out here. And I mean just that. Those staff guys have never built a damned thing in their lives. I know what I've got to do, and I'll get it done. Marsh knows what he's doing, too, but he has to work through his staff jackals. They're all afraid of him, and they take everything he says at face value. Listen, if I'd told Mason that we haven't even started B Building, he'd go straight to Marsh's handlers, get them all stirred up, and we'd be finished. Every damned staff smart-aleck in The Company would be telling us what to do and tripping all over themselves. We'd never get the job done. Besides, even if they decide to come on out now—let's say they start thinking about it tonight—nobody would arrive for a week anyhow. Get the contractor in here, Stanley, and we'll start moving on the B Building shell; we've got the bucks for it now. And, what the hell, those staff guys can't tell 25 percent finished from 75 or 80 percent, for that matter."

The moral of this chapter is: "Lie to your boss when it suits your purposes," right?

Wrong. At least mostly wrong. The moral is: "Manage the situation." And especially with your superiors. Let's try another illustration from another context. Bill Whyte—the William F. Whyte of Street Corner Society—has a story he likes to tell about the restaurant business—"The Crying Waitress," he calls it. There's a particular restaurant in a big city, a place to go to get something to eat, and then get out. It's a very busy place, not some gourmet hideaway. People don't go there for the cuisine; they go because it's quick and convenient.

Being hectic and crowded at dinner, it's tough on the waiters and waitresses. One of them, Nancy, just can't take it; things are always going wrong. Orders are getting mixed up, customers are nasty—and she ends up in tears just about every day. Another waitress, Magda, does okay. She gets through the evening with relatively few problems, no tears, and pretty good tips besides.

How come? The easiest explanation is that Magda can take it, and Nancy can't. But that's too easy, and Whyte was never one for personality theories. So he looks a little closer at the *situation*, at the way that Magda goes about her job.

Stanley has had one hell of a day, didn't leave the office until 6:45. He collapses into a booth, exhausted. Magda is right there. "Good evening, sir. Tough day? How about a drink? Martinis are the special tonight—a double for the price of a single."

"Uh . . ." says Stanley. "Well, I . . . uh, I really like bourbon better."

"Sure. I'll get you a special martini that's so special, it'll be a double bourbon." Off she goes. She knows the bartender, so she gets Stanley a double for the price of a single. While he's drinking it, she comes back." Like to order, sir? The prime rib is terrific tonight . . ." Why not? Stanley likes prime rib as well as anything. And so it goes.

What Magda is doing is managing the situation. She keeps the customers from having to think too much, makes the decisions for them. After all, most of her customers are indifferent anyway; they wouldn't be at that restaurant if they were gourmets. And they're tired, to boot. The truth is, they'd *rather* she made the decisions for them, and if she can get a drink into them first, so much the better. The less muss and fuss, the happier they are.

So that's the plan of attack: drink first (double if possible), suggest what's available and fast, rather than what's best, or, worse yet, what the customer *really* wants (most of them don't have a real craving for anything on the menu, at least not until after they make their choice). But always manage the relationship so that customers don't set their hearts on a dish only to find out that the restaurant is all out of it, or that they'll have to wait another half hour till it's ready.

There is an important lesson for leadership behavior here, in both these instances. And it has nothing to do with managing subordinates. It's just this: if you let others set the agenda for you, then you can't control the consequences. Don't worry about who is *supposed* to manage the situation; you manage it.

33

By Your Works Shall Ye Be Known

M r. Marsh's office will need this by Tuesday, Stanley. So you've got to get right on it. We've got to be sure The Company is doing its best to compensate our top technical contributors properly."

Ted's manner was fittingly important/urgent as he explained to Stanley what was needed on his special assignment.

"These people are the backbone of The Company's technical thrust," Ted explained. "All have been nominated as outstanding technical contributors by their own top management. So naturally Mr. Marsh wants to make sure that they are being compensated ('paid,' Stanley translated to himself) appropriately."

Ted departed, leaving Stanley with a list of twenty-one outstanding contributors and the assignment to unearth the personnel data necessary to determine whether or not the people on the list were being "appropriately compensated"—whatever that might mean.

It did not take Stanley very long to find out what those words *did* mean, and mostly by contrary example. For here was an outstanding contributor who was given only a C rating by his manager in his last performance review. (The Company's merit rating system ran A, B, C, D, and out, not unlike those used in the school systems.) Another was rated B by his manager—not bad but not outstanding—with summary comments indicating that the man needed to improve his technical skills to qualify for his next promotion. And then there were other cases, those who were, in fact, rated A but who were underpaid by anyone's standards. Stanley pondered the situation for a while and came to a conclusion: "Something's wrong here."

Perhaps some research was indicated. With that in mind, Stanley looked up Drew Bolt, Group Manager of Plant Engineering at Pawtucket, for one of Pawtucket's finest was on the list. Briefly, the process of forming "the list" was sequential and hierarchical, with four levels of management involved—Department, Group, Function, and the Plant Manager. Each higher level picks two or three names from the lists submitted from below. Finally, the Plant Manager selects one or possibly two names to be sent on to New York.

"So that's my assignment, Drew," Stanley was saying, "to try to get a better handle on what seems to be, uh, a difference between what these people should be paid and what they actually are paid." Then, handing Bolt the memo from Ted, "Here, this guy is one of yours, I'm pretty sure, A. S. Barker, right?"

Bolt eyed the list, frowning, "Why yes, that's right. But something's wrong here, Stan. My guy isn't on this list."

"Um, I guess that's because he wasn't picked higher up, Drew," Stanley observed brightly,

"No, no, that's not what I mean," Bolt growled. "I mean, yes, Al Barker is one of our people, but not one of the ones I sent up."

"Why not?" Stanley has a genius for missing the point.

"Why not?! How the hell would I know? I sent up Greg Mendel and Eve Curie. Barker's a good man—don't get me wrong. But this program's aimed at the individual technical contributor, the one who otherwise doesn't get into the corporate spotlight."

Stanley left with Bolt muttering to himself about just once doing something right and went to look up Bonnie, who knew just about everyone. Maybe she'd have a clue.

"What do you know about this guy, Bonnie, this A. Sayles Barker? Mr. Bolt says he works here."

"Oh, Al. Everyone knows Al Barker. Honestly, he's the nicest guy. And he knows all the big words. He always helps us with our letters and things. And he's going to be something in The Company some day, too. You just know it by looking at him. And you know . . ."

From what followed, Stanley was able to construct part of the story. And through subsequent consultations with second-and third-level staff people (the "assistants to"), he was able to piece together the rest. The process by which you become an outstanding contributor—at least for some—is this.

The first-level managers, the ones on the firing line, have a pretty good sense of who their technical hotshots are. Oh, they don't always have an outstanding contributor, but they almost always nominate someone. After all, they want to give one of their own people at least a shot at it. These names are then sent up to the Group Managers (next level). They are a little farther from the action, but still pretty knowledgeable. They knock off the obvious weak ones and send one, two, or three names to the function managers (next level), who aren't quite so knowledgeable; same process there, and then on up to the Plant Manager who isn't knowledgeable at all. The Plant Manager then okays one, possibly two, names; these are sent to New York to appear on the final list.

What Stanley found was that it is these last two stops, Function and Plant, where the process goes awry. The names that reach Function level are usually, though not always, those of quiet, competent, technical citizens known only to their own managers and, through an occasional flash of brilliance, to other quiet, competent technicians. But at the upper levels, different criteria are brought to bear by managers, whose different responsibilities necessitate a different perspective. And that's the scenario.

Barker's no dummy, make no mistake about that, but he isn't, and doesn't even *want* to be, a top technical man. Like anyone with sense, he wants to get into top management some day, and probably will. He's good with words, makes a good appearance, and has poise. He knows how to make his point and isn't easily flustered.

These are ideal qualities for the person who will make the technical presentation—the vital communication link between the troops in the technical trenches and middle management. And who would you guess is the worst at the Technical Presentation? Right. The technical people. They're not too good with words in the first place, but they're death with the top management. After all, they don't give a damn about sales or dollars or market share or anything but the beautiful technical details—in *infinite* detail.

So Al Barker makes the presentations. He's got the style, enough of the facts; he's got the right answers, and he delivers well. Above all, he likes to do it, and he knows how to present himself.

Now you're starting to see, are you? Sure. The Division Manager gets the list, looks it over, and thinks, "Say, where's Al Barker?" Turns out Barker made a really top-notch (crisp and hard-hitting, in Ted's words) presentation yesterday.

"Well, that won't do. This fellow's got to be one of our real comers. Let's see, he's in Bolts outfit, isn't he? Uh, I'll just cross off this Gregory Mendel, whoever he is, and put in Barker. Yes sir, he's a real comer. Wonder how Bolt missed him?"

And with this process taking place again at the next level, and throughout The Company, the result in inevitable.

Why is it inevitable, you say? It is inevitable because of who is involved. These top and middle managers have been away from the technical firing line for a long time. They don't have the same perspective any more, if they ever did in the first place. In any event, their role now is to make decisions about alternative programs based on a broad set of criteria, only one of which is technical excellence. They are busy people (at least to their way of thinking) and don't have the time or inclination to be buried under an avalanche of detail. They want the necessary facts, answers to a few key questions, and a balanced (again from the management perspective) presentation. So Al Barker strikes a resonant chord. He's "got his head screwed on right."

The problem, you see, is that it's one thing for Marsh's office to say "let's make up a list of our outstanding contributors," and quite another to do it. As with any complicated decision, the facts do *not* speak for themselves. It is not even clear what facts, or *whose* facts, to use. And after the facts are selected according to one set of criteria, they are judged on the basis of different, though equally valid, criteria.

What makes it seem deceptively simple at the outset is the existence of one or two individuals, those one-in-a-million, who have it all or who have produced something of unquestionable genius at the right time. But the problem is that they *are* one-in-a-million. So the ultimate judgement comes to rest with top management who, consciously or unconsciously, like to see a little "balance" in their technical people.

The net result? As usual, the quiet, competent technician gets passed over, and the one with the management flair, the one with the look of a winner, comes out on top again.

34

Management By Objectives Or The Million Dollar Misunderstanding

The thing to remember gentlemen, and ladies," announced Ted Shelby, "is that no matter how high up in The Company we are, we are all subordinates to *someone*." Twenty-six superior/subordinates murmured their agreement; Ted was addressing the Subordinate Readiness Session, level 5, on *Management By Objectives*.

"From this perspective," he went on, "it becomes crystal clear that superiors and subordinates up and down the line must have a clearly spelled-out understanding of what is expected of each. I might add that this comes out loud and clear in our interviews with top-management subordinates. Briefly stated, the objective of Management By Objectives is to eliminate totally all possibilities of misunderstanding between superiors and subordinates, and to assure that we all have a crisp and hard-hitting set of objectives to measure ourselves against. We don't want the kind of situation at year's end where someone says, 'But I didn't know . . .' No sir, no excuses. We got where we are today through tough, two-fisted management—fair, but tough. And that's the way we want to keep it. If you can't take the heat, get out of the kitchen, right?" This last remark earned him a round of applause.

"Now, I want each of you to have the opportunity to talk to a plant manager in person. I want each of you to get a hands-on feeling for how this program works."

As a new management trainee, Lesley was assigned to interview Ben Franklyn, the Plant Manager at the old plant in Pawtucket. Several days later she drove up there and was ushered into Ben Franklyn's office. "So you're the gal that Shelby sent to get some 'hands-on' experience with Management By Objectives?" Ben pronounced the words with exaggerated clarity, as he did with words he found distasteful. And because it was a staff-generated program, you already know that he found it distasteful. "You would probably like to see my objectives as Plant Manager. I hope you've got a little time today, because they need some explanation.

"You know, the staffers who write these things up, why, I don't believe they've ever been in a plant in their lives, except when Mr. Marsh makes one of his speeches here. These things are clear and—what's that word they use—'objective' (distaste again) to them only because they haven't got the first goddamned idea of what goes on in a manufacturing plant. Here, look at this."

Lesley pulled her chair over to Ben's big desk, and Ben opened up a file and spread out some papers and graphs. "Now," said Ben, pulling out a sheet titled "Production Objectives," "These are more or less okay, even though I don't have any real control over them. Let's take this one: 'Scrap as percentage of finished product.' Know how I handled that one? I inspect all the raw material coming in twice as careful as I used to. That's because it isn't only what my guys do; a lot depends on the job they do in the foundry at Fayetteville. It used to be that I could play ball with those guys; if the stuff they sent wasn't completely lousy, I'd give it a try. But not now. Now I just send it back unless it's top grade. What else can I do? It's a waste of time and money, but I make my objective.

"Here's another one: 'Production man-hours as percentage of standard time.' Now, that one's easy enough to meet. Maybe you don't always get your production up, but you can look okay if you . . ." Ben went on to describe his procedures for claiming downtime on machines and a lot of other things that Lesley didn't understand, except that they didn't sound very productive. Next, Ben pulled out a set of objectives labeled "Behavioral."

"I know you're going to find these perfectly clear, just like me—har," Ben started off. "Here, look at these . . ." There followed major headings such as "Morale," "Subordinate Readiness," "Interpersonal Sensitivity," and the like. Ben took a sarcastic tone: ". . . 'shall act to improve employee-manager relationships at all levels of plant management.' And if you like that one, there's plenty more. Look, I can't even keep track of all my 'behavioral objectives,' let alone make sure I'm on target. And I don't think top management really cares about most of these anyway—at least not until somebody gets excited about something."

"Then why don't we use just the objectives that really count?" Lesley asked.

"Why?" said Ben. "Because what I've got here on my desk is the whole catalog of excuses our plant 'lawyers' have given in the past to explain why they didn't hit the target on the objectives that really count. But here, look at this. This is what I really wanted to show you. What's today, December 20, right? Okay, "now here's my expenses as percentage of budget—108 percent. That's fine—they give us a leeway of 10 percent. And take it from me, I busted my tail to hold it there. So, yesterday, what comes down to me from New York? This!"

Ben is holding a sheet with a lot of figures on it; but Lesley was never much at accounting and looks mystified. "Let me tell you about this," says Ben. "If you read between the figures, what it says is 'Mr. Franklyn, you now have a cool million bucks of additional expense as of December 19. We regret that this may cause you to miss your expense objective.'"

Lesley doesn't have to say, "I don't get it," because it is written all over her face.

"This is the work of the big financial brains in New York," Ben explains. "They did some brand new forecasts of next year's business and found they had just received a big hunk of unanticipated cash this year and a lot of other stuff I don't understand too well. But the result of it—*that* I understand all too well. They've written off some stuff early, reallocated some expenses here and there— mostly here—to make our 'tax picture' look better."

"But what could happen from that?" asked Les. "Surely, anybody can see that your missing the objective is simply a misunderstanding."

"Anybody who wants to see it that way will," said Ben. "And if anybody finds that it's convenient to forget it, they'll do that, too. But sooner or later, *nobody* will remember how it happened. All that's in the books is that I missed the objective.

"It's the same with the rest of the objectives. You can't possibly meet them all, and they'll do what they've always done anyhow— find some way to give you the boot if they don't like something you've done. Only now it looks better—'no misunderstandings,' 'clear objective criteria,' (here he did a good imitation of Ted Shelby). Ted says there's a lot of meat here, but I say that meat's baloney!"

What Ben means is that "Management By Objectives" sounds good if you're on the end that's evaluating it, not on the end that's trying to do it. What if the objectives don't hold still? What if the people up above perpetrate a "misunderstanding" or two on you? And, even barring unforeseen problems, how good you look may have more to do with how well you juggle your budget estimates than how well you actually manage.

The real value of such measures is to provide an objective definition of failure after the fact. At some later date you "realize" that objectives three, six, and eight are really the important ones, not one, two, and five. It is a very convenient "management tool."

The Pearl

Another Company's *doing* it, I tell you. Doing it and beating us right in our own backyard! The CATCHUP task force is having another meeting, this time on the feasibility of CARP (Cybernation and Automation Readiness Project). In addition to the CATCHUP regulars, some of the top technical people in The Company are also present, as well as several of Marsh's top staff aides (Marsh's "handlers," as they are known)—in this case, the corporate technical staffers.

"You may *think* Another Company can beat us on this, but you couldn't be more wrong!" This is a reply to the claim from one of the corporate staff types by Kerry Drake. He continues. "*We* can't do it, *they* can't do it, *nobody* in the whole goddamned industry can do it! And yes, I *do* know that we have the technical knowhow to completely automate and cybernate a manufacturing plant. But I know some other things, too. I know I can pay someone a few bucks an hour to carry pieces from one machine to another and feed them in with the proper order and orientation. And I also know that it will cost a few *million* bucks to design a machine to do the same thing, plus many bucks an hour for a technician to keep it running right. That's what I know for sure!"

Another of the corporate staffers says, "If that's so, then how is Another Company doing it?"

"They're not *doing* it, goddamn it! They're *trying* to do it," replies Kerry. "Can't you get that distinction through your thick skull?"

"Well, Kerry," says another of Marsh's handlers, "at least they've got a better attitude about it than what we seem to have here. And listen, I don't think you understand how badly Marsh wants this." Ted Shelby's attention had been wandering, but no longer. His ears perked up as the staff man continued. "Mr. Marsh feels that CARP will symbolize The Company's technical excellence in the marketplace. In our position we can't give our critics anything to shoot at. And if Another Company beats us on this . . ."

Ted knew an Opportunity when he saw one. The remainder of the meeting became a process of Ted's getting himself appointed as operating chief for CARP, despite continuing protest from the assembled technical hands. Ted told them that he saw a way to get this thing done, but that he would need special powers to round up the facilities and technical talent to push ahead. It was finally agreed that this could be done if Ted's project proposal and schedules looked okay to The Corporate Review Committee.

The meeting broke up, and Stanley caught up with Ben Franklyn as he was leaving. "What do *you* think about this, Ben?"

"I think what Kerry thinks. That's something I've learned over the years," said Ben. "If it's something to do with production engineering, and Kerry says it doesn't make sense, then there's no way it's going to work. We're going to lose our tail on this one."

Yet, in not too long a time, the following memo was circulated:

To: All CARP Personnel

From: CARP Project Director

The first product line is on stream at our experimental facility at Flagstaff. You will be proud to know that we beat our schedule by six days. Our permanent facility at Phoenix is 70 percent complete, and we can look forward to a startup date there in three to four months.

Looks like we are well ahead of Another Company now.

(signed) Ted Shelby

cc: Mr. Marsh et al.

In the ensuing months, Ted generates furious activity—technical missions, conferences, plant visits, the whole works. Experimental activity at Flagstaff is furious. Demonstration lines are set up, and a steady stream of Company brass comes to see them in action. A beautiful new "facility" at Phoenix is now complete, and 50 percent of the equipment is installed. Everything looks great. And each new accomplishment is heralded, of course, by a flood of memos.

Even so, there are doubters. Some people, for example, are saying that it's one thing to run individual lines under total automation, maybe even two or three lines in tandem, but an entire manufacturing plant is another matter.

The Company Clarion thought enough of the event, and some related events, to feature it on the front page.

SHELBY TO TAKE OVER AS CORPORATE DIRECTOR OF PLANS AND CONTROLS

Edward Wilson Shelby IV will be leaving his successful project CARP for a new responsibility in Corporate Plans and Controls. In announcing this promotion, the office of M. M. Marsh cited today's pressing need for a comprehensive, company-wide program of plans and controls for the medium-term outlook. Shelby's experience as prime mover for CARP makes him the obvious candidate to head up this new program. In Marsh's own words, "we've an urgent need to take a long, hard look at tightening up our budgeting procedures and making crisper, more hard-hitting decisions."

So it was that Ted Shelby was separated from CARP at the penultimate phase. People said it was tough luck for Ted not to be able to stay on long enough to realize the fruits of his efforts. But Ted himself seem stoical enough about it.

And then there were the few who knew that Ted had himself been instrumental in developing the need for, and philosophy of, the new Office of Plans and Controls. In fact, he had pretty much created his new position. Dr. Faust was one of the people who knew this, and he shared his observations, as he sometimes did, with Stanley.

"But what did he really accomplish anyway?" Stanley asked. "You know as well as I that what Ted mainly did was stir up a lot of people, create a lot of publicity, and make some good people awfully unhappy. And now he's leaving. Who's fooling who around here? The real work of CARP is still to be done."

Faust puffed on his pipe. "Well, Stanley, I *do* know that, and then again, I don't know it. The end of this story hasn't been written yet, so I would not venture to guess what it might be. Yet whatever the outcome, there will be something of interest to be learned here."

Stanley wondered what *that* might mean, but it was obvious that Faust wasn't going to elaborate at present. Faust continued: "What did Ted accomplish? The first thing one has to recognize is that organizations like The Company are full of Cassandras. It is always easier to find a dozen reasons why something cannot be done than it is to find one good way to do it. I do not know why this should be so, but it is. Perhaps no one wants to fail, and *before* one does something, the possibilities for failure are more obvious than the possibilities for success. But one will never do anything unless he tries, so someone must get things stirred up—a shaker, a mover, an irritant. I call it the 'pearl theory.'" Faust paused to let the proper questions form in Stanley's mind.

"If you leave an oyster alone, it's a commonplace thing. It's content. But if you put a grain of sand into it, it gets all stirred up. The sand starts it working, and the result of its labors will be a pearl —something far from commonplace. As an analogy, consider The Company. This corporate oyster needs a grain of sand now and again to bring out a pearl of accomplishment. The grain of sand doesn't make the pearl all by itself, but the pearl wouldn't happen without it."

Faust looked quite satisfied with his explication of his "pearl theory," Of course, he hadn't pointed out that not every grain of sand results in a pearl, .nor does every oyster live through the process.

BOX 9

THE SAGA OF THE IBM PC—PART II

On March 12, 1985, the IBM corporate headquarters announced that Don Estridge, who had headed the Entry Systems Division since its inception, was being moved to Armonk (IBM HQ) to become Vice President of Manufacturing, a corporate staff job. Noting the move in its Business People section, the *New York Times* reported the comments of industry analysts and IBM insiders.

Insiders, the article noted, saw the move as an indication that Estridge was slated for movement into top corporate leadership. Industry analysts were not so sure, however, noting the PC-jr. flop and the problems plaguing the PC-AT. Still, through "a spokesman," IBM denied officially that this could be interpreted as anything but a promotion.

Scarcely two weeks later IBM took the computer world by surprise in announcing its intention to stop producing the PC jr. For while the PC jr. had sold well at a much reduced price of nine hundred dollars, analysts felt that IBM was not making a sufficient profit at that figure to justify production. The article reporting the halt speculated further on the reasons and timing of the Estridge move.

Apparently irritated by such industry and media speculation, an IBM Senior Vice President attempted to set the record straight on April 2. A *New York Times* story quotes that executive as saying that IBM has been "misinterpreted." However, he also announced that IBM would begin making its own hard disk drives for the PC-AT. The reports that Estridge had been transferred because of these problems were nonetheless termed as "gossip" and "rubbish." Estridge, he is quoted as saying, was "a hero in the IBM company." But that executive also is quoted as having said that in his new staff position Estridge was "being broadened . . . in recognition of the success he achieved."

The other shoe fell several months later when, on June 14, 1985, IBM announced that it was moving the now 200 member headquarters staff of the Entry Systems Division to Montvale, New Jersey, scarcely a few minutes removed from IBM headquarters in Armonk as the corporate crow flies. The reason given for the move was that this would facilitate the division's working more closely with the rest of IBM. The *Wall Street Journal* article featuring the move also described Estridge's replacement as more of a "company man," and elsewhere characterized his new position as "lower-profile." Obviously, the Entry Systems Division was being reined in to fit better within IBM's corporate culture.

In August of 1985 Don Estridge was one of the 130 passengers who lost their lives in the tragic Delta Airlines crash at Dallas-Fort Worth. IBM President John Akers eulogized him as "a man of vision whose skill and leadership helped guide IBM's personal-computer business to success."

Source: *New York Times*, November 19, 1984, p. D1; March 13, 1985, p. D2; March 20, 1985, p. D1; April 2, 1985, p. D1; *Wall Street Journal*, June 14, 1985, p.8; August 5, 1985, p.3.

36

Most Valuable Player

I've called you all together today to announce an important personnel change." The Pawtucket Plant Manager continued, "Our good friend and Mill Superintendent, Ben Franklyn, has just been named Superintendent of our new automated facility at Phoenix. Congratulations, Ben. This is a big opportunity for you. I'm sure we all remember when . . ." Here he went into a warm reminiscence of Ben's accomplishments and the good times they had all had together. Ben seemed pleased by the speech, but he didn't say much about his impending opportunity.

So now we look ahead to *The Company Clarion* for the story of how Ben's big opportunity did work out. Over the next six months the *Clarion* featured the following Company newsclips:

Franklyn will be taking over from Edward W. Shelby IV, with responsibility for making Project CARP fully operational.

There has been some unavoidable delay at Phoenix due to problems encountered in articulating the worker-machine interface . . . (which meant that the old mill hands in plant operations were having none of letting a computer do their jobs for them).

Full realization of the potential of the CARP project at the Phoenix facility will be delayed until current problems with system breakdowns and unreliability are licked . . .

The presidents representing four union locals having jurisdiction over the Phoenix plant were in agreement that key items in the upcoming contract negotiations would involve current problems with displacement of jobs and new job categories.

. . . Another Company recently announced that it has dropped its project of cybernating and automating a production facility, leaving The Company without any significant competition in this vital area . . .

The decision has been reached to o   perate the new facility at Phoenix as a semi-automated plant, with several model lines operated on a fully cybernated basis . . .

There were a number of rumors floating around The Company regarding the CARP project at Phoenix. A lot of people were surprised at just how much Shelby had been on top of it. After all, if an old hand like Ben Franklyn couldn't bring it off, Shelby must have had more management talent than had previously been suspected. Too bad they'd transferred Ted.

Another story was that The Company had put out so much publicity on CARP, mostly through Ted Shelby's doing, that there was no choice but to follow through, then salvage what it could. And with The Company, there were always the legal considerations.

At any rate, Ben Franklyn finally ended up more or less off the hook. The consensus was that it had just been too big a job, even for Ben. The technical people were heard to say, "We told you so," but not too loudly. As for Ben, it was back to Pawtucket with a suitable Company announcement about changes in plans.

"What I don't understand," Stanley said to Dr. Faust, "is how they let Ted Shelby get away with this fiasco. He got the whole thing started with a bunch of promises he didn't have to live with. I don't know why we didn't keep him on CARP to see it through. I'll bet he knew all the time that it wouldn't work."

"I wouldn't jump to any conclusions about what Ted Shelby did or did not believe," said Dr. Faust. "In fact, my opinion is that he *did* believe there was a chance of success. But that's beside the point. You can't leave a man like Shelby in one place too long—he's too valuable."

"Too valuable?!" Stanley choked. "You've got to be kidding! Here's a guy who goes against the best technical brains in The Company, promises something he can't deliver, creates a hell of a mess, but takes the credit before he bails out to save his own skin— and you say he's *too valuable* to leave on the job? The only reason he took it on in the first place was because he knew Marsh wanted it so badly he could taste it."

Faust let Stanley stew for a moment while he paused to light his pipe. His final pronouncements were always more effective when preceded by time for thought punctuated by puffs of smoke. Finally he began. "Your facts are correct, essentially, but your conclusion is flawed. First, give Ted credit for what he excels in—launching new programs. And though you appear to be in awe of technical arguments, be aware that the technical people are not always right, even when their arguments *are*. They forget the fact that once one has made the decision to go ahead, he often finds ways of getting the job done that never occurred to him earlier. Shall we say that there is added motivation to find a solution.

"Also, there are certain projects that, from the perspective of top management, are too important *not* to attempt. That is where the value of a Shelby must be appreciated. Make no mistake, Ted knows how to bring people together and get them moving. And yes, I know that he is not good at following through, but there are others to do that. You need someone who is willing and ready to take risks, to bet on the long shots—but you must protect him from the consequences of his failures."

"But what if everybody did that?" said Stanley. "What if . . ."

"I wouldn't worry about that," said Faust. "First, there are not many people who are willing to take that kind of risk; and The Company would not let them."

"But I thought you just said . . ."

"I said that you need *people* like that, not an organization like that. Obviously, one cannot afford to have everyone running about, stirring things up. Evidently you have forgotten some of our previous discussion. There are right and wrong decisions, true. But enough energy and enthusiasm in following up can often make right decisions out of what, by all appearances, were wrong ones. In a situation involving a real decision, there is usually a wide margin of error either way.

"There are times when one must have someone to push ahead with certainty, to say, 'come, we can do it.' And one must protect such people from failure, give them a certain immunity from the facts.

"But this is not like committing everything on a long shot. In a corporate environment, rarely do these 'long shots' result in total losses. But when they win, there are great gains that can be realized. Our problem is that people are timid enough already. If punishment for a failure like CARP were swift, sure, and drastic, one would see fewer CARPs to be sure, but not many advances. So when one finds someone like Shelby with a certain flair for getting risky projects underway, one protects him; moves him where he is needed. He's too valuable to go down with the ship."

Section Six

Actions Speak Louder Than Words

Communication as Myth, Symbol, and Ritual

How do we get to know what we think we know about organizations? This is the theme that runs throughout *The Ropes*. But in this part, we will meet the question head on and talk about the process of communication, the attempt by one party to get another party to believe or do something. The interest here is not in plain old garden-variety communication, conveying necessary information from one person to another. It is important to do this, but it's just not very interesting.

No, what we want to look at here is the kind of communication that is used to maintain, build, or perhaps change the culture of the organization. This kind of communication supports the structure of authority and organization, it reaffirms the mission and purpose of the organization, and it reasserts the cornerstone corporate values of efficiency and effectiveness. This type of communication strives at all times to make the existing corporate structure and hierarchy of authority appear as a "natural" fact rather than a contrived and constructed one.

An example may help clarify the last point. Consider this "corporate news bulletin."

NEW CORPORATE STAFF, EXECUTIVE APPOINTMENTS ANNOUNCED

Company Chairman M. M. Marsh today announced the creation of a new corporate staff: Technical Personnel Development.

The new group will promote the technical vitality of the Company's professional engineering, technology, and scientific communities throughout the world and will work to enhance the exchange of technical information among the Company's laboratories and its business units.

Company Vice President Blake D. DeKalb has been appointed Vice President, Technical Personnel Development, to head the new staff. Succeeding Mr. DeKalb as Vice President, Engineering, Systems and Technology, is Company Vice President Marshall B. Mason.

Commenting on the new corporate staff, Mr. Marsh said, "Company leadership in our fast-moving industry is heavily dependent on our ability to help our technical people to maintain professional vitality and to ensure open communications among our engineers, scientists, and businesspeople. I think this is an important milestone along that road."

This one has been carefully massaged by the Corporate Communications folks. It has been prepared in such a way that it is factually correct, but in substance totally misleading. What has actually taken place is the following: Blake DeKalb is a Company old-timer. At one time a brilliant engineer, he is responsible for some of The Company's major business successes. But time has passed, and he is thought to be no longer equal to that important Vice Presidency of Engineering, Systems, and Technology. So he is being replaced by someone who is believed to be more up to date. Undoubtedly, that technical personnel development function will be useful. But surely The Company hasn't just discovered the need for it. And surely it is not a promotion—notice the "appointed"—to move from a vital function to an ancillary one. Finally, the big pep talk from Marsh about the importance of this new function is so much window dressing. After all, personnel is personnel, and The Company doesn't live or die by that function.

Then why all the fuss? One thing every human organization —be it a corporation or a nation—must have is the acceptance by its members that its leaders have a legitimate, or justified, right to direct the organization's affairs. In democracies, this is achieved through the electoral process. If you don't like the current bunch of rascals, you can throw them out and bring in a new bunch of rascals.

But it's different in autocracies, where there is a single ruling group not subject to the direct will of those being ruled. Leadership in these organizations, to the extent that such organizations are stable, gains legitimacy through adherence to a belief system, an ideology that sets forth a set of guiding values and a statement of the right and proper means for attaining these. Examples are the classless society of Marxism-Leninism and the Book of Mao. The structure of authority and organization of these autocracies is explained as "natural," a result of the pursuit of lofty goals—"building socialism"—within the framework set forth. Every action taken is also justified by these values.

Still there's a catch. Because the leadership structure is justified by these beliefs alone (occasionally with a bit of support from the police) "deviation" from the proclaimed true path is seen as potentially undermining leadership authority. For this reason, errors are covered up, history rewritten, and occasional scapegoats singled out as having caused problems because they departed from the system. Above all, the myth is maintained that the *theory of the system* is itself error free, even though an occasional individual may deviate from the prescribed orthodoxy. Not the least reason for the collapse of the former Soviet Union was the "perestroika" initiative taken by Gorbachev. This opening up and restructuring (literally) admitted that the old system was not what people had been taught to believe. As a consequence, the natural next question must be, "Well, if not this, then why any of it?"

Now in case you hadn't guessed, corporations are not democracies. Although the average corporate citizen is free to cross borders, there is just one more of the same at the next stop. That is why a great deal of fuss is made to cover up corporate error and deviation from the values of the corporate culture—values that include reward in proportion to performance, upward mobility through the ranks of the hierarchy commensurate with performance, and the twin banners of efficiency and effectiveness. This is why The *Company Clarion* and its bulletins read more like *Pravda* (translation—Truth), or *The People's Daily*, than the *New York Daily News*. It is just that they are pursuing pretty much the same ends.

Notice that much of corporate communication is one directional. Subordinates are required to convey information up the line, but reciprocity down the line is not required. Victor Thompson has pointed out that this is the key mechanism in the "creation of awe."

> Incumbents of high office are held in awe because they are in touch with the mysteries and magic of such office . . . Since one knows less and less about the activities of superordinates the farther away in the hierarchy they are, the greater is the awe in which he holds them . . . The hierarchy is a highly restricted system of communication, with much information coming in to each position; but the amount sent out to subordinates . . . for strategic and other reasons is always limited. There results an increasing vagueness as to the activities at each level as one mounts the hierarchy, and this vagueness supports the prestige ranking which we call the status system.[3]

At least one reason this process works is that there aren't any knowledgeable Company Democrats and Republicans to tell you what "Marsh is really doing," or that he is the one directly responsible for the fact that we have fallen way behind in this or that race. It appears that just this fact is responsible for the demise of the first phase of the H. Ross Perot candidacy in 1992. Mr. Perot, it seems, didn't take kindly to the sniping of the Republican "dirty tricksters" and the press. Well, he just wasn't used to that sort of thing. In phase two, the "campaign commercial" phase, Perot adopted an approach that insulated him from such scurrilous stuff as open disagreement with him.

Communication is often symbolic. Dress, language, manner, and physical props—vital elements of the dramaturgy of the corporate stage—all contribute to what we "know" about our organization. Rank in the status hierarchy is carefully correlated with office size, furniture, and incidental office appointments such as pictures or water carafes. Indeed, there is a group of people who "manage" these things. And Mr. Marsh's personal secretary, Marsha Mason, also has an office befitting her importance in The Company scheme of things.

Edward W. Shelby, IV has mastered the corporate dramaturgy of The Company. Impeccably dressed in a three-piece suit (he uses the same tailor as Mr. Marsh!), Ted has cultivated the no-nonsense crispness of manner favored in The Company and in many such organizations. Ted's look and tone communicate a well-honed sense of urgency and, if need be, the willingness to play hardball. Although Ted casts himself as a strategic thinker, he avoids being viewed as too egg-heady or think-tanky. Plans gone awry haven't failed; they just require some fine-tuning.

Corporate cant also favors sports metaphors that convey activity and competitiveness. That hardball thing. Corporate managers, in discussing pending deals, speak of "going for the double play," or, if they miss, "at least getting the out at second." Another refers to being "blind sided" (football) by an unexpected maneuver. And there's the "full court press" of the hostile takeover.

No need to go on, although it's fun. The point is that these aren't just random individual preferences for phraseology. No, this is the stuff of corporate culture. Beliefs, attitudes, and motives abound in every act and word. They have a purpose. And that purpose is to reaffirm the belief system and values that support the status hierarchy that is the leadership of the organization.

Coffee Break

Can you imagine the nerve? Honestly, some people in this Company really need a lesson in manners. Who does he think he is?"

This last question stuck firmly in Ted's mind as Bonnie described her encounter in a Corporate Headquarters elevator. Bonnie was outraged.

"And without so much as an 'excuse me,' mind you, he *pushes* himself into our crowded elevator and spills half the coffee. So I told him he ought to be more careful."

Ted's interest was indeed starting to grow. Bonnie had just come back from "outside" with a carton loaded with coffee. Company policy (in *this* building, Mr. *Marsh's* policy) frowns on going out for coffee. Looks bad. So a coffee cart comes through once a day in the morning, presumably to wake you up, and that's it. But that's not it for the coffee-addicted faithful of The Company. They need an afternoon kick as well. So in keeping with the spirit, if not the letter, of Company policy, Ted has Bonnie go out for afternoon coffee for his section.

"So then he starts giving me this lecture, all about profits and stockholders. *Honestly!* Where do I think The Company would be if we all took the afternoon off? The nerve!"

Ted grew visibly apprehensive.

"Well, I wasn't going to take any more of that, so I told him. I said they get tired in the afternoon, and this helps them work better. And this way they don't have to go out themselves. We do it all the time. Everyone does.

"So then he asks me where I work. Can you *imagine?*"

Ted blanched. "You didn't tell him, did you?" But he knew the answer.

"Of *course*, I did. And then he got off the elevator on the 28th floor."

"Oh, my God." Bonnie had never seen Ted more agitated. "Bonnie, do you—do you, ah, have you ever seen Mr. Marsh? Do you know what he looks like? You don't? Would you describe this person to me?"

The next day Ted was on tenterhooks all day. What should he do? A personal note to Mr. Marsh? No, that wasn't it. But what? The following day Ted was even more sure the hammer would fall (why hadn't it fallen already?).

Then, that afternoon, an unprecedented event took place. The coffee wagon! For the second time that day! Accompanying the wagon was a sheaf of announcements—(take one).

> It has come to my attention that scheduling a second coffee run in the afternoon may be necessary. In keeping with Company policy you are expected as usual to remain at your desks during this period.
>
> M. M. Marsh

Ted could hardly believe it. How could Bonnie bring off in a few minutes something that the personnel specialists had been trying to do for a year?

The answer? Probably because, as a lower participant, Bonnie's directness and honesty are evident, and because she clearly has nothing personal to gain from the outcome. (Also, she has nothing to lose by speaking out on a matter of such trivial importance as this.) While Ted Shelby is chary of "rocking the boat," Bonnie (correctly) saw no harm that could befall her for voicing an honest, innocent opinion (although, if she'd known it was Mr. Marsh himself, she might not have been *quite* so forthright).

Society Of Equals

Ted Shelby doesn't make very many mistakes, but . . .

"Hey," said Ted, leaning in through the door, "got a minute? I'm restructuring my office. Have a look."

Stanley is always interested in Ted Shelby's new ideas. For if there is anyone Stanley wants to do as well as, it is Edward W. Shelby IV. Stanley follows Ted back to his office and stops, nonplussed.

Restructured is right! Gone are Ted's size B (Junior Exec.) walnut veneer desk and furniture, and his telephone table. In fact, the room is practically empty save for a large, round, stark white cafeteria table and the half-dozen padded vinyl swivel chairs that surround it.

"Isn't it a beauty! As far as I know, I'm the first in the plant to innovate this. The shape is the crucial factor here—no front or rear, no status problems. We can all sit there and communicate more effectively."

We? Communicate? Effectively? Well, it seems that Ted has been attending a series of Executive Development Seminars given by Dr. Faust. The theme of the seminars was—you guessed it—"participative management." Edward W. Shelby IV has always liked to think of himself as a practitioner of democratic management. And when you are Ted Shelby III's son, you can afford to think things like that.

"Don't you see," says Ted, managing his best sincere/intense attitude, "the main thing wrong with current mainstream management practice is that the principal communication channel is down-the-line oriented. We send our messages down to you people, but we often neglect the full feedback potential. But just because we have management responsibilities doesn't necessarily mean that we have the same kind of hands-on understanding as the people below us (Stanley duly noted the word, 'necessarily'). So, as I see the situation, what is needed is a two-way communication network: down-the-line *and* up-the-line.

"You people have a lot of good ideas, I'm sure, and there is no reason why you shouldn't input them directly to management. But for years, no one thought about that! So here we all sit, behind our desks, giving the impression that we know it all, when we could be managing 72 percent more effectively (Ted must have taken notes, thinks Stanley) if we just cut out that artificial barrier."

"That's what the cafeteria table is for?" Stanley says.

"Yes!" says Ted. "It's high time management people admit we don't have all the answers.

"Let's take an extreme example . . . the folks who run those machines out there. I'll bet that any one of them knows a thing or two that I've never thought of. So . . . (sweeping his arm around the "restructured" office) so that's the point of this. What we have here is a full-feedback communication net. It's a lot like 'skip-level sensing,' where workers can communicate directly with higher management. Anyone and everyone will be able to sit right here in my office, together, on equal ground. You, me, Ben (maybe), Lesley, Kerry, Bonnie, our production people. The management process will receive direct input from all participants."

"That certainly is an innovation around here," says Stanley.

A few days later, Stanley passed by Ted Shelby's office and was surprised that Ted's desk, furniture, and telephone table were back where they used to be. The white cafeteria table had vanished. He backpedaled to the door and asked, "Say, Ted, what happened to the table?"

"Er . . . Kerry suggested that the cafeteria probably had a better use for it." And without engaging Stanley's gaze, Ted mumbled something about overcrowding. Stanley couldn't tell whether Ted meant crowds in the cafeteria or his office, but didn't think it made much difference. Stanley, still curious about the unrestructuring, went to Bonnie for enlightment. "What," he asked, "happened to Shelby's round table?"

"That table we were supposed to sit around and input things?" she said. "All I know is, about two days after he had it put in, Mr. Drake came walking through here. He looked in that office, and then he sort of stopped and went back—and he looked in there for a long time. Then he came over to me, and you know how his face sort of gets red when he's really mad? Well, he was. And when he talked to me, I don't think he actually opened his mouth; and I could barely hear him, he was talking so low. 'Have *that* removed,' he says, 'Now. Have *Mr.* Shelby's furniture put back in his office. Have *Mr.* Shelby see me.'"

You may be saying to yourself, Why is Kerry so upset? It's not as though Ted has really committed a major error. He hasn't "cost The Company money."

Well, I guess it depends on how you look at it. Ted's right, you know. That office *is* a "full-feedback" communications device. It's just that the feedback isn't the kind that Ted lately envisions. The management office is one of the chief props in the Company dramaturgy of authority, and as such helps a great deal in the "creation of awe."

Picture the aboriginal men's hut. Then imagine one of the tribal leaders leading a group of young boys through the sacrosanct interior and saying, "See? What did I tell you? There's nothing but this old hut, and there's a bunch of masks that we wear, and here's the chief's throne. It's just a chair with some zebra skins wrapped around it. Really, there's nothing special at all about the men's hut."

No, that wouldn't happen. Everybody knows: It's the men's hut. Occasionally Dr. Faust or Ted Shelby might have a lapse of memory, but Kerry or Ben Franklyn will be quick to set them straight. A company office bespeaks privilege and achievement. It is an important symbol of leadership authority in the hierarchy of The Company.

BOX 10

PRESIDENT CARTER ATTACKED BY RABBIT?

One otherwise unremarkable morning in August of 1979 I came upon a story in the *New York Times* that I found truly incredible. President Jimmy Carter had been set upon by a hissing, tooth gnashing, "attack rabbit" while fishing from a canoe in a lake near his home. The gist of the headline and the article was that the President had been forced to drive off the beast with his paddle when it had threatened to climb into the canoe after him.

My own feeling was one of disbelief, yet the story lingered on for several days in local papers and news reports. What was going on here? Had the President lost his wits?

But now the truth is out. The reporter who wrote the story has come clean. It seems that he first heard the tale from a secondary source, not the President himself. The original piece was a very brief one of the sort intended for gossipy filler, and sent out over the AP wire service. What the reporter had never envisioned was the response of broadcasters and editors throughout the nation. The Washington Post carried it on the front page with the headline, "Rabbit Attacks President." The reporter says he has an entire scrapbook of cartoons and stories about the "Killer Rabbit" incident.

Why such a response? True, mid-August doesn't generate much news, but that really doesn't account for it. No, the answer seems to be that the image of the President of the United States being threatened by a swimming rodent was the perfect symbolism for the Carter administration, beset as it was at the time by failure and the inability to control even its own party members in Congress. The attack rabbit metaphor communicated directly what all America seems deeply to have felt—this administration is utterly and hopelessly incapable of effective action.

Source: *Wall Street Journal,* May 19, 1984, p. 21.

Praise/Criticism

Ted Shelby opened up the morning session of participants in the Phase Three, Section II, Group I of the "Subordinate Readiness Program: Production Workers." "Gentlemen and ladies," he said, "Stanley has come in this morning to take over this session. He is our expert on employee relations on the assembly line, and that is the topic today. Stanley, the session is all yours."

Stanley, having finally broken from the embrace of his personal Iron Maiden, Ben Franklyn's information system, has been working with Ted for almost a year now. But he still bears the imprint of his technical background. To put it bluntly, he isn't the world's greatest showman. He knows his stuff, but he has trouble putting it over. At every opportunity he seeks security in charts and numbers, and had tended, as he evolved this session over the months, to build more and more charts and numbers into his presentation. He doesn't have to engage his audience if he just talks facts, so he reads the numbers from the charts, pokes at them with a pointer, and says as little as possible about what they mean.

". . . and so we see here that Class A assemblers who—and I quote: 'accept instructions eagerly and intelligently—have a tendency to move up faster in pay grade than those who do not. Eighty-seven percent of assemblers who scored lower than 25 percent went up a grade in less than 6 months, compared to only 43 percent of assemblers with scores higher than 50 percent. Remember that low scores indicate high instruction-acceptance, and that high scores indicate low instruction-acceptance. That is, where the chart is going up, it is actually going down, etc., etc. . . ." Stanley really worked very hard at his sessions, but sometimes it was painful to watch.

Stanley's troubles were not lost on Ted Shelby. Given the situation and his responsibility for it, you might have thought that Ted would have tried to straighten Stanley out early in the program. But

Ted didn't like interpersonal conflict, and Stanley was pretty defensive about his sessions, not being sure that he wanted to do that kind of thing anyway. Criticism from Ted would be certain to precipitate a confrontation; he knew that Stanley's reaction would be something like: "What do you mean, 'go easy on the numbers'? Look, I'm the expert on this topic, and what do you know about it? What makes you think your way is better anyhow? If that's how you feel, you can take your Subordinate Readiness Program and shove it, for all I care. I'm going back to production where we talk facts, not B.S."

Ted simply had no stomach for that sort of thing. People like praise. Accentuate the positive. Catch more flies with honey than with vinegar, etc. So from the very beginning . . . "Good show, Stanley. The way you handled that question about Subordinate Responsiveness was terrific. It was your *best talk yet.*"

This went on for almost a year when Stanley finally burst into Ted's office and said, "I quit! You must really think I'm some kind of idiot!" Stanley hadn't been drinking, but he had been indulging in what Elton Mayo quaintly termed pessimistic revery. He was really fuming. "The very first time I did that session you said, 'Good show, Stan.' Okay. I knew it wasn't that great, but I appreciated your wanting me to feel good. The next time you told me it was better than my first one, and I think it was. But, it's been how many times now? And each time," Stanley mimicked Ted's supersincere delivery, ". . . your best talk yet, Stan." Well, if the last was my best then the first one was really lousy, and you've been lying like hell to me right from the beginning!"

What Ted had in fact communicated to Stanley was not that Stanley was doing a good job. No, it was that Ted was unwilling to put in the effort to help Stanley do the job better. Ted's words said one thing, but they were counterfeit. His behavior sent the real message.

* * *

Whenever Stanley got back to Pawtucket, he invariably stopped up to see his old buddies on the fifth floor. Today, as he entered the big drafting room, Claude Gilliam and Lesley were having a heated discussion. Stanley approached the pair with some circumspection, not knowing what he might be getting into.

"I don't get it, I *don't* get it. You'd think Claude would get a kick out of this. Why is he getting so excited?" Lesley was talking half to Claude and half to Stanley. It turned out that Lesley had just been chewed out by Kerry Drake—who is an expert at that. Lesley was willing to admit that she was wrong, that Kerry had a good point, but Lesley didn't see the necessity of Kerry's doing it the way he did. Stanley, of course, knew that Kerry *had* only one way, and that was it.

The spat developed when Claude commented that Lesley shouldn't complain, that actually she was very lucky. That sort of thing never happened to Claude. Lesley was in no mood to take any needling, especially when it didn't make any sense to her.

Hearing all this, Stanley made an attempt at reconciliation. With as much good humor as possible, he recounted the time that Kerry really skinned him on that construction job. Lesley and Stanley laughed it off, but Claude became even more insistent.

"Sure, you think it's funny. But then, how could you understand?"

Uh oh, thought Stanley. Here we go with that "black experience" stuff again. Stanley had gotten to know Claude well enough in the past to have a couple of friendly arguments about that sort of thing. For Claude was one of The Company's first wave of "Equal Opportunity employees." This was a way of saying that if The Government hadn't found ways of making The Company hire black professional people, The Company probably wouldn't have gotten around to it for some time. Nevertheless, in fairness to The Company, once they decided to do it, they were going to do it right. And they were trying.

It isn't that The Company never had any black employees, even professional black employees; but typically they were "white" blacks: except for the accident of skin color there wasn't any difference between them and the rest of the people in The Company. But Claude was black; black in speech, dress, appearance, and in a thousand and one minor ways that told you that Claude hadn't a close white acquaintance until he became a student at the Polytechnic Institute. But back to Stanley, Lesley, and Claude.

"No, you *don't* understand. You don't understand because nobody's ever treated you the way they treat me. Look at Ted. Know what I am to Ted? I'm Ted's nigger." Stanley and Lesley blanched at the word. Claude enjoyed the reaction.

"That's the way he thinks about me, I mean." And pointing to Stan, "He thinks about you as you. But me, all he sees, all he can think of, is that I'm a black man. No, I don't mean it that strong—but it's always there.

"And you know what? He's scared to death of me. What if I fail? How will it look? They'll think he can't get along with Equal Opportunity employees (Claude added an ironic emphasis.)

"Why the hell is he so afraid I'm going to fail? I got through Tech okay and everything I got, I got the hard way—working my ass off to learn what all you dudes knew in high school. So what's he so worried about?

"I'll tell you. He's worried 'cause I don't talk right, I don't sound right, and I don't act right. I guess I don't look too good to him, either. That's what I mean when I say, how could you understand? How *could* you?

"Ted just knows there are things I can't do, so he's not going to give me the chance to fail. He does what he thinks is helping me out. They all do, more or less. Don't give me anything too tough to do. Make excuses for me. No criticism. Never, never chew me out. See, I'm just not going to get the chance that you dudes get, so how do I learn? Everything I do is always fine. And then, finally, the time comes when I've been here a while and I've been promoted—and when that time comes they turn out to be right after all. I can't do these things 'cause no one's ever let me and no one's ever given me an honest reaming out when I've screwed up. Then they say, 'See, just like we thought. It's the way it is with them.'"

And there you have it. Unfortunately, Claude is right on target. Ted is prejudiced. Not in a conscious, nasty, malevolent way, no; it's unconscious, well-meaning, and stupid. The crazy thing is that Ted, as in all the affairs of The Company, wants what The Company wants, wants black professionals and managers, wants Claude to succeed. The irony is that Ted *is* trying to help Claude. But he is afraid that Claude will fail, and he doesn't want that to happen. So the way he helps only ensures that, sooner or later, Claude will fail. Expectations frequently lead to the fact.

Bite Of The Apple

40

By Company custom, Personnel and Communications had an office party at year end. No, not an "Office Party," The Company didn't believe in them. This was more like a pep rally. It provided a time for mutual appreciation and congratulations for the good work done over the past year—a time of good fellowship.

Ted especially liked this year-end solidarity ritual. "You know, Stan," he said, "there's a bright future for you in The Company. I've watched you grow over the past year, and I want you to know, personally, that Company Personnel is really pleased with the job you've been doing."

At times like this Ted could be genuine and likable. Perhaps this was because, on such occasions, his own ambitions, those of The Company, and those of the people he worked with were all one. No matter. Ted was in an expansive mood.

Spotting Lesley, Ted went over to spread good will, "How's the new whiz of corporate communications?" he began. Then, putting his arm around her shoulder, "You know, Les, I think there's a bright future . . ."

"Would you mind removing *that*?" she interrupted in an icy tone, slipping out from under the offending arm.

"Why, er—I'm sorry, but . . ." Stunned, Ted fumbled for words for a moment, then abruptly walked off. Now he was genuinely angry—a rare thing for Ted. Grabbing Stanley by the arm and dragging him into his office, Ted vented his emotions.

"Just who in the hell does *she* think she *is*? Please remove that?! Goddamn right I'll remove *that*. Here I'm just trying to be . . . be, just trying to show her that we *care* about all our people, and she's got to pull some wise-ass stunt like that. I don't give a damn if I never say two words to her again. What the hell do *I* care?"

Boy, was Ted hot, thought Stanley, wondering just what it was that made him so. He'd seen Ted take far more malicious putdowns in corporate staff sessions and stay cool as a cucumber. Finally Ted did simmer down, apologized to Stanley for losing his "cool," and left. Still, Stanley was curious, so when he spotted Pat Jones over by the library he'd figured he'd get a professional opinion.

As Stanley related the incident to Pat she chuckled. "It would have been worth it to see some genuine emotion from your boss. You know, I think that's at the root of it right there."

"What is?" Stan asked.

"Genuine emotion, feelings. You know Ted as well as I do, don't you? Most of the time he's wearing a mask, playing a part. He's not hurt personally in those meetings, because, well, I suppose it's just a game he's involved in.

"But you've seen him here, too. He really comes out from behind that mask at these things. And yes, he's expressing genuine emotion. So in a way, he's vulnerable as he seldom is otherwise. That's why, when his actions are misinterpreted, as it seems to me they were, he's hurt, confused, and embarrassed in a way he's unprepared for." Pat paused, thoughtful for a moment. "Oh well, no real harm done I suppose." Yet her tone suggested she only half believed it.

When Stanley found Lesley, she looked extremely agitated. "I guess I really screwed that up?" Stanley didn't help much by saying that she probably had. Then she continued. "Honestly, I didn't mean to insult him, but I hardly know the man at all. Why should he be so familiar with me? He gave me the creeps, that's all."

"But he was just trying to be friendly, Les."

"I don't see how you can be so sure," she countered.

"Okay, then don't believe me if that's the way you want it. Anyway, what's the difference if he is?" Stanley was getting a little indignant over what he considered to be Lesley's puritanical attitude. "Don't tell me you've never had a guy make a pass at you before."

"You jerk, don't you understand?" Lesley exploded. She was agitated and unsure about the earlier incident. Stanley wasn't helping. "This is business, work . . . my career! *You* (finger pointing) don't have to fight it every day, trying to convince everybody that you're not just here until you find a husband or whatever. *You* don't have to try to figure out whether someone thinks you're really doing a good job or if he's just trying to get on your good side so he can take you to bed some night . . ."

"Oh, Les, come on, come off it, will you? You make it sound like the whole damn Company's got nothing on their mind but your body!" Then he suddenly changed his tone, "Look, would it help if I said that I think I *do* understand, that I think you do face a problem that I don't? But could I also give you some advice?"

"Well, what kind?"

"Friendly."

"Okay."

"Look, I think I know you pretty well, but a lot of other people around here don't. You're getting yourself a reputation as somebody with a chip on her shoulder." Lesley started to protest, but Stanley continued, "Hey, it's no skin off my nose, you can do what you want —*you're* the one who's going to have to work with these guys. But when they're looking for people they want to work with in task groups, they're *not* going to be looking in your direction. Relax a little. You're a big girl. You know how to take care of yourself."

Easy enough to say, Lesley thought to herself, and probably pretty sound advice. More than anything, she wanted to be taken seriously as a career professional in The Company. And to move ahead, she had to know that praise for her work was genuine. Still, Stanley was right, too. So what to do? The rules of conduct in the men's hut have been derived from historically male relationships. What now? Ted was embarrassed because he *was* abiding by the rules, and as he saw it, Lesley was not.

Well, folks, what would *you* do?

Spacemen

Stan settled back in the chair in his temporary office.

Comfortable enough, he thought. Because his initial assignment had been to help out Dr. Faust in the first stages of developing The Program, Stanley had been temporarily assigned space in Faust's former office. And although Faust had spent a good deal of his time here during leave from The University, that leave was now over—hence, the available space.

However, within a day or so one of the people from Plant Administration (Stanley was later to learn that in Plant common parlance, they were called "Spacemen") happened by, looked around, paused, looked at Stanley, and spoke.

"Doesn't Dr. Faust use this office?"

Answer: yes.

"Er, I mean, this isn't Dr. Faust's personal office any longer, is it?"

Answer: yes. No, it isn't.

"Well, then, that won't do." And he left.

"What won't do?" The question was left unanswered—but not for long.

Next day the "Spaceman" returned.

"We're going to replace your furniture," he said flatly. "If you've got anything in the desk, take it out and pile it over there. The men will be by in a couple of minutes."

"Uh, would you mind if I asked you what's going on?"

"Well, this isn't the right furniture for you, so we're changing it." At this point, two workmen entered, lifted the desk, turned it on its side, grunted out of the office down a narrow stairway, muttering and cursing *sotto voce*.

"Not the right furniture?"

"No, this is for an Assistant Area Manager."

More grunting, muttering, cursing, this time up the stairway. The workmen entered with a new desk and walked out with an unknown (to Stanley) item. The new desk looked pretty much the same to Stanley. Well, it was a little smaller and light green instead of pastel pink or mauve or whatever that color is, and its vinyl top looked like plastic instead of simulated woodgrain plastic.

"Well, that's it," said the Spaceman. "We don't have the right chair right now so we're going to let you keep this one. Oops, almost missed that!" The Spaceman grabbed the carafe and left.

Later on, Stanley commiserated with Bonnie.

"What puzzles me, Bonnie, is why go through all the trouble, when I'm only going to be here maybe a month more?"

"Oh, but you've got to be fair! What would people think if you had the good furniture and everybody else had the other? And you couldn't give everyone the good furniture. My goodness, just think what that would cost." Her expression revealed that Bonnie was just now thinking what that would cost.

"No, Bonnie, I don't mean that. I mean, I really don't give a damn what furniture they give me, but why *bother* just for a lousy couple of weeks?"

"Oh, but it is important," Bonnie swept her hand around the secretarial cubicle. "Just last month Ginny Szekely and I thought it would be nice if we had a little rug in here to keep down the printer terminal noise. So we got one. The next day the man from Plant Administration came by and said we had to take it out. We asked him why, and he told us it was a safety hazard. 'A *safety hazard?*' we said. 'Yes,' he says. 'And besides, how would The Plant look if everyone put whatever they wanted wherever they wanted it? No, that wouldn't look right, and it wouldn't be fair to the others who worked hard trying to make The Plant look nice. No,' he says, 'the rug will have to go, girls.' Then we . . ."

"Uh, excuse me, Bonnie, I'm going to be late for a meeting." More confused than ever, Stanley left for his meeting with Ted. Up the elevator, down the hall . . . hey, what's this? Furniture piled in the hall, and sitting in the chair, Blake DeKalb, Manager of Mill Maintenance Engineering, known to Stanley as left fielder on The Plant softball team (good hit—no field).

"Hey, Blake, what's up? Taking a little work break?" Inside the office, noises of banging, ripping, and thumping.

"Very funny. C'mere." And taking Stanley through the door, "You're a bright young kid—let me show you something." Inside, the workers had just finished rolling up the carpet, exposing the shiny vinyl tile beneath. Right now they were attacking the modular painted steel partitions that constitute the office walls.

"Know what they're doing? They're 'un-managering' me!"

"They're *what?*"

"Un-managering me. You see, first the Spacemen take up the rug, then they turn a 9×15 office into an 8×10 by sliding those partitions 1 foot one way and 5 feet the other way. They take your table and three of your chairs. But what hurts most is when they take your Company Managers Manual and take you off the mailing list. It's like defrocking a priest or ripping the epaulet from an officer's uniform. Before, you got to know things a day or two before everybody else. Now you wait with the rest of them."

"My God! What did you do?"

"Nothing, nothing." DeKalb went on to explain that his small Mill Maintenance Engineering Department had been "consolidated" with Mill Maintenance proper. Although he still had the same job, same pay, same functions, he was technically no longer a manager.

"So, because you no longer need the space to hold meetings, you get the standard staff office. And because the standard hunk of 9×15 carpet won't fit in 8×10, they take that too—at least that's how the Spacemen put it. But that sounds fishy to me. I've called Ted . . ."

My God! Ted! thinks Stanley—the meeting. "See you later, Blake."

"I'm afraid you'll have to wait a while, Stanley, Mr. Shelby is on the phone now."

Stan is seated close enough to Ted's office to overhear parts of a lengthy conversation. Ted, in charge of Plant Administration, has apparently been taking some heat from DeKalb.

"I'm just asking you to get this guy off my back! Won't you just try . . .

"I know it's not your responsibility, Mason, but he's driving me crazy. Listen, last night he called me at two A.M., and I had to talk with him for an hour trying to explain why he can't keep his old office . . .

"Yes, I *know* we make no exceptions, but he says it's not his fault that we decided to eliminate the position . . .

"Of course, I *understand* that it's silly of him to be so upset. I know it doesn't mean anything . . .

"Certainly, we'd all move where we had to for the good of The Company . . ."

It seemed to Stanley that this wasn't going to end soon, so he asked Bonnie, "Is there something you can tell me? Doesn't look like Ted is going to be through for a while."

"Sure. I think Mr. Shelby just wanted to tell you that your new assignment has been okayed upstairs, and that you've been assigned new space here on the fourth floor. You can start moving your things into 421B any time."

Wow, thought Stanley, fourth floor, with Plant Management!

As Ted's new Administrative Assistant, he couldn't be far from here. So why ask Bonnie? He'll just find the office himself.

Pretty nice up here, thought Stanley, who had just started noticing such things. Carpets, windows, paneling.

"Now let's see . . . 421. Ah, there it is." Stan approached a large room. "No, that can't be it, that says 'Conference' on the door. Oh yeah. Bonnie said 421B. Got to be here somewhere . . . Oh-oh! That door says 421A *and* B." (Actually, it read 421A,B.)

Inside a standard (for this floor) 9×15 were not one, but *two* low-rank green desks, only one work table, two chairs, *no* carpet. A two-man office! The only office like it on the entire fourth floor.

A tight little ball of disappointment started to form in the pit of Stanley's stomach. What would people think? What about the guys on the softball team? How could he work in here with management people, when they'd know right away he couldn't have much to say about anything?

Stanley had learned a great deal that day. And, as with many educational experiences, it hadn't been exactly pleasant for him.

42 | Extra Effort

Mr. Marsh is just concluding his address to The Company Foremen's Club. Most of Plant Management is there. "Extra effort," he says, "is what made The Company what it is today. Don't take failure as a final answer. When it looks like all is lost, that's when you should come back and try twice as hard. I'm sure you all remember the time we fell behind on . . . etc., etc."

During his speech, Mr. Marsh has alluded to production difficulties on the M-Machine line, making it abundantly clear that he wasn't happy about the fact that The Plant had not met the deadline. As usual, things had been held up in production engineering. Typically, the Development Engineers hadn't given much thought as to whether the machine they'd designed could be produced easily. In this case, it couldn't. So, for weeks the project had been hung up in production engineering, waiting for, among other things, a few key decisions from the development people.

Because of these problems, Dr. Faust had been called in as a Management Consultant to "get things straightened out," and rumors were flying that heads would roll unless things got straightened out pronto. Stanley, Faust's former student, was assigned to help Dr. Faust get the paperwork together.

"The President's office wants to get to the bottom of this," said Ted Shelby with the concerned/crisp tone that he had decided was best for this situation. "I've been given the authority to open whatever doors may be necessary to help you get us out of the woods. Stanley, your job is to see that Dr. Faust gets whatever documents and clerical support he needs. Don't forget, this is our chance to put in that little extra effort and beat this problem." With this last remark, Ted Shelby strode decisively from the room.

"Well, what do we do, Dr. Faust?" asked Stanley.

"First of all, dig out all the correspondence, weekly progress reports, expenditures, and whatever other documentation looks relevant. Put it all together and bring it to me."

About a week later Stanley brought in a stack of papers. "There's something funny going on, all right," he said. "You know, I was on that project, and it's a fact that lots of Ben Franklyn's Production Engineers were just sitting on their hands doing nothing. He was waiting for some decisions on the M-Machine from the Development Section. But look here—he's had his Production Engineers on *overtime* for the last two months, nights, and Saturdays! If you want to know where the problem is, it's right there. Franklyn doesn't care about how he spends The Company's money."

"Possibly, but actually I think not," mused Faust.

"How can you say that?" asked Stanley, bewildered. "You're trying to tell me that having people sit around on overtime with nothing to do helps The Company? Come on, Doc."

"No," said Dr. Faust, "what's wrong is something else, probably unavoidable, but no one's fault really. I'll try to make that clear in my report, although I don't expect they'll believe it. They'll wind up pointing the finger at someone; they always do, no matter what. And that's what Ben Franklyn knows that you don't know."

"I don't understand what you're driving at," said Stanley.

Dr. Faust paused to light his pipe. "Tell me what you would have done if you were in Ben Franklyn's shoes."

"That's easy," said Stanley. He is always eager to tackle the things he knows least about—and maybe that's why. "It's obvious from this pile of correspondence that Ben Franklyn knew this would happen all along. See, here's his early memo to the Office of the Vice President of Design and Development. He called it perfectly. So, if I were him . . ."

"He," Dr. Faust interrupted.

"So if I were he, I'd simply take this memo, make X many copies, send them around to everybody concerned, and I'd be home free."

"Wrong, dead wrong," said Dr. Faust. "That's a good strategy only if someone else has the responsibility for getting the job done. If that's the case, you circulate the memo to show that you warned him but he wouldn't listen. Now let's say that Ben Franklyn tries that. He says, 'I told you all along that this project wouldn't go.' Then what?"

"Oh, I get it." Stanley exclaimed. "Then they say, 'Ha, this guy never really tried. He never put in that extra effort to push it through. He never believed in it from the beginning. What we need in that job is someone who carries his part of The Company load, not some backbiter who points the finger at somebody else when he never did his own share in the first place.'"

"So you do see it, then. And what to make of the overtime?"

"Let's see . . . . Ben can't just *say* that he's tried his hardest, he's got to be able to *prove* it. He knows that they'll look at the records, and that the records don't show what his people have actually *done*—just how many hours of overtime they've been paid for. So he had his Production Engineers sitting around forty hours a week plus ten extra hours on overtime so he can say . . ."

"Exactly!" said Faust. "When Shelby makes his report to the President's office, Franklyn will be spotless. He will be on record as having given his . . . (here Faust winced) . . . ah, 'extra effort.' Yes, it cost The Company some money, but he did all that he could."

Stanley thought for a moment, then delivered his final assessment, "It's true then, Dr. Faust, isn't it—I mean, what they say about actions speaking louder than words?"

"LEADERSHIP NOW": THE NEW TEAM SPIRIT AT GM

As the year 1993 broke, General Motors was envisioning the permanent closure of twenty of its production facilities. Projections for market share were at a modern era low, and the motors giant was still struggling to get back in the black. Additionally, GM's increasingly active board had fired Roger Smith's successor, Bob Stempel, after a brief stint as Chairman and given his successor marching orders for dramatic moves in cost cutting and further "downsizing." Dealings with the union were couched in terms of sharing the pain.

And yet just four years earlier, with Chairman Smith still very much in command the outlook had been very different, at least superficially. The talk was of a newly realized teamwork, of a revitalization—no, a *rebirth*—of the notoriously autocratic GM culture into a sensitive, participative approach to management. In short, the talk was of "Leadership Now."

Management development experts were brought in to guide in the move toward participative management styles. Twenty five hundred GM executives attended sessions to enable them to communicate in an open and caring manner. Smith himself and his top seventeen executives participated in sessions whose description fits that of a sensitivity training group. The hope throughout was that increased sensitivity to, and hence understanding of, the concerns of others at lower rungs of the hierarchy would bring increased teamwork, and in consequence, productivity.

And indeed, improvements in productivity were noted, as were some signal successes in union-management joint activities. Still, there were skeptics. One union official pointed out that basically not much had changed, except that management had become more sophisticated in its approach, less directly autocratic. Other skeptics pointed to the motivational power of fear, noting that with permanent layoffs on the horizon, incentives for increased productivity already were abundant. "Leadership Now" was little more than window dressing.

Well, we *do* know the end of this story. GM is still struggling, and "Leadership Now" is history. The moral? Probably that there is no such thing as a quick fix, that changing a firmly entrenched management culture is no easy trick, and especially when there are so many other problems to deal with.

Source: *Wall Street Journal*, December 12, 1989, p. A1; September 21, 1992, p. A3.

43 Incredible

It's not that Ted and Ben don't like each other (although as a matter of fact, they don't); it's the way it is with cats and dogs. God intended them to do very different things. And as experience with normal, healthy cats and dogs has shown, when they are placed in the same room the fur will fly.

And so it was that a certain amount of fur littered the conference table in room S-211, Corporate Headquarters, where Ted, Ben, his staff, the staff people from New York, and one of Marsh's handlers were discussing the latest program to help Ben run his plant. The topic of discussion, if we may call it that, was Ted's newest wrinkle on subordinate readiness—his GOALSETTER program— GOAL SETting Through Exchanged Roles. Ben, for his part, was getting more impatient. Of course, Ben had been born impatient. But there were production problems at Pawtucket. The big, new rolling mill was down, and nobody could figure out why. So Ben was in no mood for subordinate readiness.

"Ben, we realize that the decision on this is entirely up to you. But it's a two-way street. With every other plant in The Company (not quite true) really starting to get some mileage out of modern behavioral technology, I don't understand why it is that we always have to drag you into the twentieth century . . ." Ted had broken with his usual decorum with that, but for a change, he wasn't acting. He had a big stake in this program, and Ben, as usual, had turned out to be his main stumbling block. But then, Ben never noticed things like this anyway. Ted went on.

"I don't know why you're unwilling to accept the facts we have about Goal Setting Through Exchanged Roles." Ted's tone was urgent/agitated. "Our trial run at Paducah showed that subordinates set goals 20 percent higher in the role exchange situation. Now that's good enough for us, and it's good enough for Mr. Marsh." There was just a hint of hopeful uncertainty in that last statement.

Now it was Ben's turn. "Listen, I'm the first one to admit that I don't know a damn thing about your behavioral technology, if that's what you call it. And it's not likely I ever will. But I *do* know something about getting a product out the door. And what I know is that I'm goddamned well not going to get a product out the door with all my managers and half my millhands sitting around and getting confused about who's boss so they can decide what they ought to get done next year. I can tell you what they'll get done that way—not a damned thing. And what's more, I'll tell you who sets the goals. Me. That's just the way it is, and that's the way it's going to be."

"Now just a minute, Ben. That's a distortion of what our program is all about." One of Ted's staffers was talking. "We're not trying to confuse anyone. Quite the opposite. It's a healthy thing for the workers to step into their manager's role and vice versa. It helps them see their problems more clearly. That's why we observe the phenomenon of increased goal expectation and saliency." (This was a psychologist speaking.)

It was Ted's turn again. "I hate to say this, Ben, but it seems to me that you're deliberately distorting the character of this program just to find reasons for not doing it. But it's up to you. As we said earlier, if you just don't want the program—if that's your reason, that you just don't want it—then say so. We can't force it on you. But I have to say that I think you're being unreasonable."

"Unreasonable!" Ben exploded, his face reddening. But then slowly, and most unusually, Ben slipped into a thoughtful calm. It must have taken enormous willpower for him, but those who knew the old Ben Franklyn, could sense that it was a calm like that in the eye of a hurricane.

Ben started to speak slowly and deliberately. A crease of humor showed about his eyes and there was a hint of irony in his speech.

"Unreasonable. I guess you all know that I spent a lot of time in this Company as a mill hand before the old man (Marsh, Sr.) made me a foreman. And you know, I've been a mill Foreman, mill Superintendent, and now Plant Manager. I've had to learn everything the hard way. And maybe I don't talk quite right, and maybe I'm a little rough at times. And maybe that's why they sent me first to middle-management school and then, since I've been Plant Manager, to executive school.

"Now maybe that didn't make much difference but, you know, I did learn one thing: as I said, I came up a mill hand—and back then when I heard something that was horseshit, I used to say, 'horseshit'! At executive school they told me that didn't sound so good, that instead of saying 'horseshit' I should say 'incredible.' Well, Ted, what you've just suggested to me—well, it's incredible."

With that, the meeting dissolved in laughter, and not much more business was transacted.

From the standpoint of communication, Ben could have handled this in a number of ways. But in choosing this fashion, Ben achieved at least two things indirectly that might have been difficult to put directly into words. First, he has symbolically isolated Ted from the rest of the group by having all participate in a joke at Ted's expense. Second, Ben has brought the flow of the meeting to a halt, providing a handy opportunity to redirect the agenda. Not bad!

MY OBJECT ALL SUBLIME I SHALL ACHIEVE IN TIME

POWER, STRATIFICATION, AND MANAGERIAL MOBILITY

The title of this part is taken directly from a line in Sir William Gilbert's libretto for the operetta *The Mikado*. It is a remarkable spoof on the fads and foibles of nineteenth-century Britain, set, of course, in Japan. In the scene from which the line is taken, the all-powerful emperor of Japan, the Mikado, is musing over the possibility of making the punishment fit the crime (for example, the pool shark condemned for all eternity to play on "a cloth untrue, with a twisted cue and elliptical billiard balls").

The targets of Gilbert's satirical jibes were chiefly the system of status and power in Britain and the British obsession with class. The notion of punishment fitting the crime, for example, runs through early attempts to reform the harsh British justice system. A British liberal, Jeremy Bentham, proposed what he termed his "felicity calculus," contrived so that the criminal would suffer punishment in exact proportion to the weight of the offense. Not one bit more, not one bit less.

The idea behind this is that a justice system that is perceived to be just better supports the existing structure of power and privilege, of class. This is because, since the beginning of time, the justice system has been applied primarily to the underclasses. The more just the justice system, the less likely is protest endangering the entire class system it supports.

So now we come to organizations. Organizations, like societies, are systems of status and power. And they are class systems. By that I mean that Jimmy Szekely doesn't have a snowball's chance in hell of moving up the ranks to become a Corporate Director. Neither do any of the secretaries, clerks, or countless others who lack the proper credentials. Not unlike society, organizations have class systems that act to restrict and maintain the structure of power and privilege.

But just what *is* power? Those little boxes on the organization chart depicting the management hierarchy have power, for example. Just the boxes. The people in those boxes exercise the power inherent in the position, but if they leave that position they lose that power. Yet *individuals* also have power. People are said to have power when we believe that they have the ability to bring about or change the course of future events. The chairpersons of important committees in the U.S. legislature are spoken of as powerful, because their backing is necessary to enact desired legislation. They can make it happen or not.

But it's a different kind of power from that of a formal management position. That is, they cannot decide by themselves. Rather, they must convince a group of others to go along with the proposed legislation. The exercise of this kind of power is commonly referred to as political "horse trading." It is a game whose rules say that if I do something for you, then you must do something for me, when and if I ask. Sociologists call that the norm of reciprocity. And if you don't play by those rules, you won't get the chance to play at all. Which, in turn, means that you will be an ineffective representative for your constituency.

So the exercise of power involves at least two things, though not necessarily both: first, being in a position that allows a measure of control over a particular set of events and outcomes that are important to others; and second, the existence of a network of people who stand to gain or lose from those outcomes, and who adhere to that norm of reciprocity.

In the section on leadership I claimed that relationships with direct subordinates were less important to successful leadership than relationships with superiors and peers in other parts of the organization—relationships up the line and diagonally and laterally across the line. To put it another way, the most important relationships are those that don't involve power derived directly from the formal hierarchy of the organization. Here is an illustration. I've drawn a diagram of three levels of management, with each position in the top levels having five subordinate managers. All told there are 5×5 or 25 first- to second-level power relationships, plus 5 second- to third-level ones, giving a total of 30 formal power relationships. The third-level manager also has formal power over those 25 first-level managers, so add another 25 to the 30, giving 55 formal power relationships.

How many different lateral and diagonal relationships can you find? For starters, each of those 25 first-level managers can relate horizontally to one another. In consequence, the total number of different pairs of twenty-five people equals $n(n-1)/2$ or 300! Then there are lateral relationships among the second-level managers and quite a few more diagonal relationships. By my calculation I get a final total of 410, roughly eight times the number of formal power relationships. So there you have one measure of the importance of these lateral and diagonal relationships. Of course, there is the possibility that many of these are never actually used, so they shouldn't really count.

But I'm not so sure. The production manager, for example, who wants a favor from personnel, a slight "bending" of personnel policy, will find it impossible to do this through formal channels. But if he or she has previously done a favor for the personnel manager, then it is probably going to be granted. The same follows for relationships between engineering and production, and so on.

The point is that any ninny can wield the club of formal power that the superior holds over the subordinate. Well, almost any. But it takes skill and attention to build a network of "political" power relationships. And that, I think, is the primary reason why those lateral and diagonal relationships are key to leadership success. My buddy, Fred Goldner, once did a study of managerial advancement in a large corporation in which he compared managerial beliefs at an earlier period to promotions upward five years later.[1] What he found was that the recognition of the importance of these lateral and diagonal relationships was a major factor that differentiated those who made it big from those who didn't. So it's not just a matter of opinion.

Where does power come from? First, formal power resides in those boxes depicting positions in the management hierarchy. It involves the right to hand out rewards and punishments to subordinates and to make certain kinds of decisions. But the power that is held by individuals, let's call it *informal* power, is another matter. What do we know about it? How does someone come to have informal power?

ORGANIZATION CHART

THIRD LEVEL

ETC., ETC   SECOND LEVEL

FIRST LEVEL

To begin with, it is important to recognize that power is largely in the eye of the beholder. If others in your organization believe that you can make things happen, chances are that you can, because they will be willing to do what you ask. But that doesn't answer the question of how you get to that point, does it? One factor is certainly the recognition that you have knowledge or expertise in some necessary activity. This might be something as mundane as a detailed knowledge of a complex filing system, or as esoteric as the ins and outs of the tax system.

A second factor is a friendship network, people for whom you have done things and who, in turn, are willing to do things for you. Building this network takes a little doing in the beginning, going out of your way to find things to do for people that make their jobs a little easier. It also requires proven loyalty, people coming to understand that they can count on you to come through when they need something.

Another factor comes only with time. And that is occupying a position in some function critical to the successful day-to-day activities of the organization, especially a position where "bending the rules" can be of major benefit to some distressed fellow worker. So now you've got some real horses to trade, and you're in the big time.

Finally, never, *never* give anything away without at least the implicit understanding of an IOU. Experienced politicians will also instruct you never to let a transgressor go unpunished, no matter how long it may take. And they will tell you to make *that* explicit. When you object, saying that this is a rather nasty and small-minded way to behave, they'll say, "Well, suit yourself, but we're talking about power, not a popularity contest." To be perfectly honest with you, I wouldn't want you to behave that way, either. But I've seen it, and I think you should understand why it happens. Remember, power is in the eye of the beholder. So knowing that punishment for "disloyal" acts is certain sooner or later may be just as important in establishing informal power as is the horse trading of favors.

So far no mention has been made of the term *authority*, although that is the term used in organizations in connection with the formal power relationships we have been talking about. Authority is used to denote that the superior is authorized to issue directives to designated subordinates within the legal written rules and regulations of the organization. In complementary fashion, those subordinates recognize that such requests from superiors are justified or legitimate within the legal system of the organization. Consequently, the exercise of legitimate power in superior/subordinate relationships is termed authority and is built into the class system of the organization together with the recognized right of superiors to hand out formal rewards and punishments.

So now we have come full circle back to the opening theme of this part: the class system of societies and organizations and its role in preserving the structure of authority and organization (as well as power and privilege). The opportunity to advance within the managerial ranks of the organization—the opportunity for upward mobility—is a major factor in preserving the class system of organizations, and this is why I have linked power and mobility in this part.

And just how are they related?

First, superiors have considerable power over upwardly mobile subordinates like Ted Shelby. Ted will toe the line, you can count on it. Why? Because Ted is going for the "whole bag of marbles." It is true that he and many others like him will never make it to the very top, but that's not the point. The point is that they all *think* they will. And they will do whatever they're asked to keep themselves in the good graces of those who make the decisions as to who moves up and who does not. You might say that mobility is a great motivator.

Conversely, people who aren't going anywhere and know it, and who don't care, or like it that way, are tougher customers to deal with than the Ted Shelbys. Superiors don't have that much power over them, and that can create problems. Most of these people, provided that they are doing their jobs reasonably well, can get away with things that approximate insubordination.

Second, those people who have been identified as hot shots—stars, comers, fast-trackers, call them what you will—*because* they are evidently on the move, also gain a measure of power. This is embodied in the corporate dictum, "better watch out how you treat her, she may be your boss someday!"

And then there are the so-called lower organizational participants, the lower classes of the organizational society. For some of the reasons just mentioned (although they don't wield formal power), these lower participants have considerably more *informal* power than you would think. That will be one of the main topics in the next section dealing with power.

A final word. I don't pretend here that I have done much more than introduce the topic of power, for it is a most complex topic that is not easily understood. Consequently, the section that follows is intended to give you some food for thought about the many faces of power in organizations like The Company.

The Race Is Not To The Swift, Nor The Battle To The Strong

Mobility and the Power of Lower
Organizational Participants

In the opening essay of this part, I noted that Sir William Gilbert's zaniest plots satirized the British class system. Let's continue with that theme. In *HMS Pinafore* we find a tale of true love thwarted by the class system. The daughter of the captain of the Pinafore would marry one of its common seamen, but the match is impossible because of the great difference in the social "rank and station" of each. However, as their woes deepen, a former nursemaid announces that for years she has held the guilty secret that the seaman, Ralph Rackstraw, and the captain were switched as babes, with no one knowing it had happened but herself. Upon hearing this, Sir Joseph, First Lord of the Admiralty comments, "then am I to understand . . . that Ralph is really the captain and the captain, Ralph?" Yes, he is. So as the story ends, Ralph is now dressed in the captain's uniform, and the former captain is dressed as a seaman. Their trials ended, the happy couple embrace. Through an incredible twist of fate, they are free at last to wed.

One gets the feeling that Gilbert has exaggerated the rigidity of the British class system a bit, but only a bit. The point is that the emphasis on class, and the limitation of the opportunities available to those of lower rank, maintain the structure of power and privilege enjoyed by the upper classes. Still, the maintenance of the class system requires at least a grudging acknowledgement of the legitimacy of such a system by those lower on the social ladder. The privileged, in their turn, are saddled with certain obligations. Second sons must serve military careers, third sons must join the clergy, and so forth. Daughters must "marry well." In their turn, of course, these obligations do their bit to buttress the class system. The recent contretemps of the British royal family—Charlie and Di—is not in the least due to their failure to uphold their obligations as the exemplars of this archaic system.

As has been said, organizations have class systems. The military is a good, clear-cut example. There are two classes of officers, commissioned—the lieutenants, captains, and majors, for example, and the noncommissioned—the corporals and various levels of sergeant. Each class has its own career ladder, but they are completely separate and distinct. You do not become a commissioned officer after "graduating" from the top of the noncommissioned officer career ladder.

Business organizations have similar class systems. Here there are distinctions made between professionals and nonprofessionals, a distinction based mainly on certification, on the possession of a college degree. Again, like the military, each has a career ladder, but one does not lead to the other.

How's that? How about Ben Franklyn? Well, you are right, but Ben is really a holdover from the old days when college graduates were rare and didn't go to work in factories. But yes, it still does happen; the fact that every now and then someone does move up through the ranks is a good demonstration that it is indeed a rarity.

It was noted earlier that opportunity for upward mobility is a motivator. Let's elaborate on that. A professional person starting out in a large organization is anticipating a career. This career has ordered stages, with increased responsibility accompanied by increased privilege and pay. In past decades, at least, this was one of the greatest motivators for the management professional. You might ask yourself, "Why are these young, upwardly mobile professionals putting in those twelve-hour days and seventy- to eighty-hour weeks?" "Wall Street" aside, not primarily for their current salaries. For there are plenty of "grumpies" (gray upper management professionals) who are no longer on the move, but who make more and possibly do less. One answer has got to be that these young professionals are motivated by the anticipation of *future* rewards. Therefore, this system of staged upward mobility—in the past, at least—has been a smart economic move for organizations. The motivation derived from staged advancement allows deferring a part of the salary bill to later years.

My best evidence for this is the 1990s binge of downsizing (Ted likes to call it "right-sizing"). Surely there's more to this than the sudden insight that large corporations have bloat in the midsection. And if you read the various business publications, you will find clear voice to these feelings of, yes, *betrayal* among these fired middle managers. They know full well that their corporations are reneging on that implicit promise of rewards to come later for service rendered now.

But back to the point. It is these anticipated long-term career benefits that keep the Ted Shelbys running and make them very responsive to management directives. Still, the system is not without its problems.

For one thing, the nature of managerial mobility resembles a tournament more than a contest, a tennis tournament more than a marathon foot race.[2] I'll explain. In the marathon *contest*, some runners do drop out; they never reach the goal. But others do, at their own pace. The opportunity to reach the goal remains for all who persevere, regardless of how long it takes. But a *tournament* presents a different arrangement. Once you've lost, you are out. Players who lose in the first round don't get another chance to compete for the second level. And of those who do advance to the second, some will never reach the third, and so on.

In the analogy to organizations, you should think of a lifetime career as participating in a tournament, and of career progress as being broken into time periods or stages like levels in a tournament. Those professionals who don't gain promotion into management during the initial time period, say within the first five to seven years, are out of the tournament. They will never again be considered for a management position. Given the size and growth rate of the organization, this group might be relatively small at this point. Similarly, those first-level managers who are not promoted in the next time period are also dropped from the tournament. And this may be a considerably larger group. (Note that the only claim made here is that the mobility patterns observed in large organizations *resemble* this tournament pattern, not that management has planned it as a tournament, nor that there aren't good reasons for such a pattern to appear. The people who fail promotion at any stage may just be the ones who lack sufficient motivation or skill to go further.)

But the pattern in itself is important. It means that at every managerial stage there are people who are "plateaued," who will no longer be motivated by the possibilities of advancement up the ladder of pay, power, and privilege. And why is this important? Remember what's been said about power. Formal power stems in large measure from control over rewards and punishments. Well, what have you got for plateaued managers? They are not going anywhere, and they know it. And no, you cannot fire them all, either. Besides, most are doing their jobs middling well, so how would you justify firing? As a result, these managers can be difficult people to deal with. They are just not as responsive to the wishes of superiors as are the Ted Shelbys, and that causes problems.

The same kind of problem is presented by managers in key jobs who opt out of the mobility tournament (call it the "rat race" if you'd like). The plant manager who is doing a good job otherwise but does not want to move up to division or corporate is an example. Ditto the sales manager who just loves the town and the branch office and is making excellent commissions besides. The problem with these people is that you can't threaten them, and there's nothing they want that you can give them. They are a thorn in the side of superiors, who often need to get some special project under-way because *their* bosses want those projects—and they *do* want to move ahead.

For another thing, having been in their jobs a long time, these stationary managers have had an opportunity to build an extensive network of personal relationships giving them considerable *informal* power. This makes them even more difficult to deal with. This is at least one of the reasons upper-level management tries to move such people on up the ladder, or laterally. Although it's generally explained that this is necessary to allow a younger person to gain the experi-ence of that position—which probably is true—there is an equally valid but unstated reason: management also is avoiding a potential problem.

So that is one link between power and mobility.

But what of all those folks in the lower ranks of the organi-zation, the noncoms and foot soldiers, the so-called lower organiza-tional participants? These lower participants often have abbreviated career ladders of their own and can come to wield a considerable amount of power. Just why this is so is a major topic of this section.[3]

Lower participants are interesting in several ways. They are not going anywhere in the mobility tournament, and they know it. Why, they weren't even invited to participate in the tournament in the first place! Except in times of economic recession, there are lots of similar jobs around. A good secretary can probably walk out the door today and find at least as good a job somewhere else tomorrow. So there's not much to lose. That is why the superior's power over such people is limited.

On the other hand, some lower participants are in positions to wield informal power far above what you might expect. I'm thinking of people like executive secretaries, dispatching clerks, computer op-erators, purchasing clerks, and so on. For those of you who have seen *M*A*S*H*, "Radar" Riley is the consummate lower participant. Let's take a look at just where this power comes from.

To begin with, like the nonmobile middle manager, most sea-soned lower participants have held their jobs a long time. They have probably seen a good half dozen or so bosses come and go. And because these bosses *are* participants in the mobility tournament, they are usually too busy to attend to the administrivia of getting the actual work done. No, bosses make decisions and attend to the big picture, and they spend a lot of time building political con-stituencies in other departments and functions. The lower partici-pant is in the position to send out a lot of routine memos, place a lot of routine work orders, make a lot of routine appointments (and just as important, deny others), and the like.

Right here we have two reasons for lower participant power: (1) expert knowledge in some speciality area that is attainable only through long experience and (2) the lack of interest on the part of the superior in performing the day-to-day details of the work. The result is that the lower participant is in a position to grant special favors to others in return for things they may desire. The old horse-trading game again.

Next, lower participants are often in a central position in the communication network. In fact, just *because* they are not in the competition of the mobility tournament, they are allowed access to organizational secrets that their bosses would never willingly share with potential competitors. For example, secretaries who take minutes and type memos are privy to the plans and personal programs of lots of high-ranking people. Note that secretaries *do* get to attend those meetings from which managerial subordinates are customarily barred. If knowledge is power, then the strategically placed lower participant is powerful indeed.

A remaining source of power is what has been termed "bureaupathic adherence to rules." Few organizations could function at all if every bureaucratic rule and regulation were observed to the letter. Therefore, woe to the superior who offends the lower participant, usually by way of abruptness of manner or arrogance. From long experience, the lower participant knows all the rules and how to get around them. But in this case, punishment due the offending superior consists of dredging up every obscure rule and procedure and following them to the letter. In consequence, entombed in paper and harried beyond endurance, superiors will realize the error of their ways; avenged, the lower participant will return the shop to normal.

So there you have it. Power and mobility are related in lots of different ways and offer lots of different opportunities for alert organizational participants, both upper and lower. So let's get back to the folks in The Company and watch as Stanley is given a lesson in the etiquette of horse trading.

44

Your Job? My Reputation!

"**F**or the life of me, Stan, what I simply can't understand is why Ted just doesn't get Marsh's office to drop the hammer on him." The speaker was Sherman March, one of Ted's young assistants in the burgeoning Subordinate Readiness Program.

"I know how you feel, Sherm," said Stanley. "Franklyn can do that to you. But even if Mr. Marsh was willing to order Ben to go along with us, why, we'd still come out losers. Ben's got a memory like an elephant, and sooner or later he'd pay us back. That's the way he operates. Come to think of it, I guess that's the way they all operate. So we win this battle, but we'd lose the war."

With that, Sherm just threw up his hands, muttered something about kitchens and taking heat, and walked out.

Well, maybe it wasn't so obvious, Stanley mused to himself. And maybe some people have to learn for themselves. God knows, he thought, I do. He could chuckle now at the memory of some of his own instructional episodes. But one in particular from Dr. Faust stood out from the others.

"Now look," Stanley was saying, his eyes flashing, "I'm fully aware that Mr. Marsh wants it that way! But that's not what we all agreed on when this project was launched, and Mr. Marsh can't change his mind now. We'll do it like we said, or not at all!"

Stanley is having a heated argument with his mentor, Dr. Faust, of The University. Faust, Chairman of The Department, had been approached by The Company to recommend somebody to head up The Project, and he had named Stanley. Stanley had seen some of the correspondence involved in his selection and had found it flattering in the extreme. Faust had even told a meeting of top management that they were lucky indeed to have a young man of Stanley's calibre. Stanley had even begun to believe it.

Stanley's first task had been to write up a project description. "This is basic, not applied, research," he had emphasized. Once begun, it was strictly hands off. It was to be understood from the start that no concrete outcomes were to be expected for several years, if then. Progress reports would be issued twice a year, but on no account was anyone to ask the project group to justify its existence every couple of months. The reasons for this filled several pages.

Stanley submitted his project description, and after the usual "whys" and "what ifs" and "have you talked to so-and-so," it was accepted, all tied up with blue ribbons and promises. The budget, a generous one, was approved after a suitable number of recycles, and the project was on its way. Stanley was to direct it; Professor Faust to be retained as Consultant.

Only eight months into The Project, Stanley and his mentor had fallen into bitter disagreement.

"Absolutely not!" said Stanley. "I will not do it! This is *exactly* what we were trying to avoid in the first place. I made that perfectly clear in the project description. There isn't any product yet, and there won't be for years; and everybody agreed to The Project on that basis. Taking this new direction will . . . why, it's selling out!"

"Well," Professor Faust replied testily, "I'm afraid you don't have much choice. New York is asking some very pointed questions. We're going to have to come up with something, show them something!"

"No, I don't agree," said Stanley. "Tell them to read the project description. Mr. Marsh okayed it himself."

Faust was becoming agitated. "I think you fail to understand. It is *not* up to you. We simply *must* show them something. The New York people are taking a very hard look at this project."

"Let them, let them," barked Stanley. And staring Faust in the eye, "If it comes right down to it, I'll lay my job on the line!"

Faust exploded. "*What?* Your *job?* It may be your job, but it's *my reputation!*" With that he grabbed his briefcase and stormed out the door, leaving a bewildered Stanley.

Good grief, thought Stanley, could Faust possibly have meant what he just said? But then, he must have. Faust doesn't jest. What an egocentric perspective! Here I am, willing to lay it all on the line, and all he worries about is his connection with this project. As if it's any skin off his nose—with all the consulting he does, he'd never miss this one. After all, *I'm* the guy who's responsible.

This is a *very* good story to tell over drinks, and during the next few months Stanley gets a lot of mileage out of it. Yet the time will come when Stanley realizes that he has missed the point once again.

Stanley doesn't understand his relationship with Professor Faust. Faust has recommended Stanley for the job because Stanley is available, not because he fits the description that Faust has given to the executive committee. And right there, Faust's reputation is working for Stanley. If Faust, the Consultant, says that Stanley is the right man for the job, then, by God, he is! Faust recognizes that no job ever requires more than about 25 percent of what it pleases management to believe, so there isn't *that* much risk of failure, even with Stanley at the helm.

Faust, when asked, must find someone for the job, someone with whom he has a plausible connection—preferably, a graduate of The Department. Stanley's mistake, a familiar one for him at this stage in his career, lies in accepting as truth statements that are made to fulfill necessary ritual requirements. And from his understandably egocentric perspective (he, not Faust, is the guilty one here), he fails again to see that there are thousands of Stanleys and thousands of Projects in this world, but few Professor Fausts. In truth, Faust's reputation *is* more important (yes, even to Stanley) than Stanley's current job. Since Stanley is where he is as a direct result of Faust's stated judgment, it is in the best interests of both to demonstrate the correctness of that judgment. Certainly Stanley wants to look good in his new position. But more to the point, he is obligated to aid in making Dr. Faust look good as well.

Ted's Boy

Stanley carefully marked the page in *Fortune* before turning off the reading lamp and turning in for the night. Yes, it was another story about the "fast-track" and those irrepressible fasttrackers. Well, he knew from personal experience what the fast-track was, all right—it was whatever he was not on.

No, that wasn't quite right either. He'd moved up out of the plant rather quickly. The first time, at least. Then off to New York. The old memories came flooding back. His first few encounters with Ted Shelby and the others. Stanley drifted off to sleep reliving his first years with The Company.

"Why don't you check that out with Ted Shelby over in Industrial Engineering, Stan? He's probably got the answer to your question." The speaker? Why, just about everyone he had asked a question, or so it seemed at the time.

Okay, why not? He had a question about making some critical path estimates in planning a project that was coming up. "Hey, Ted, got a minute?" said Stanley, poking his head into Shelby's office. "I've got a question about CPM."

"Why certainly, Stan. Here, have a seat. Now, just what can I do for you today?" Ted's self-presentation was calculated to produce the effect of a senior person who was willing to go out of his way to help a junior one.

Stanley went on to lay out the problem as he saw it, the possible options, and the points where his inexperience led him to need help. Yet as the meeting progressed, his attention wandered to speculation about Ted himself. For one thing, although he held a second-level management position accompanied by suitably impressive office space, Ted was no more than two or three years older than Stanley. At least, that was his impression. In Stanley's tight little world of the time, Shelby was clearly the competition.

"Do you see my point, Stan?" Ted asked.

"Er, I guess I'm not so sure I do, Ted. Just that last, I mean." Indeed, though Stanley had only been half listening, he hadn't heard much from Ted that seemed helpful.

For most of their nearly hour-long meeting, it seemed to Stanley that Ted had spoken in generalities—"on the one hand, but on the other," type of stuff. On several points, when Stanley tried to pin Ted down to specifics, Ted always wriggled free with a statement like, "But of course, that's a question of project specifics and not for me to say" or, "I think you'll find that your own project people will have to tackle that, but it's just a matter of details, really." Therefore not worthy of the attention of one such as Edward Wilson Shelby IV, Stanley added to himself.

The meeting over, Ted was graciously superior in bidding Stanley, "Stop by any time. I'm always glad to help."

Some help, muttered Stanley to himself. Fact was that he hadn't learned anything he didn't already know. So this was the competition, eh? Well, the competition just ain't that good, he smiled to himself. Still, Ted's got to have *something* on the ball, doesn't he? he thought. He didn't get where he is on the basis of the opinions of guys like me. He must know what he's doing—he wouldn't be there if he didn't.

Hey, I bet old Chuck Toole's got a handle on him. Toole was the Mill Master Mechanic. A company old-timer just a year or so away from retirement, Chuck had been everywhere, seen everything, and knew just about everybody of any consequence in The Company.

"Say, Chuck, I've just been over talking with Ted Shelby. I wonder if you could give me some advice?"

"Who? Ted Shelby?" Chuck seemed surprised. Then the light went on. "Oh, *that* Ted Shelby. You mean Ted's boy."

"Ted's boy?"

"Yeah, Ted Shelby III's son. Ted set up the original Expandrium line at Paducah."

"You mean Ted's Dad is Plant Manager at Paducah?" Stanley's jaw dropped.

"Not any more. That was years ago, just before they made him general manager of the Pacific region. Sort of a big change from Kentucky, I guess, but people figured that the way he set up the Expandrium division in the South, he could probably handle about anything that came his way. Haven't you heard about Ted Shelby? Well, you're new here. He's on the Board now. He was our Chief Operating Officer before he retired. Look him up in an Annual Report if you're interested. He and Marsh, well, hell, it's practically their company, if you want to know the truth. Those two guys damn near did the whole thing themselves. Best of friends, too. When little

Ed was born, it was at his baptism, I understand, Marsh looked at him and said to Ted, "I can tell this young man has a great future with The Company."

At this stage in his life, Stanley is impatient. In this respect he is a typical, ambitious young person. But contrary to myth, most of those people "up there" were not Plant Managers by age thirty—one or two, perhaps, but not all by any means. It all takes time, and sometimes you move faster than others. One year is no time at all in this context, and five years isn't much. Sometimes you can leapfrog and sometimes you can't. But five years is not nearly as long a time at thirty-five as it is at twenty-five.

And Stanley has learned one other thing from this incident. You're never sure why some people are where they are. A wide range of abilities determines your advancement. A good style and technical ability are both important, and these are usually visible abilities. But other less-visible abilities, such as the ability to pick the right parents, can be important, too.

46

Rightsizing

"I dunno, Ted," Lesley was saying, "First of all, the very name of this program sounds like a contradiction of what you're saying, and second, I'm not really sure that 'rightsizing' is going to sound as good to Company people as it does to your Wall Street stock watchers."

Lesley (Corporate Communications Program Manager) and Ted (Corporate Director for Human Resources Development) are meeting to discuss the proper "spin" to put on the announcement of Ted's new SPRINT program (Staff Productivity Retrenchment INiTiative). They had been tossing around slogans like "SPRINT to the finish line" in reference to early retirement. (Nope, too negative).

"Rightsizing may sound good on the Street," she went on, "but to our people it means staff management layoffs. And it raises the question of how come we got it wrong in the first place?"

"But that's just the beauty of it. Don't you see that?" Ted gushed. "The point is that *no one* is at fault here. It's an adjustment—a timely adjustment—the rightsized management staff for today's modern business environment." Ted went on to rattle off the current key phrases, "global competition," "electronic workplace," "instant communications network."

"Staff management now have the tools for a quantum leap in productivity, that's what SPRINT's all about, and that's why rightsizing *is* the right word."

Oh brother, thought Les. But she said, "Um, well, if you see it that way, Ted. It's not Communications' job to tell you what to say, just to make sure you get your ideas across the way you want to." Not that she believed it.

Later that week Les was having what she and Stanley called their "lack of power lunch." Every Friday noon they took a long lunch to compare notes on the week past. It was primarily a gripe session, or "necessary therapy." Necessary because The Company required a stiff upper lip from its staff managers in times of adver-

229

sity. A positive attitude and bitching were not compatible, so these gnawing negativisms had to be shared in trusted company.

"Does he *really* think that Company people are going to buy that line?" Les was saying. "I mean, look, times are tough. The Wall Street wolves are howling for The Company's staff blood. Now. So call it what you like, look at it any way you will, The Company is going to be laying off staff managers. You know that, and I know that, so why pretend otherwise?"

Stanley repressed the thought that maybe Les had been in communications a bit too long and mused, "Yeah, I know exactly what you mean, Les. Fact is, I can't say that I'm not a little worried myself. The lucky guys are getting early retirement. But you and me . . .

"With us they say, (and here Stanley adopted his 'Shelby voice') we're phasing out your position. But in keeping with Company policy we've got another employment opportunity for you at our Depot in Duluth. You'll be handling our Expandrium applications hotline. I understand that it's less responsibility, but there will be no cut in compensation."

"Why, *thank you*, Mr. Shelby . . ."

Then Les continued, "That's just it, isn't it, Stan. Sure you have a job. And I guess it's something. But it's the end, really. You can hang on and hate it; or you can tell them to shove it, so at least you don't have to move; or you can go to Duluth and start sending out a flood of resumés."

"Well, you won't have to move if you can still afford the rent, that is." Stanley added.

Needless to say, Lesley and Stanley didn't add much joy to their day that noon. But it was therapy. In point of fact, neither had much to worry about. Both had received "excellent" performance ratings last go-round (excellent but not the coveted "outstanding") and were secure, at least for the time being. What troubled them was, in fact, their loyalty to The Company.

The Company wanted honesty from its people, and, in turn, had been exceptionally honest with them. You could feel good about working for The Company. But this was different. Well, maybe it just seemed different. But, damn it, something about what was going on seemed to be a betrayal of trust. Something bordering on the unethical. It was in times like these that Stanley sought out the counsel of the good doctor.

As Stanley explained Ted's version of rightsizing, Faust nodded. "You do understand, of course, that it is Ted's responsibility to put these developments in the best possible corporate light," he began. "And that would be as a dynamic response by The Company to . . . how to put it . . . *positive* developments in today's business environment, as opposed to Company management oversights."

"Right. So you agree, then? This is just a big smokescreen to hide management's screwups."

"When did I say that? In point of fact I think management has little direct responsibility in this, except to the extent that in good times it is quite difficult to properly anticipate the bad.

"And The Company is not alone in being unprepared for this. Oh, the usual cycles of expansion and—ah—consolidation, present no problem. Hourly workers generally have borne the burden of this. But staff management has had little to fear, until now, that is.

"After all, staff management *is* the management. Managers commonly understand the implicit guarantee of security in exchange for loyalty, of putting the good of the organization ahead of one's own— in certain instances."

"Yeah, and now management's reneging on that deal. That's just my point, Doc."

"Am I to understand by that, that you do *not* consider yourself a member of management?"

"Why, I mean . . . of course I do. But . . ."

"But these are those others, the 'management' to whom you have entrusted your future. Yes, and they recognize that.

"But what options have they for protecting that trust. Let The Company flounder into Chapter 11? That wouldn't help you. Sell off parts of The Company as independent business units and put you at the mercy of the new owners, with whom you have no bargain, implicit or explicit. And early retirement is no option for you.

"What then? Triage, save the most able and let the others go. That's been done, and highly despised. It's implemented through the merit rank ordering of the staff management in each unit."

"Like they say, heaven help the hindmost," Stanley muttered.

"So as I say, what then? Job reassignment, adjustments through natural attrition in The Company's internal labor market. Unfortunately, just as in the external labor market, there are—ah— temporary dislocations in supply and demand. Yet it seems to management to be the best way, since it honors that implicit bargain."

"And also might persuade a few additional people to leave," Stanley added. "You know, Doc, it's a funny thing, but sometimes I think, wouldn't it just be better to fire us flat out than to try to convince us that it's all being done for our own good?"

Friday Go To Meetin'

Ted strode by briskly wearing his best urgent/serious look.

"This is the big one," he was telling a compatriot, "we're down to the crunch, systemswise. New York is going to be asking some pretty pointed questions soon, so we've got to get our ducks lined up."

As Ted moved on, Stanley thought, "What now? What's the big crisis this week?" By all appearances Ted's career is strung together with a neverending series of crucial events. He moves from one to the next, making the most of each by getting to know the right people on a first-name basis.

Ted is also the office Stakhanovite, a model for capitalist emulation. He is there when you get there, there when you leave, and there when you don't have to be. This has always puzzled Stanley, for to his way of looking at things, the office is not the most desirable place to be. Unlike the mill floor, nothing *real* ever seems to happen there. And there is nothing that Ted has to do on the average work day that couldn't be handled in, say, three or four hours of honest application. It seems to Stanley that Ted spends most of the day wandering around socializing.

Stanley's musings end temporarily as he arrives at Ben Franklyn's office. He has been assigned to pull together the facts for Ted, who will then edit and rearrange them ("massaging" the facts, Ted calls it). And Ben has some of the crucial facts.

"This is another one of Ted's Things-That-Can't-Wait, is it?" Ben growled. "Let me tell you something, son. I've been with The Company for forty years now, and there's something for the life of me that I'll never understand. We *never* seem to have the time or money to do it right in the first place, but we *always* seem to have whatever it takes to bail us out when we get in trouble. I don't understand why in hell we can't . . ."

Ben, obviously primed to talk, is interrupted by the phone.

"Mr. Mason for you, Mr. Franklyn," Bonnie calls in. (Marshall Mason is Corporate Director of Plant Manufacturing Automation.) "Meeting? There is? . . . Tonight you say . . . uh, today's Friday. No, I won't be able to make it. I promised my family I would take them to church tonight . . . Yes, I do understand that . . . No, I don't need to think it over . . . Yes, I know, I do accept that." Ben is now holding the phone about 3 inches from his ear. "How about first thing Monday? . . . Oh c'mon, you know better than that . . . Well, I can do this. If you're still in session, I can make it by eleven . . . No? Not good enough? . . . No. No, you won't."

If Stanley could have heard both sides, here is what he would have learned. First, Mason (basically a staff-type like Ted Shelby) is preparing for the witch hunt brewing in New York (more staff types of the Corporate variety). So he's called a meeting of all involved management the soonest he can. Because of other commitments, this turns out to be eight o'clock Friday evening. Franklyn (through his secretary) has already told Mason's secretary that he cannot make it.

No good. So Mason "gets on the horn" to put the squeeze on Ben—to "communicate his sense of urgency." But Ben isn't buying. To him this is just more staff nonsense whipped up by people who don't have any real work to do. They can't do anything over the weekend anyway, so why not wait until Monday A.M.?

Mason isn't used to this. After all, management is a seven-days-a-week, twenty-four-hours-a-day proposition. "We're always on call. That's what it takes to keep The Company a step ahead." So he tells Ben to think it over and call him back in a half hour. Presumably, with a little time to ponder it, Ben will come to realize the enormity of his refusal and will come in with the right report. But actually, Mason is upping the level of implied threat and providing a face-saving mechanism for capitulation (think it over and call me back). Ben counters with his own proposal to be there by eleven P.M. Presumably Mason, therefore, will understand that Ben is not just avoiding his duty and will accept his proposal as sufficient. But again, what is really being done is that Ben is providing Mason with a face-saving way of backing off, a symbol of submission, "turning the neck." And now Mason isn't buying, so finally, "No, that's not good enough. We've got to have your input. See you tonight at eight." This last was followed by Ben's refusal.

What is going on here? A battle of wills? Dereliction of duty? Possibly. Mason (who really isn't such a bad fellow) is probably more astonished than anything else. He's gotten himself into this situation because it never occurred to him that Ben would flatly and finally refuse. In his eighteen years with The Company, from staff trainee on up, he had *never* seen anyone in a responsible management position refuse to attend an important meeting for personal reasons.

Ted's reaction is also revealing. Stanley left Ben's office with the information and was now with Ted getting an item-by-item rundown.

"But I don't have a good grasp of what this means for us manufacturingwise, Stanley. It's not clear how we're supposed to interface on this one . . . Well, we don't have time to work it out now. I'll toss the ball to Ben tonight."

"Uh, if you mean Mr. Franklyn, well—uh, I've got an idea he isn't going to be at your meeting tonight."

"Where did you get a crazy idea like that? Of course he'll be there—he's got to be! We've all got to be right on top of this thing."

"Uh, it might be a good idea to call him, Ted."

Ted did and found out for himself.

"Can you beat that, he isn't going! And there's a lesson for you, Stan. Have you ever wondered why after forty years Franklyn hasn't made it beyond Mill Superintendent?" (Of course, he hadn't. From where Stanley stood, Ben's job looked impressive enough.) "He's got no sense of urgency, that's why. The people who make it to the top in this Company are the people who are always willing to give a little more than the next one: the Marshes, the Masons (the Shelbys. Ted's look said it for him). These people care about The Company, and The Company takes care of them."

Symbolic acts communicate a great deal. How does anyone know that Ted Shelby is a hotshot young manager? After all, few people ever get to see what he actually does. Well, there are ways.

"That young Shelby, a real comer. Right on the top of things, you can bet. Many a time I've thought I closed the building down, but Shelby's still there hammering away at it." And . . .

"I'd feel better if we got on it right away, sir. Dollarwise we're not talking a whole lot but I like to treat The Company's money as I would my own. How about this evening? We can grab a bite in the cafeteria and get right on it . . . if that's okay with *you*, Mr. Mason."

Dedication, zest for work, a sense of urgency—these are management qualities. But there are difficult qualities to display with actual work, for the simple reason that, in most cases, the actual work does not require them. That is why these attributes must be displayed symbolically by the aspiring manager. But what Ted and Mason fail to understand (how could they?) is that Franklyn has no interest in a higher management position. He'd rather be shot than work with a bunch of corporate "staff busybodies," and in New York, of all places! With this in mind, you can take the analysis from here by yourself.

BOX 12

TOO MUCH OF A GOOD THING, PERHAPS?

On July 9, 1980, the *New York Times* reported that Jane Cahill Pfeiffer had been relieved of her duties as Chairman of NBC. The firing incident was not without some rancor. Apparently in an effort to get Cahill Pfeiffer to resign, executives at NBC had leaked the news to the press that her resignation was imminent. But she denied all rumors, saying that if they want to fire her they'll have to do it themselves. Interestingly, though Cahill Pfeiffer was Chairman at NBC, she in fact reported to the President.

There is no question that Jane Cahill Pfeiffer is an exceptional woman. In the early 1970s at thirty-nine, she had moved to the position of Vice-President for Corporate Communications in the IBM corporation. T. J. Watson, Jr. is on record as calling her one of the most competent executives who had ever worked for him. But NBC is not IBM, and therein lies at least part of the tale.

After graduating from the University of Maryland, Cahill Pfeiffer had spent a brief period in a religious order. That and her no-nonsense management style would later at NBC earn her the soubriquet, "Atilla the Flying Nun." For various reasons she left IBM after a brilliant twenty-year career. Following several interim ventures Ms. Pfeiffer was appointed Chairman of the National Broadcasting Company. And scarcely a year after that came the epic event that eventually was to end her career at NBC—the unit managers scandal.

Unit managers are essentially in-house travel agents for the broadcasting and camera crews who travel the world in search of stories. They arrange for accommodations, the rental of necessary equipment, and generally pay the bills incurred by production crews. However, as Cahill Pfeiffer soon discovered, a substantial portion of this money customarily went unaccounted for.

- **Item:** One unit manager laid out twenty thousand dollars for rental on a piece of equipment which later turned out not to exist.
- **Item:** Expense money paid for landscaping one unit manager's garden.
- **Item:** Expense vouchers routinely inflated and, on occasion, simply invented.
- **Item:** One unit manager "lost" a valise containing thirty-eight thousand dollars in cash, which presumably was intended to grease the palms of foreign petty functionaries.

All in all, it seems that on the order of one million dollars remained unaccounted for over the course of several years. Cahill Pfeiffer's first reaction was to fire the lot of them. However, executives of parent RCA objected. But Cahill Pfeiffer was not to be mollified. Such things were undreamed of in IBM, and considerably lesser offenses met with swift punishment. So Cahill Pfeiffer undertook her own investigation. First came a team from Price Waterhouse to audit the books. Then a hit squad of Wall Street lawyers. With evidence thus assembled, she swept into action. You were involved personally in the dealings? Fired, for reasons of guilt. You knew about it but did nothing? Fired, for reasons of complicity. You know nothing of it, at all? Fired, for reasons of incompetence. A veritable corporate inquisition at the behest of Atilla the Nun! When her "investigation" was finally complete, the price tag ran between four and five million dollars. Like sending in the whole damned marines to rescue a treed cat, one executive is said to have commented.

Understandably, the incident left a bitter residue among the middle managers of NBC. Consequently, later in the year Cahill Pfeiffer came up with a morale-building scheme, or so she thought. The plan was to fly in nine-hundred or so top managers, assemble them in a large studio, serve up coffee and doughnuts with a few motivational speeches, and then top it off with a group singing of Christmas carols! Never mind that NBC executives would by far have preferred a case or two of scotch, nor that probably half of them were Jewish. That was the IBM way.

Well, Christmas Day came and went without that particular pep rally, and you already know the end of the story.

Source: *New York Times*, July 9, 1980, p. 1; M. Ver Meulen, "The Corporate Face of Jane Cahill Pfeiffer," *Savvy*, 1, May, 1980, p. 24ff.

Ghosting For Gain

What follows is a simple, yet in-structive application of the power of lower participants. This game is easily played. You follow a universal principle: busy executives are too busy to write all of their own memos. Sergeants write those letters signed "The Commanding General," just as obscure staff specialists write those magazine articles attributed to Mr. Marsh. And, of course, the President of the United States has a staff of ghosts who contrive his most moving phrases, his most powerful speeches. Recall, it was staff speech writer Peggy Noonan who coined the now unforgettable 1988 presidential promise, "Read my lips, *no new taxes!*"

One of Ted Shelby's most productive ideas as assistant to the Manager for Personnel Development was his Subordinate Readiness Program. That is, it was productive for Stanley. Inconceivable? Here is how it all transpired.

When Ted first came up with the Subordinate Readiness idea, he wasn't all that enthusiastic about it himself. Ted preferred working with management, and the higher the better. Still, this was another Opportunity and a new program—and that spelled Edward Wilson Shelby IV.

Amazingly, Kerry Drake (the Production Manager) also favored this program. Not that he was worried about getting his subordinates to do what they were supposed to do, that has never been a problem for Kerry. What he liked about the program was that, unlike the other programs Ted Shelby customarily inflicted on him, this one at least left his *managers* alone. And he couldn't see Ted Shelby doing anything to the rank and file with this program that might result in any permanent damage.

So neither Ted nor Kerry felt strongly enough about the program to want to do much about it themselves. Kerry, as usual, just didn't want to be bothered with Shelby's nonsense. And Ted was more interested in *management.* You spend your time with other executives, not subordinates, is one of Ted's rules of thumb.

The next day Ted Shelby got together with Stanley. "I think there's a major place for you in this new Subordinate Readiness project," Ted began in his best earnest/executive tone. We're ready to get underway, and there's a crying need for someone to keep the program on course—schedule room arrangements, make sure that all the materials for the sessions are in order—that kind of thing. It's probably going to eat up some of your time, but I'd sure appreciate it. Tell you what, why don't you hop over to production and ask Kerry if there's anything more that needs to be done on his end. You handle it. Naturally, I'll be available if you need a decision," Ted concluded.

With that, Stanley marched off dutifully to get things lined up with Kerry. But Kerry himself had little time for this kind of thing: he endured rather than supported Ted's programs, and only because he was well aware that his own effectiveness rating would suffer if he couldn't show some kind of ongoing personnel development activity.

"Because you're Shelby's liaison on this, Stan," Kerry began, "I wonder if you could also do some things for us—scheduling, room arrangements, that kind of thing. I know you're plenty busy already, but Jimmie (Administrative Assistant) is completely tied up on the inventory right now, and I'd really appreciate your help. Why don't you draft a memo from me to Shelby saying that as far as we're concerned, things are ready to go."

So the memo was sent over in Kerry's name, nowhere mentioning Stanley's own involvement. A day or so later, Ted pulled out his memo from Kerry and handed it to Stanley.

"The first thing I'd like you to do is answer this. Kerry says he's ready to go. Tell him so am I, and that next week is fine, if he can line up the conference room for Thursday and Friday. I'll handle getting the word out to his people. Oh, and one other thing, he's really cooperating with me on this program, and it's something I'd like to encourage—so make sure we take a positive tone on this." (Ted uses phrases like "positive tone" to avoid having to do the work of figuring out what he really wants.)

Stanley took the memo back to the office and looked it over. It was the memo he'd written for Kerry the day before! Well, answering it should be simple enough, and by the way of "positive tone" he added at the end: "Incidentally, it looks like this program is really shaping up well. Keep up the good work!"

Two days later Stanley was again in Kerry's office. "I see you've got everything lined up for that program of Shelby's," Kerry told him, "and I'd like you to draft another memo for me, telling him when and where. He's being pretty good about this program—said that he was impressed with the job that we're doing—so let's try and encourage him. Put something in the memo about how I appreciate the effort at his end, that should do it. There's one thing that bothers me though. He has a session scheduled for Subordinate Sensitivity, and I just don't see how I can spare the people for that one. Any ideas?"

"Maybe there's some way he could do that session while everybody's on the job," Stanley suggested.

"Hmm," said Kerry, ". . . put that in the memo. Make sure you get that 'on-the-job' business in the title. That will appeal to him. Here's his last memo, for reference."

Stanley could scarcely believe his eyes; it was word for word the same memo he'd drafted for Ted two days before! He didn't say anything about it, but did just what Kerry had asked him to do, "On-the-Job Subordinate Sensitivity," he called it. And when it came to the part about complimenting the effort at Ted's end, he made sure to be duly complimentary.

A couple of days later, Ted Shelby called Stanley into his office and said, "Kerry came up with a great idea, On-the-Job Subordinate Sensitivity, he calls it. What a concept! Teach our people while they're on the line! I'd like you to draft a memo for me right away telling him this looks like a real breakthrough, and that I'm all for it. Say, and send a carbon to Mr. Marsh's office. We might as well let him know what a dynamite program we're putting together here and what a great job Kerry's people are doing on it." He gave Stanley Kerry's last memo, which Stanley really didn't need, having written it himself only a couple of days before. Stanley was only too happy to take pencil in hand and . . .

By now you've got the idea. Stanley is bouncing good things about himself back and forth between two people whose good opinions are valuable to him. And, not knowing of Stanley's involvement at the other end, each is genuinely impressed. So Stanley is getting good mileage out of this.

Is Stanley being dishonest here? No, not really, because if he weren't doing a good job at both ends he couldn't get away with this sort of trick. And if he is doing a good job, it doesn't really make any difference whether he says so or Kerry says so, as long as Ted Shelby *thinks* Kerry says so—and vice versa.

The occasion won't often arise where you find yourself writing such memos back and forth. But often enough you will find yourself writing material in which it is easy enough to slip in a good word on your own behalf. As long as it is grounded in truth, where is the harm?

Finally, remember the value of the file and the personnel dossier. Even when memory has long-since faded (a year or two perhaps), those letters in Stanley's personnel folder will give eloquent testimony to his competence and, hence, his readiness for the next management "opportunity."

49 Don't Ask

Thinking back on it, if it hadn't been for a peculiar turn of phrase by Mr. Marsh, Ted Shelby might never have become the author of The Company's Subordinate Readiness Program. But I find this incident instructive for other reasons.

Perhaps you will, too.

"Hey, Stanley," said Ted Shelby, "would you take care of this for me? I'm pretty busy, and I think it's something that you can handle as well as I." He gave Stanley a sheaf of papers.

Stanley shuffled through it. "What do you want me to do?" he asked.

"You can figure it out," said Ted. "No problem."

Later in the day Stanley looks at the papers more closely. At the bottom is a seven-page article copied from *The Academy of Management Review* on "Managerial Subordination." Attached to the article is a small mound of paper. Leafing through to the bottom, Stanley finds a brief note from The Office of the President addressed to the Vice President in Charge of Personnel. The 3×5 stapled to the memo says, "Ralph, please exercise on this at your earliest opportunity. Marsh."

Layered over Mr. Marsh's 3×5 is another from The Office of the Vice President in Charge of Personnel, this addressed to the Personnel Director. This says, "Sheila, let's exercise on this. Ralph." And on top of this is attached still another memo, from Personnel Director—Corporate Staff, which says: "I think we ought to 'exercise' on this at our earliest opportunity. Sheila." This memo is addressed to the Director of Management Development.

The penultimate layer is the memo from the Director of Management Development to Ted Shelby, which says: "Ted, I'd like you to 'exercise' on this. This is something Mr. Marsh wants now."

The final link of the chain connecting Stanley and Mr. Marsh comes from Assistant to the Director for Training Programs—Edward W. Shelby IV. It says: "Stanley, please 'exercise' on this."

Stanley is puzzled by the word "exercise," it doesn't make any sense to him in this context. So he takes it to Lesley, and the two of them puzzle over it for half an hour. Still, they can't come up with any notion of what any of those people mean by "exercise on this."

Finally he goes back to Ted Shelby. "Ted," he asks, "just what in God's name did you mean when you said 'exercise on this'?"

Ted is smiling at him. "Why, Stanley, I'd have thought that a bright fellow like you would have been able to figure that out."

"No," said Stanley, "I don't have a clue, and it seems as though nobody else around here knows either, at least from the look of those 3×5's."

"What *does* it mean?"

"I don't know," said Ted, "and you're probably right that nobody else does either, except maybe Mr. Marsh."

"Well, then why didn't anybody ask him what he meant? Why pass the buck all the way down the line?"

"Good idea," Ted laughed. "So do this for me. Head right up to the seventeenth floor and get Marsh's reading on this."

"Er . . . I, ah . . . do you *really* think it's such a good idea? I mean . . ."

Ted leaned back in his chair. "Of course it isn't. If it was, we wouldn't be in this spot now, would we."

"But here, let me tell you a little story." Edward W. Shelby IV had a lot of stories about The Company. "Way back during the war most of our buildings were thrown up in a hurry. Pawtucket had just been completed—one of those corrugated steel jobs. I was there with my dad when Mr. Marsh (Sr.) went on an inspection tour of one of those buildings. You know the kind, corrugated sheet bolted through the structural members. Naturally, the nuts on the inside show, and naturally, they turned every which way. Well, Mr. Marsh says, 'That looks terrible!' And that very night the Plant Manager sends in a crew on overtime to straighten out the nuts and get them all turned in alignment. A week later, they were all like ducks in a row."

"I don't get the connection." Stanley looks really puzzled now.

"The point is that no one wants to ask a question of the top management. If you have to ask a question, the implication is that either you are stupid (because you didn't understand what management said) or that management is stupid (because they didn't make themselves clear.) So when Mr. Marsh says, 'That looks terrible,' he might have meant the nuts, or he might have meant the whole plant, and he might not even have meant to be taken seriously. But the Plant Manager wasn't about to ask and take the chance of looking foolish."

"Oh," said Stanley, "then all those people passed that memo down because they didn't want to stick their neck out, and maybe guess wrong on what Marsh meant by 'exercise on this.'"

"Right," said Ted, "but after I gave the memos to you,· I got some ideas. It looks to me like we just might have something here. We know that Mr. Marsh likes it—or at least, he knows about it. And that's a pretty good start." Ted took the pile of memos back from Stanley and went to his desk to start drawing up guidelines for his forthcoming "Subordinate Readiness Program."

We already know how the "Subordinate Readiness Program" turned out—very profitably for Ted, and for Stanley. But that is another story. The lesson from this tale is more for the Mr. Marshes of the world than for the Teds and the Stanleys: "It is easy to abuse your power." Since subordinates don't want to be put into the position of questioning what the boss says, the boss must be careful lest offhand remarks be put into effect. And even more important, the boss has got to be aware that the Shelbys and Stanleys have stopped asking these kinds of questions, that they are likely to get a great deal more "exercise" than was ever intended if the boss doesn't take the trouble to make the message clear.

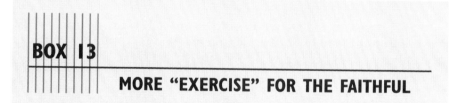

BOX 13

MORE "EXERCISE" FOR THE FAITHFUL

Not too many years ago G. Gordon Liddy was an invited speaker on the Penn State Campus. Liddy, of course, is best known for his role in the Watergate break-in, which ultimately led to the resignation of President Nixon.

Having served his prison sentence, and, thus, with his credentials established, Liddy has become a regular on the speechmaking circuit, commenting on his observations of life in official Washington.

While such "war stories" are undoubtedly embellished, one in particular struck me as having the ring of truth. The subject in this case was J. Edgar Hoover, who for years was chief of the Federal Bureau of Investigation. Hoover, a life-long bachelor, personally oversaw and directed every detail of the FBI operation. Nothing was done without his full knowledge and direction. Indeed, Liddy referred to Hoover as "awesome," one of the most dominant personalities ever in the United States.

One of the management devices that Hoover used to maintain his power was the two-page memo. Nothing longer would be accepted. He also had precise guidelines for the size of the margins on these memos, because this was where he wrote his response. Occasionally in attempting to cram additional information within the two-page limit, subordinates resorted to cheating on the margins.

The aftermath of one such attempt was recounted by Liddy. In this instance, Hoover refused to comment on the memo and sent it back to the subordinate simply with the admonition "watch the borders . . . Hoover." The result was considerable confusion within the originating department, especially because the memo had absolutely nothing to do with the borders of the United States. Still, not one person could be found who was willing to approach the imperious Hoover and ask him to explain exactly what he meant by the ambiguous message.

So in awe were subordinates of this man, and so unapproachable was he by subordinates, that they always carried out what they thought he meant, or at least what they sincerely hoped he meant. The result in this case was that the FBI sent thirty-seven additional special agents to our border with Mexico, and an additional twenty-five to our border with Canada. As Liddy put it, "no one knew why, but if the Director said to watch the borders, we are going to watch the borders until its safe to go back to Washington."

Was Liddy embellishing the story a bit? Perhaps. But in some ways, factual or not, the folklore of an organization often speaks more truth than a truly factual account.

Note: This incident is also recounted in *Secrecy and Power: The Life of J. Edgar Hoover*, by Richard Gid Powers. New York: The Free Press, 1987.

50

Point Of No Return

"Can you beat that?" Lesley was mumbling to herself. She turned and, tossing the crumpled paper ball at the wastepaper basket, exulted, "Two!"

"Can you beat what, Les?" Stanley, passing through the Corporate Communications Department, had his interest piqued.

"Oh, hi, Stan. Nothing really. Besides, you know we're not supposed to talk about Company announcements until they're announced."

Stanley, now genuinely interested, had to engage in a little information bartering before Lesley would fill him in.

"I've been working on the announcement of this Franklyn guy's promotion for about a week. That (pointing at the successful basket) was the eighth try. For some reason they wanted it just right. And *now* they tell me forget it. Seems he's not going to get the job after all."

"What job, Les?"

"Oh, Corporate Director for Manufacturing. But why would they go through all the trouble of preparing an announcement if they weren't sure they were going to give it to him, Stan?"

That question stumped Stanley as well, so, you guessed it—the next time he ran into Dr. Faust he requested another reading of the Corporate tea leaves.

"So that surprises you does it?" mused Faust, "Well, it should not. You still have the same problem, I'm afraid."

Silence. Faust knocked out his pipe and reamed it over the massive ashtray on his desk. Stanley waited. Then, "You are over-fond of making assumptions. Otherwise, the facts are clear enough. So let us proceed first with the facts. What do you know about Ben and Pawtucket that seems related to this?"

"Uh, let's see, well, The Company's going to install the PIP program there."

"Assumption," Faust barked.

"The Company is *trying* to install the PIP program at Paw-tucket," Stanley corrected. Faust nodded.

"And Ben says 'over my dead body'—ah—I mean, he actually says 'not while I'm Plant Manager.'"

"Go on."

"But that's just what I don't get. Why are they thinking of pro-moting him when he's making all kinds of trouble for them?"

"The *facts*, please," with an exaggerated air of patience.

"Uh, let's see. Ben's been at Pawtucket twenty-six years now. Well, it's his home. And he's doing a good job. I've heard people say that lots of times."

"Correct."

"Okay, so they decide to promote him because he's done a good job, but now he fouls the whole thing up and they change their minds."

"Assumption. False conclusion. Assumption." And then with a mock sigh of despair, "I can see that you are not as—ah—organiza-tionally mature as I had thought. But these things take time.

"Assumption one: that they, whomever that may be, decided to promote Ben because he is doing a good job. False conclusion: that Ben—er—'fouled up' his chances by his rejection of PIP. Assump-tion: that 'they' withdrew the promotion. Obviously you fail to under-stand. Let me give you a little help. Do you think Ben would like the Corporate life here?"

"Oh, Lord no! He'd . . ."

"Yes, of course, and so?"

"So he never would have taken that promotion in the first place. Then why ? . . ." Stanley mulled over the facts momentarily, then, "So someone was twisting his arm. Figure they give him some-thing he can't resist, get him out of Pawtucket, then zap! PIP. But whoever it was didn't know Ben very well."

"Curiously enough, that seems to have been the case."

"But he really has to take it, doesn't he? I mean, if push comes to shove can't they just say, 'It's this or out!'"

"Fire him? Much too crude, and impossible, really. And no one in The Company *has* to take a promotion. Of course, it is highly unusual not to. Moving ahead is the reason most are here. But fire him? Marsh wouldn't hear of it. How would it look? You said it your-self: Pawtucket is one of our most productive facilities. And many people in this Company are personally loyal to Ben."

"Well, if all this is true, then what I can't see is why they just don't leave him alone, let him do it his way?"

"No, no you do not understand. Mr. Marsh *does* want this pro-gram very badly, just as badly as his Plant Managers do *not* want it. Now they will fall in line, partly because they do want that next promotion and partly because they have been told that *all* plants are participating. Yes, you see the problem. Now, my guess is that Marsh has given his Vice President for Production direct responsibility for the success of PIP, so it's really *his* problem. And what is he going to tell Marsh? 'I can't get Franklyn to fall in line.' Oh no. He knows the answer to that. They all do. Marsh says, 'That's *your* problem. If you can't handle it, I'll get someone in here who can.' You've got to realize that Mr. Marsh probably values Ben more than this Vice President. He can always get another Vice President, but effective Plant Managers are a rare commodity."

Stanley frowned. "You make it sound as though Ben can get away with anything he wants to."

"It may sound that way, but that is not what I said, of course. Ben is in a strong position primarily because there is nothing The Company can give him that he does not already have. He's well-off financially, he wants to stay in Pawtucket, and he thinks Plant Manager is a more important job than President. So the usual—ah, motivational tools do not apply.

"But he's only resistant, not immune. He's in an unstable position now, and he will have to give on something. My guess would be that he will take some modified version of PIP with the objectionable features removed. In return, I think he will have to make some promises about productivity increases that may be difficult to keep. I don't know. This thing is far from being over."

With that, Dr. Faust seemed to tire of the discussion, looked at his watch, and abruptly walked off.

51

Haste Makes Waste

Braang! The phone slammed down in an obvious display of evil temper and spleen.

"I can't believe it. I just *cannot* believe it. Three weeks! Three weeks and Data Analysis still doesn't have that job for me. You know how long it takes to do that on the computer?"

Stanley nodded appreciatively, although, in fact, he had no idea how long or what job.

"Two point three seconds, that's how long. Two thousand three hundred milliseconds, and they can't get it done in three weeks. Three weeks!"

At this point Stanley cut in hoping to avoid further rendering of temporal equivalents.

"I know it seems a long time to wait, Lesley, but The Computer Department is busy, and that job of yours probably has a pretty low priority. And you've got to remember it takes more time to set up a job than to run it."

"Hell, that's just it. I'd do it myself and get it done faster—but they won't let me."

"Of course they won't. You still need a mainframe to work that database, and if everybody like you were let loose running around in the Computer Room, things would be so fouled up that nothing would get done."

"Say, you sound like you're on his side. Listen, what I want to know is, does this guy work for The Company or not? If he does, then why doesn't somebody shape him up or get rid of him?"

"Lesley, you don't have it as bad as you think. Let me tell you a story about how bad it really can be."

Stanley wandered back in memory to his student days when he had accompanied the redoubtable Dr. Faust on a visit to The Agency. Actually, The Agency was one of a number of government agencies involved in the highly unpopular venture of giving money away.

Why *un*popular, you ask? Simply because you can never make friends by giving things away. Your constituents have only complaints: they should have gotten more than they did; this one should have received but that one not; or the money didn't arrive on time . . .

But this is digression. The Agency was a large agency and gave away lots of money to lots of people. And the process was the usual one for such agencies; that is, on regular schedule, checks were sent out through the mail to The Agency's "customers." This business of giving money away is very political, and, as we've said, the customers of The Agency are frequently unhappy and complain to people in The Government—who consequently make life miserable for the people who run The Agency.

But back to the point. Stanley vividly recalls the despair and resentment expressed to Dr. Faust during his visit to improve the "administrative efficiency" of The Agency.

"Is it your customary practice here to tally these forms off by hand from the carbon copy?" Faust was incredulous as he queried the Section Chief of Vital Statistics and Control.

"Yes, it is our practice," came the sullen reply.

"I—ah—I mean, wouldn't it seem, ah—more direct to compile these statistics by machine-processing methods?"

"It would." This time the chief did not so much as glance at Faust.

"Ah, well, I hate to ask the obvious question. I'm sure that . . ."

Faust was cut off sharply.

"You're going to say that you're sure there's a good reason why we do it this way, aren't you? Well, there isn't."

Faust cleared his throat, paused, and started to fill his pipe. Always good in an emergency, thought Stanley.

"Ah, thank you for your time, sir. Would it be all right if we stop back again and talk a bit?"

"If you want to."

As Faust and Stanley passed down the hall to the elevator, they caught a brief conversation.

"Got that report for me yet?"

"Not yet."

"Any idea when? We've got to have those numbers. It's been two months."

"Sorry, you'll have to ask Kenny. Two weeks, two months, two years—who knows?"

"But can't you *do* something? Tell Sypher it's important. We can't move until we've got that stuff."

The other speaker made a strange choking sound and just walked away.

"Well," said Dr. Faust, "now I think we are making some progress." Their appointment with the Director for Administration was revealing, for Faust now had some pointed questions. "I get the feeling that your group is completely overburdened by paperwork," Dr. Faust began. "Now, my guess is that you know this as well as I, and that you also know what to do about it—but for some reason you can't."

"Yes, you are quite right, Dr. Faust. Obviously, the answer to our paperwork problem is machine processing. But it actually takes more time to do it that way than the way we do it now.

"You see, our problem is that all our machine capacity is taken up getting these payment checks out. I've talked this over with Kenny Sypher, our Chief of Computation, and he says that there is just no give in the system."

"But might you not run an extra shift?"

"We run three shifts right now."

Now Faust is really incredulous.

"On that machine, *three* shifts, and you're running to *capacity*?"

"That's what Kenny tells me. You know, Dr. Faust, you really have no idea what a time-consuming job it is getting those checks out. You ought to go down and talk to Sypher!"

"Ah, I probably shall. But first, couldn't you rent time on another machine. Wouldn't that solve your problem?"

"No, I've tried that. First, I have no money in my budget for that, and because we have our own machine, regulations won't allow it. Next, I have no positions in my organization outside of Sypher's shop for people to do that kind of work, so I'm right back where I started. No, I'm afraid this problem is just something I've got to live with."

Later, Stanley and Faust did visit Kenny Sypher and learned a great deal, but not from Kenny. His discourse on the "details of his operation" was an exercise in total obfuscation. But they did learn that Kenny's key personnel were "my guys"—brought up from the ranks, totally secure and totally loyal, knowing key parts, but only *parts* of the total operation. No one talked to anyone in Machine Operations unless and until they cleared it with Kenny Sypher.

"Well, what is your diagnosis, Stanley my boy?" Dr. Faust seemed incongruously jovial as he leaned back to light his pipe. He obviously was enjoying something.

"I'd say this Sypher is the fly in the ointment, Dr. Faust. Listen, I don't care how big the job is, with that machine he's just got to have time to help out. He's either incompetent or, unwilling or probably, he's both.

"But still, I can't figure out why he's not willing to help out, why he drags his feet so much. Some of those people we talked to waited three months for piddling little jobs that could easily be squeezed in within a day or two."

"And what effect do you suppose that would have?" Dr. Faust was leading Stanley ahead.

"Well, certainly things would get done faster and better."

"And . . . ?"

"And what?"

"Ah, how would others react?"

"Well, they'd—yeah, I guess they would. They'd say, let's get Sypher to do this. And they'd dream up new things to do, too. "No problem, Sypher can run it off for us this afternoon.'"

"Precisely."

Stanley is now racing ahead in the excitement of discovery.

"So he puts them to the test. If they really need something, they'll keep after it. If not, forget it. After all, haste makes waste. He figures most of the things people ask for are just matters of convenience anyway, no harm done. And it makes his job a lot easier."

"Well, you do understand then."

"I do, and yet I don't. I guess I forgot the reason why we're here in the first place. A lot of things don't get done around here, and we know that Sypher is the reason. Now that can't be lost on the Director either. Why doesn't she get rid of him."

Again, strangely, Faust was smiling.

"Indeed, why not?"

"Oh, I know he can't be fired—Civil Service regulations. But remove him?"

"How would The Agency get its job done without him?" posed Dr. Faust. "Remember, his—ah, 'guys' are intensely loyal—owe their jobs to Mr. Sypher. And none of them knows the entire operation. In fact, key parts exist in only one place, Sypher's head."

"I guess I do see. So if we dump Sypher the whole operation grinds to a halt for a few weeks or a month and . . ."

"And, the tempest breaks loose when the money is not delivered," Faust interjected, "and the one who is to blame is the Director."

"Who can be fired," Stanley completed. "Well, let's see. We can't set up a parallel operation—no way to justify that because you've already got one, and you would have to admit you were doing a lousy management job. You can't get to his subordinates, because you're really got nothing to give them, and they're under Kenny's thumb anyway.

"But look, why doesn't the Director lay it on the line? Kenny can't just ignore her, or directly disobey an order."

"Yes," said Faust, "in a formal sense she certainly does have the authority to do that. But look at the game, think about the pay-off matrix. The Director can order this 'extra' work to be done or not. Kenny can choose to do it or not. But he can also influence the outcomes. He prepares a memorandum in answer to the Director's order. This memorandum cites the order and points to the fact that

Machine Operations is currently so close to capacity that in event of an unforeseen machine breakdown, checks to The Agency's—ah—customers, could be delayed two weeks or more. Of course, there would be more to that memorandum, but you can fill in the details for yourself."

"Okay. And I think I see something else, too. The Director can't be sure but she's got to suspect that the chance of 'unforeseen' machine breakdown gets pretty high if she pushes that order. So Sypher's in the catbird seat there."

"Quite right. The Director's maximum loss comes under the condition of ordering the extra work. Being a minimaxer, she will avoid that condition."

"But one thing still bothers me. Doesn't Sypher know that he can be caught if someone, say an outside expert, is called in to report on what goes on? Why doesn't that keep him honest?"

"I never said the man was not honest, Stanley, nor do we know that he has actually done anything. It is simply that the possibility exists. As for your outside expert—how much did we learn about Machine Operations in our tour?"

"Well, not too much, but we didn't have much time."

"Ah, time. It *would* take time to learn the operation and then to verify what had happened, wouldn't it? And you could not call in an expert until after a disaster had occurred, could you? By then, where do you think The Director would be? Relieved of her duties, of course. But wouldn't she be cleared eventually? Possibly, possibly not. In a very real sense, she would be responsible for the political turmoil resulting from the incident, so reappointment would be unlikely."

"All right, you've got me. I guess there is nothing that can be done. But honestly, you've been acting as though you're enjoying this. I'd think you'd be pretty unhappy about it."

"Perhaps, Stanley, perhaps I should be. Yet I've always found pleasure in viewing the work of a consummate artist."

There But For The Grace Of God Go I

Power, Status, and Cooling out the Mark

How many of you have heard the term "confidence game?" Good. But I certainly hope that none of you have been involved personally. Basically, the confidence game is a series of steps in which the victim, or "mark," is deprived of cash or property.

In step one, the mark learns that he or she can make a real killing, either by obtaining something for far less than it is worth, or by doubling or tripling his or her money in a day or two. The only catch is that there is something shady about the deal. The "operators" who run the game usually pretend to have inside information that makes the killing possible. So step one is the mark accepting the "play."

Step two is some form of confidence building activity: for example, letting the mark hold the operator's stake in the play during the time the mark rounds up his or her own stake.

Step three is the "sting," where the mark is liberated from his or her cash. Angry and humiliated, the mark contemplates action. Even more than money, it is the loss of self-esteem that motivates the mark to action.

Step four, therefore, is the "coolout." One of the operators, posing as a fellow victim, plays the role of the "cooler." The cooler's job is to convince the mark to accept the loss stoically, without protest. The reasons given are: (a) it wasn't such a dumb thing to do to begin with. It could have happened to anyone—like me—and I am taking it philosophically; and (b) it really was an illegal scheme, you know. If we go to the police, *we* might be the ones arrested. So let's cut our losses and just chalk it up to experience. Come on, I'll buy you a drink.

You might think that these things couldn't happen to reasonably intelligent people. But guess again. You may not remember "Abscam," but following that scam you could have seen on TV, from a hidden camera, a U.S. senator taking bags of money from phoney oil sheiks presumably as payment for future favors. Unfortunately, Uncle Sam was the operator of that game.

The corporate variety of the coolout isn't part of a confidence game, but it has the identical purpose: to provide the mark with face-saving reasons for having been deprived of status or position. In the corporate coolout ritual, the coolers are everywhere: they are everyone who understands the corporate culture and its proper attitudes, values, and motives.

The purpose? Maintenance of the class system and preservation of the structure of power and privilege—what else? By providing the mark with face-saving explanations for the benefit of those viewing the play, the coolout makes protest unlikely and keeps the mark from questioning the legitimacy of the system of power and privilege.

And what occasions the need for the coolout in the first place? Look at it this way. First, there are lots of losers in the mobility tournament. There have to be. It is the old "all chiefs, no Indians" dilemma. True, some don't care, but others do. And they could present problems.

Another reason is that there are always some problem people, managers who are otherwise productive but won't go along with upper-management wishes. Or maybe they have allied themselves politically with a faction that has lost out; maybe time and technology have passed them by, and they are obsolete. These are the people who, as Kerry puts it, will be "transmoted"—transferred and demoted.

Yes, it is true that in our recent hard economic times we have witnessed corporations firing hundreds of managers, planning to fire literally tens of thousands more white collar workers, and drastically curtailing or terminating the activities of entire divisions. And they get away with it. But that's an impersonal thing. Because everyone gets it in the neck, and the explanation is self-evident, there is no need for the coolout. The situation is responsible.

Ah, but individuals are another matter. Here we must reckon with the principles of perception and attribution. Leaders—managers—are perceived as personally responsible for the successes and failures of their organizations. So transmotion, in its raw and naked form, is seen by observers as a result of personal shortcomings.

What, then, to do with the humiliated manager who shouts, "Foul play! I didn't deserve what happened to me. It's the rotten system—I never had a chance!" Because the engines of corporate effort are fueled by motivation derived from belief in the fairness of the system of performance and mobility, this presents a problem. Remember, others are watching. Each thinks, "There, but for the grace of God, go I." Hence, the attention given the coolout. It is necessary for no less a reason than to preserve the corporate culture and its central myth that effort and ability translate into performance, and performance into advancement upward through the ranks of power, privilege, and pecuniary advantage.

You may have heard of the "Peter Principle." There was a time when it was a clever, if trendy explanation for the widely perceived incompetence among top managers. In a nutshell: people are successively promoted until they finally reach their level of incompetence. But while the principle was seen by most as a dismal prediction, it has always struck me as a reaffirmation of faith in the corporate system, a completely logical derivation of our most cherished of corporate myths! In actuality it is the corporate version of Bentham's "Felicity Calculus" applied to the justice of the corporate reward system: each is promoted in exact proportion to his ability.

The introductory story about Ben Franklyn's move from Plant Manager to Corporate Safety Director is an example. To the uninitiated, any move to corporate headquarters is a move up. So something good has happened to Ben. Experienced readers of the corporate tea leaves will not be so sure. Plant Managers are more important people than corporate directors of safety, especially "newly created" ones. Still, you can never be sure. The corporate communications people have taken care of that. So as Fred Goldner put it, there is an inherent *ambiguity* built into the coolout ritual.[4]

Another feature of the dramaturgy of the coolout is the ritual statements from friends and coworkers. Ben is indeed "better off" or "more suited" to the new position, which he will certainly find "more rewarding." It will often give him "more time for family and friends," or golf, or fishing, or whatever. These same people will comment on how "Ben never really wanted that job in the first place," or that really, "he'd gotten to the point where he just couldn't take any more of it," or was simply "burnt out."

So there are lots of coolers, all busily explaining to each other that, whatever actually happened to Ben, it was certainly for the best in this best of all possible companies.

As pointed out by Erving Goffman, there are a number of common procedures used for cooling out the corporate mark.[5] And each has the feature of depriving the mark of the power of her or his previous position. Here are a few.

- Offering a position of similar rank, but in a function of less importance—from finance to public relations, perhaps.

- Offering a position of unique merit and prestige, but no power. The Vice President for Engineering becoming a "Distinguished Company Scientist."

- Being "kicked upstairs," possibly to a "newly created" function, but with no power. Sound familiar?

- Allowing the mark to keep the same role, but carrying it out in a "safer" (that is, less powerful) context. For example, moving a sales manager from a crucial territory to a routine, less important one, where he or she functions essentially as an order taker.

Very often the transmoted mark is offered a bribe to accept the change without "squawking." This bribe is commonly in the form of allowing the mark to pretend that it was he or she who had taken the initiative in the matter. This introduces further ambiguity into the interpretation of the situation.

Oh, my, I seem to be running on again. But there is one more point to illustrate. So please bear with me.

As said earlier, the class system of organizations is divided along professional and nonprofessional lines. But there are some important exceptions: organizations whose work force is made up primarily of college-educated professionals. These are the product development laboratories, hospitals, and technical sales organizations, to name a few.

What is the shape of the mobility tournament now, for the majority of these people cannot possibly be placed in management positions? Oh, I know, some people will protest that these are technical professionals, deeply involved in their work, who have no aspirations to become managers. Don't believe that for a minute. They're human, aren't they? And management is where the power is, isn't it? So there are going to be lots of unhappy people in these organizations.

The best proof of this that I can offer is the fact that many organizations of this type have adopted the structural innovation of an alternative, parallel ladder of advancement for nonsupervisory professionals. This "dual hierarchy" of management has a ladder of advancement for "administrative" management, and another, parallel management ladder for "individual contributors." And . . . well, no need to describe it now. In just a minute you'll see how Ted, Faust, and Stanley look at it.

But technical people are no dopes. So organizations have had some difficulty in convincing those "individual contributors" that they have not been had in this promotional con game. The coolout in this case is performed by both management and professional career counselors—coolers, if you will—retained by The Company for just this purpose. The coolout follows this sequence of steps.[6]

- **Gradual disengagement.** People identified as future "individual contributors" are urged to see this status as more fitting. Self-assessment is encouraged, and evidence of performance given, to suggest that the alternative status is more appropriate.

- **Objective denial.** Appraisals and other "objective" data such as personality and interest inventories provide the professional with accumulating evidence that it is he or she, rather than the organization, who is responsible. These procedures are generally handled by the professional counseling coolers and help to detach the organization and its managers from the emotional aspects of the cooling out process.

- **Agents of consolation.** The career counseling coolers are ever available to explain patiently to unaccepting professionals the necessity for changing their intentions. "They believe in the value of alternative careers . . . and are practiced in consoling."[7]

- **Avoidance of standards.** All discussion of the dual advancement system avoids reference to standards that allow only one set of criteria for success. Rather, it is continually emphasized that many kinds of ability are valuable, and both types of "managers" are necessary.

Proper placement is key, standards are relative. For the system to be effective, it is necessary for management and their cooling counselors to believe in it. When you get right down to it, what is the alternative?

All right, as I promised, here's how Ted explains these matters to the uninitiated of The Company, and how Cal Kulas, Dr. Faust, and Stanley react.

52

All For The Best In This Best Of All Possible Worlds

Up toward the front of the seminar room were the usual paraphernalia required for a presentation. Since this was a repeat act, Ted had gone multimedia, with sound, CD-ROM, gorgeous 3-D charts, and, of course, Ted himself. Older technologies included the portable microphone that dangled from a cord, and the water jug. Up above a sign read WELCOME ABOARD, and a little beneath that it said, "Orientation Seminar—New Technical Personnel."

Toward the rear of the seminar room sat the new technical personnel. The general understanding was that they were here to learn something about The Company's general personnel policies, and in particular about a scheme called the "Dual Ladder of Management Opportunity."

Ted, exuding an unusually crisp and hard-hitting appearance, strode into the room, and the general murmur diminished appropriately. Ted was fresh from a tour of duty as Personnel Manager of The Research Laboratory and had fittingly fresh insights into the process of research management. He was here at the Portland Plant to deliver the orientation seminar for newly recruited engineers. You must understand that The Company has literally hordes of these technical people, all college graduates, and all expecting some day to become laboratory managers at the very least. But people in The Company know that this is not going to happen, there's no way it could. In consequence of this inevitability, The Company had introduced its "dual ladder" of management opportunity. Let's listen to Ted:

"Welcome aboard. I'm sure you know that you are the most carefully selected crew of young technical people in the country today. (Murmur of approval.) We've hired top-notch technical people like you because The Company knows that without you we can't remain Number One. And we know something else. We know that we've got to reward superior performance by recognition of that performance. I want you all to know right here and now that every one of you is management material, and if you do your job as we think you will, you're going to be in management in the next five or six years. (Another murmur of approval).

"In most companies that might be a problem. Because in most companies, management means supervision; it means that you've got to stop doing what we hired you to do in the first place—technical innovation." Ted paused for a minute to let that sink in. Then, with a dramatic sweep of his hand (and a click of the remote controller) the multimedia blitz commenced. In resonant tones the disembodied voice declaimed,

> We in The Company must ensure that our 'individual contributors' don't get saddled with the supervisory drudgery that usually goes with management. That is why we've developed the dual ladder of management opportunity. (screen graphic). What we show you today represents the distillation of the most recent innovative management ideas available.

At this point—I swear it's true—the audio background featured some vaguely heroic sounding march music, while a graphic appeared showing a tuning fork with some little boxes below and more little boxes above in parallel arrangement. As each box in turn was highlighted, the phantom voice continued.

> Here we have our usual premanagement positions, our entry grade, our engineer, and our associate engineer positions. As you can see, these represent levels of achievement. We expect every successful engineer to be promoted to the associate grade when she or he has achieved the necessary experience. (mercifully the music fades).

> For those who distinguish themselves by their achievements, we have three additional levels of management opportunity. Let's take a look at the usual *supervisory* side first. Here we have three levels of *professional* achievement. And over here (highlighting shifts) we have three equivalent levels of *professional* achievement for our *staff* management. (murmurs of interest and puzzlement from the assembled newcomers).

> What have we achieved? Nothing less than arranging our ladder of advancement so that you *will not be forced* to go into supervisory administration to get management recognition. (Oh, my God, here's the march music again!)

> Our strong technical people, our *individual contributors*, keep their specialties. For that is where they make their real contribution to The Company. Professional recognition, that is the key. We are all managers, though the work is different (music fades).

Our job descriptions tell it all. Let's take the top positions here and see what is expected of our top professionals. (Descriptions now slowly scroll upward, no music).

There follow the descriptions for Division Engineer (supervisory management) and that of Engineer Consultant (staff management). As might be expected of most job descriptions, they are somewhat inflated. The position of Division Engineer stresses demonstrated capacity to direct the efforts of others, and of experience in previous supervisory positions, that of Engineer Consultant, background and technical achievement. It reads, "Ph.D. or equivalent with 10 years of experience, a level of demonstrated technical achievement rarely observed in others."

Finally, with the formal presentation over, Ted was prepared to field questions.

There were questions on salary. Answer: yes they were equal, well, in most instances they were equal. Questions on what happened if you wanted to move on a parallel between staff and supervisory management. Answer: yes, that happens. You might get tired of supervision, or you might be pressed into service as a supervisor for a particular project.

Through all this, Stanley has been sitting in the rear of the room, taking notes on the questions asked in order to give Ted feedback. He has also recorded some enthusiastic remarks from the young seminarians.

A little later Ted and Stanley are sitting in the Portland Personnel Manager's office, when his secretary announced that there was a Calvin Kulas here to see him. It seems that Kulas has some complaint or other about a promotion he was to receive, a complaint his manager felt needed to be resolved by a representative of Corporate Personnel. As it turned out, Kulas had just been told by his manager that next month he was to be promoted to first level *staff* manager. He was most unhappy about this turn of events. After a brief discussion with the Personnel Manager, they returned to the office.

"Ted, I'd like you to meet Cal Kulas, one of our engineers. He's got some questions about our dual management system. Would you mind if we took a little of your time? I've told him that we don't want to get into his personal complaint, but I think he'd get a better understanding of how our system works from the expert."

Notwithstanding these instructions, Cal did get into his personal problem. He didn't want to be promoted to staff manager. He wanted to stay on the premanagement ladder until he could get a 'real promotion to manager.' (His words.) He told them that he felt once you have been moved over to the staff side you were "branded," that your chances of getting into management weren't nearly as good. With that Ted began.

"Cal, I don't think you're looking at this in the right way. You *are* in management—staff management, not supervisory management."

But Cal was not to be put off easily. "Don't tell me that. Managers have something to manage. That's why they call them managers. And you can't be in management if you're not a manager. And you can't be a manager if there's no position to come up for promotion to. It's as simple as that. That's why I don't want to be promoted until there's a management position open. Because if I take this promotion, then maybe they won't think of me when the next *management* position opens up." Ted was sorely tempted to explain again the difference between management and supervision. It was so obvious. Why did this Kulas person persist in misunderstanding?

At this point the Personnel Manager cut in. "I don't understand why you insist on saying that promotion to staff management is being branded a failure. I think those were your words, Cal."

"Oh you don't? I'll tell you why. Look at this." Cal produced a little notebook with some statistics in it. "There's supposed to be movement back and forth, right? Well, here's the only two guys who went from manager to staff (Kulas persisted in his wrong-headed usage of the words). One of 'em I don't know, but the other I do. And I'll bet you that one is like the other. I mean, I know why Drew Bolt went the other way. He couldn't manage his way out of a paper bag. So they canned him."

Now it was Ted, eager to explain and interpret.

"Why, that's bound to happen, Cal. We make mistakes in predicting supervisory ability, certainly we do. So we want to be able to return the person to more suitable work. But to say he was, as you say, 'canned,' why, that misunderstands the logic of the whole process. The point is that we have an arrangement here that provides, ah, *flexibility* to make the best match between people and their work."

Kulas was not satisfied. "Yeah, flexibility. I suppose that's why *every* one of our Engineer Consultants (top of the staff ladder) used to be a manager until he . . ." Ted was not prepared to listen to any more.

"That's not right. You just don't have the facts. Why, right here at Portland you've got an Engineer Consultant who is one of our true technical geniuses in The Company, Gregor Mendel."

"Oh yes, I *do* know that, but he doesn't count. Look, nobody ever *sees* him. I think he's nuts. He works from nine at night until four in the morning. How many guys like that can you use, anyway?"

With this the Personnel Manager felt it necessary to intercede. "Really, Cal, I think we're getting off the track and too much into personalities. You came here with a personnel matter, didn't you?"

"Well, I did and I didn't. I guess what I wanted to do was explain to you that this dual management system you talk about is a lot of baloney, at least the way it's run here. We ought to do it right or forget it.

"Yeah, and another thing, you say that the 'staff opportunity' is equal to that of the manager. But look what happened to Drew Bolt when they unmanagered him. They took his office away!"

Ted looked concerned, "Did you? Now that would not be right."

"Of course not." Now it was the Personnel Manager's turn to get a little hot. "We simply did what is always done. Bolt didn't have supervisory responsibilities any longer, so he didn't need the space and furniture for group meetings. We changed his office from the standard A-7 to the standard A-3 layout."

"You sure did." Cal's tone was one of derision. "And I suppose he doesn't need that lousy carpet, either. Go on, tell me that it helps to keep the noise down during those group meetings."

A few days later, Stanley ran into Dr. Faust on the occasion of one of his consulting forays into New York. Stanley, eager to share his new insights, pieced together the past few days' experience for Faust. Finally, he expressed his conclusion that the dual opportunity idea simply could not work. The Company ought to do away with the whole thing, stop the sham.

"Well, let me see. I'm not sure that this dual management opportunity system is so bad as you say. Let's go over your logic.

"To begin with, tell me why you think The Company has this—ah, arrangement in the first place."

"Oh, that's easy. I think it's pretty much like they say. You've hired those people to be technical guys, not managers—I mean supervisors."

"Yes, that is what you mean. Now think a minute, Stanley. Why all the fuss? Why bother at all with this dual opportunity business? Why not just pay those people what they are worth and let it go at that?"

Stanley looked puzzled. The answer was either too obvious or too obscure. He couldn't see it.

"But that was the problem in the first place. Wasn't it?"

Faust said nothing.

"Well, wasn't it? I mean, it's because all these people went to college, and when you go to college you ought to be in management, and . . ."

"And?"

"And—uh, and, and yeah! You've got your mom and your aunt Doris and everybody asking how you're making out on the job, and did you know that Jimmie Szekely next door who never went to college is store manager of something or other—and what do you tell them? You'd like to think you're getting somewhere, but it looks like you're not. Sure, you ought to be in management by now."

"Yes. Now why is it that one is not in management?"

"But, I just told you, Dr. Faust. The Company needs these people in technical work."

"Oh yes, The Company does, though apparently not all of them. But for the sake of idle speculation, let us say that The Company did promote all into, ah—'supervisory' management."

"You *couldn't* do that. Why . . . Sure. I mean, I know there wouldn't be room for all those chiefs with no Indians . . . but that's the problem, isn't it! They all come into The Company expecting to be chiefs, and if they don't make it, why they're failures. And because The Company's got so many of 'em in the first place, why, there's going to be a lot of failures—a lot of unhappy, high-priced gripers who spend more time thinking about how they've been screwed than in doing their job."

So Stanley finally understood why the dual opportunity structure wasn't a failure at all. It was true, the opportunities weren't always equal, and the staff management side was a tempting dumping ground for a few unsatisfactory management (er, sorry, *supervisory*) types, and it *is* logically impossible to be a manager with nothing to manage. But it *was* a most satisfactory cooling-out device. The Company—wittingly, and Ted—quite unwittingly (he bought it completely, for others, of course) had redefined a situation of failure as success and had gone to great lengths to elaborate the logic of that success. And faced with the choice of defining himself a failure (under the old system) or a success (in staff management under the new system), the mark chooses the coolout. It works, all right.

53

More Bang For The Buck

Stanley was doing his best to get some sleep on the "redeye special" from New York to Los Angeles, but he'd always been uneasy with air travel (if God had wanted us to fly he'd have given us wings). Consequently, he spent the hours in a somnolent reverie. Why in hell were these research laboratories always located so far from Company Headquarters? Even when they got to L.A., there would be another three to four hours of travel by car. Oh yes, *they*: Stanley and Faust were making this trip together on a mission for the CATCHUP program. But more about that later.

Stanley had been to The Company's Research Laboratory before, and it was indeed a beautiful spot. But then, there were also beautiful spots near New York. Stanley then dozed off for what seemed like a minute, to be wakened several hours later by the groan of the hydraulic gear as the pilot lowered the flaps on the big jet. But Stanley's train of thought was right where it had been. Yes, in fact, he did know some of the reasons The Company gave for the location of this research laboratory—he had asked in preparation for this assignment. The Company wants to be, and is, number one in industrial research. But basic research is a delicate and time-consuming process, and basic researchers are delicate and time-consuming people. Or so it was thought. So one reason for the remote location was to relieve the researchers from the continual piddling inquiries by Company management as to their contribution to The Company's profit structure. Indelicate questions like that were assumed (and quite rightly) to upset delicate researchers. Because of the time, distance, and the difference in lunch hours, there were effectively only three or four hours of the day for telephone communication. The difficulty of travel made personal visits unattractive. Well, maybe the remote location was necessary.

Next day Dr. Faust and Stanley arrived at the Research Laboratory a little later than usual. They were there at the request of Ted

Shelby, who had recently been assigned as Personnel Manager. This, of course, was simply another way station along the road of Ted's personal development as a Company executive. It really didn't matter that Ted knew nothing about research. He didn't have to. After all, this was a "managerial experience," wasn't it?

Which is not to say that Ted was incompetent. Ted knew how to do certain things exceedingly well. Among these was the ability to "sniff noses and tails" as he called it, to get the lay of the land in a new situation. And it was because some of the noses and tails didn't smell quite right that Faust and Stanley were here—Faust as consultant and Stanley as support from the CATCHUP project.

"Something's wrong, something just isn't right out here," Ted was telling them. "I can't put my finger on it, but we have too many people moving through here. After all, we moved this operation out here because in our judgment this is the proper climate for research. But in the last six months, why, I think I've separated or transferred at least five or six scientists—no, make that seven. We just processed Giles Selig yesterday.

"You see what I mean? *Seven* in six months? I don't know what Kerry's thinking about, but then, these technical people don't make good managers anyway. I think we've got a chance to bring this place around." Ted was now falling into his crisp/urgent tone. "Yes, I think it's up to us. I think CATCHUP can make a real contribution here. You see, what concerns me is that these people should be unhappy about leaving here, but they don't seem to be. That's not right. Even the ones leaving The Company for The University talk about this being '*a good experience.*'"

With that, Ted suggested that Stanley and Dr. Faust spend some time interviewing scientists and their management—Stanley, the rank and file scientists, and Faust, the more sensitive management assignments.

So Stanley and Dr. Faust spent an interesting two days listening to the complaints, fears, and successes of an array of doctors of chemistry, physics, mathematics, and engineering. On the third day they got together to exchange notes. Faust was already there when Stanley entered their temporary office. He was relaxed, puffing slowly on his less-than-aromatic pipe. "Well?" he said.

"It's tough to know where to begin. Each one of these people is different in so many ways that it's hard for me to say what I found. But there is something; there is something funny here. First of all, I did talk to a couple of guys who seemed to be completely happy. They both seemed to be doing exactly what they wanted to do and doing pretty good at it."

"Well," interjected Faust. (He couldn't help himself.)

"Uh, doing pretty well at it. In fact, one of them thinks he's going to get a Nobel Prize for his work. But the others, well, I guess you could say there were two types. Or maybe three. Anyway, the rest of them don't seem to be very happy.

"See, there's this one guy I just talked to who's really got the redass . . ."

"The *what?*" Faust looked as though he'd touched something unclean. But Stanley, now into his tale, went right ahead.

"He's really burning. Thinks The Company has screwed him over (again the look of distaste from Faust) and wants to leave. Says he was promised all sorts of things that he never got. He wants to get back to basic research at The University. But he's the only one like that.

"The others, well, the others I just don't know how to describe. They're unhappy all right, but they seem to be more unhappy with themselves than with The Company. It's like they look around them and see some people doing big things and winning Nobel Prizes and stuff, and they ask, 'But what have *I* done?' They're making pretty big money, and they seem to have gotten used to it. But it's funny, you know, they seem to feel they owe The Company something. That they haven't really carried out their part of the bargain."

"Ah, yes, yes, that seems to fit." Faust wasn't listening to Stanley anymore, but puffing on his pipe slowly and staring at the ceiling. "Yes, that fits. Interesting."

Faust would say no more to Stanley other than that it seemed time to talk with Kerry Drake, manager of the research function in the laboratory.

Again, in their meeting with Drake, Faust was unusually silent. All he did was outline the basic function and mission of project CATCHUP and Ted Shelby's concerns. Of course, Drake knew most of this: it is customary to clear these things with management before proceeding. But beyond that, Faust said nothing—he just asked Stanley to fill Kerry in on his conclusions. When Stanley had finished, Faust turned to Drake and asked for his reactions to what Stanley had just said. It seemed that Faust was not going to commit himself before he had seen all the cards.

"So that's what you see, do you?" said Kerry. "Well, I can't say I disagree with you. Yes, our scientists have a certain self-image of what they are, and you (pointing to Faust) and the rest of The University people are responsible for that. When you people in the big-time universities finish with them, they think they're going to be—or they think they want to be—Nobel Prize winners. And I guess if they didn't think so, we probably wouldn't want them here.

"But hardly any of these people are going to succeed at that— partly because success in this kind of work has a strong element of chance, and partly because very few of us are Nobel calibre to begin with. Well, what that means is failure—by our standards. But we don't want to put it that way. So very few here are directly asked to leave. We want them to come to that conclusion for themselves. Some don't find what they want in The Company, and we give them a year or two to go to The University or even to Another Company if they wish. But you've seen it, most want to stay with us. They've gotten used to a good salary and the benefits and they've even gotten used to The Company. They have friends here. And you know, Stanley, you're right. They even feel a little guilty for having pulled down a good salary for a few years and given The Company nothing in return. Yes, they feel they owe The Company something. So we arrange to transfer them to a more applied kind of work at one of our other locations."

"But that doesn't make sense," Stanley blurted out. "Why does The Company want to keep failures?"

Kerry looked at Stanley but left it for Faust to say, "Did Kerry say they were failures? I don't think he did. I thought I heard him say they were failures by the standards of The Laboratory, and that is quite a different thing."

"Exactly," agreed Kerry. "That's the point. These are very talented people, make no mistake about it. But they've tried to do something that very few of us can do. We know that, but they don't. But what if we tried to tell them that in the beginning? Naturally they wouldn't listen. What if we said, 'Look, don't fool around with basic research, take a job at our plant in Pawtucket. There are lots of really important things you can do for us there.' Well, you can see, we'd never get any of them that way. And so we wait. We wait until they find out for themselves they aren't made from the stuff of Nobel winners. Yes, we let them get a taste of failure. Then they'll come to us and say, 'Isn't there something I can do in The Company that will be a little more useful than what I'm doing now?' And so we say, 'Why yes, there's this job in applied science at Pawtucket.' We need good people out there, too. But you take one of your top Ph.D's from a major technical university—we'd never get one of *those* people there in the first place. Why, they'd never give a place like Pawtucket a second thought. But in this way they do. So you see how it works."

Once again Stanley was puzzled. "Okay, now I understand that, but then why are *we* out here? Why don't you just explain that to Ted and let it go at that?"

"No, don't do that," said Kerry with a hint of anxiety in his voice. "Look, Ted won't be here all that long. By the time he's ready to leave he'll probably have figured it out for himself. But right now I don't know what he'd do if he understood the system. I want Ted to do his job, counseling our people on other job opportunities. If he actually understood the process he wouldn't be half as effective."

With that the meeting was over. All that remained to conclude a successful trip was the meeting with Ted to present the recommendations. Stanley now knew why Faust had been so noncommittal, he had understood the situation from the beginning. *His* problem was to satisfy Ted without blowing Kerry's cover. And in the end, that wasn't so difficult either.

Dr. Faust skillfully steered Ted to the conclusion that things were about as they should be, that because The Company had such high (high, but realistically high) standards for its researchers, there would be failures. It was unavoidable if excellence were to be maintained. And just as Ted was beginning to get a bit uneasy, the "solution" was delivered. Yes, a "training package."

"And it would be appropriate for this to come out under your name, of course, with myself listed as consultant. Here . . ."

With that Faust produced the first few draft pages of *Personnel Management in High Stress Environments*. Ted beamed.

What we have just witnessed is an exemplary "play" by the con artists of The Company. The Company wants its Research Laboratory, make no mistake about that. But even more, The Company wants its applied research scientists working in its production plants, "more bang for the buck" as they say. And who is to say they're wrong?

BOX 14

MORE BANG FOR THE BUCK AT BELL

The Bell Laboratories of the American Telephone and Telegraph Corporation has long enjoyed a reputation as the finest industrial research laboratory in the world. Bell labs boasts four Nobel Prize winners, among them one for the invention of the transistor, an invention that has revolutionized modern society. Though perhaps only 10 percent of Bell's budget has been devoted to pure, or basic research, still these scientists were able to pursue any line of research they chose, given that it could be related somehow to "communication."

The distinguished reputation of the laboratories made it possible for Bell to recruit top-flight basic and applied researchers from throughout the world. Having been good enough to have been recruited by Bell Laboratories is a major step in establishing a scientific career.

The engine that made possible this laissez-faire indulgence of basic researchers has been the monopoly rate base enjoyed by AT&T. Free from the concerns of direct competition, the parent company could benefit from the image of excellence projected upon it by its basic research facility.

But that era came to an end with deregulation and the breakup of the Bell system. Unburdened by the constraints set under an earlier antitrust consent decree, AT&T can now enter unregulated markets from which it previously was barred. But apparently some scientists have not reacted well to their new corporate environment. For one thing, the earlier university-like atmosphere has been replaced by one emphasizing competition, business applications, and security consciousness. All staffers are required to wear security badges bearing their photo. Long used to the free and open exchange of information, some scientists have rebelled. One replaced the photo in his ID badge with a picture of a gremlin. Others have taken the more drastic step of quitting and returning to the university environment.

Other major changes are also distressing to the staffers. For one thing, there is no more open publication. Management "watch dogs" have begun withholding approval for the publication of technical findings. Furthermore, there is pressure to come up with profit making ideas. While salary advances have been frozen for all technical staff, it is still possible for those who work out new business ventures to receive bonuses of up to 50 percent of salary.

Recruiting procedures also have been modified. Where previously little was considered beyond the potential of the recruit for technical excellence, the background of recent recruits is expected to be relevant to a field of applied science.

Source: *Wall Street Journal*, August 13, 1985, p. 6.

54 Individual Contributor

"**Y**ou mean they actually denied you the opportunity to build your management expertise . . . and on the grounds that they couldn't spare you from your job? Really!" Lesley was indignant.

The source of her indignation was the story being recounted by Holly Peño, former Manager of Architectural Applications Quality Assurance in The Company's division of the same name. Holly had recently been "transmoted" to a corporate assistant-to position, a compromise between being "reassigned" to an individual contributor position at Division, and being flat out fired. Les had gotten to know Holly in her earlier stint as technical sales trainee.

Holly's black eyes burned with the injustice of it all. "Look, look here, here's what Marsh himself has to say about our human resources development policy." Holly read excerpts from the letter accompanying the policy manual.

> Today, we face ever-increasing competition as we strive to meet the product and service needs of our customers and the financial needs of our investors. To meet this challenge, we must restate our historic commitment to human resources . . . We must encourage a participative management style founded upon open communication and employee input in the decision-making process . . . at the lowest reasonable organizational level.

Oh sister, vintage Shelby, Les thought to herself. "So you're convinced that they would have, um, handled it differently if you had been one of the boys?"

"Absolutely! Look, I'm the first one to admit that I may have made a few mistakes. But who doesn't? And 'specially when you've been brought in *explicitly* to clean up the mess that they've made. Hey, I'm a professional, and there's a job to be done.

"The problem is that management have all come up from the architectural sales side. That's a fancy way of saying that they won their spurs wheeling and dealing with construction contractors to convince them that Expandrium is a better application than their usual material. It's another way of saying that this is *really* the old boy's club of a not too enlightened kind.

"So there I am, Manager of Applications Quality Assurance—'that broad from AQUA'—telling 'em that that last batch of whatevers doesn't meet quality specs, *trying* to explain what statistical QC is all about, and them moaning that this is going to cost them business.

"'Listen up,' I say. 'These are *your* specifications, not mine. If you don't like 'em, change 'em. It's as simple as that. The reason I'm here in the first place is because of the mess that you guys have created.'"

Holly went on to describe how she had been accused of not being a team player, but Lesley was only half listening now. Holly had succeeded in lighting a brightly burning fire of feminist indignation, and Les was thinking of the next steps to be taken.

A call to Pat Jones, Director of Human Resources Research, brought a prompt meeting. ". . . so I see this as a textbook example of what's wrong for women in the corporate world," Lesley began. "Are you familiar with the situation, Pat?"

"Probably more so than you would guess. You see, Ms. Peño sent quite a detailed memo to Marsh's office. The details are unimportant, but let's just say that the memo was answered by Corporate Counsel, and that I was given a complete file to review.

"Hold on a moment, let me call Holly and get her permission to discuss her case with you. Obviously, I can't show you anything, but we can talk a bit."

"Sure. I can understand why you might be worried about her," Les replied.

"It's not Holly I'm worried about."

With permission granted, Pat proceeded to fill in some details. "Let's look at the mentoring and training issue first. Ms. Peño was hired from a similar managerial slot at Another Company, with the promise of quick movement up the ladder. And this apparently happened. Her provisional six months review is quite positive, and she is assigned significant new responsibility at the end of the first year." Pat shuffled through the past appraisals.

"But here's something interesting. Somewhere between the first and second year reviews she's been shifted under a new boss—yes, another man—who actually reports to her former boss. And here's a memo explaining that this will enable her new boss to provide the more detailed supervision that the other could not. I can't give you the details, but the record from here on makes it clear that sometime just prior to this shift, management had decided that Holly wasn't one of them."

"You mean . . ."

"Oh no, naturally it doesn't just come out and *say* that, Lesley, it's just quite clear from how things are handled. The second-, third-, and final fourth-year reviews are remarkably consistent. The second year points to some deficiencies in 'relating to clients'—internal groups—but notes her strength as an individual technical contributor. Most of her ratings are 'meets requirements,' with a sprinkling of 'meets minimum requirements.' There is a recommendation that she seek out ways of improving communications skills and to try to accomplish more working through others."

Pat leafed through more forms. "The third-year review continues the same themes, with lower ratings generally, and now a sprinkling of the 'needs improvement' category. That's the 'kiss of death' as you know. The only positive area again is specific mention of the individual contributor skills. Finally, as you know, the fourth is more of the same, with the recommendation of termination."

"Then it's just as Holly said, isn't it? They never gave her a chance! They decided they were going to dump her and that was it. So all this stuff about mentoring and human resources and stuff is just so much garbage. I'll bet if . . ."

"Now just hold on a bit. There's more. I decided it might be interesting to find out how others made out in Holly's spot. That's something experience has taught me. So I went back ten years and reviewed the personnel records of those managers.

"The first one I found, another woman, seems to have held down the position for about three years, and then was moved—at her request, it says here—to the position as Senior Quality Analyst, an individual contributor position. She was replaced by a man."

Lesley nodded vigorously.

"But he quit after less than a year. Seems he got a better offer from Another Company. At least that's what he told Personnel. *His* successor managed to hold down the job for three years, and get himself promoted to Area Sales Manager. *Sales Manager*? How that makes any sense is beyond me. Quality assurance is a technical specialty. So something strange is going on here.

"Back to normal for the fourth incumbent. Fired after repeated violations of Company policy. Something about 'misrepresenting test results.' Caught by an insider whistle-blower. Maybe that tells us something about that manager who got promoted into sales.

"And now Holly."

"So what you're telling me is that it's really an impossible job? That Holly wasn't treated differently? But still, why did management refuse to help her. I . . ."

"Why didn't they help her? The simplest answer is that management helps the ones they want to help and constructs a paper trail to justify what they decide to do with the ones they don't want to help. And it takes patience. What we see here is a decision made more than two years before the final, fatal appraisal. That's why the second-, third-, and fourth-year reviews are so consistent, to justify the action taken in the final year.

"But no job should be impossible. So there's some action that needs to be taken here. But it's something *structural*, something to do with the way this job is set up."

"Pat! You sound as though you *actually approve* of the way they treated Holly! What about mentoring, what about this 'commitment to human resources' we keep reading about? They never even lifted a finger to help her! Why, if they'd put as much time into helping Holly as they did burying her, why . . ."

55

The Threefold Way

$\mathbf{A}$nd here we are, nearly at the end of our story. Let's move ahead a few years and take a look at the finale of two distinguished careers.

Despite Dr. Faust's ominous predictions about the situation at Pawtucket, Ben weathered the storm and was made Plant Manager of the big new manufacturing plant at Portsmouth. Why? Because Marsh trusted Ben, believed in his loyalty to The Company, and felt that the technical hot shots at Portsmouth needed a bit of toning down by way of a large dose of practical experience. Ben was that large dose of practical experience. But things hadn't gone so well at Portsmouth. No, it wasn't Ben's fault. He did what he was supposed to do. But innovation is always accompanied by trouble. And then, Ben was still the bull in the china shop, and that didn't help smooth things over. He was still convinced that there was only one way to run an Expandrium mill, and he had difficulty going from that role into the role of Plant Manager at a modern, automated plant. So go back for a minute and reread the introductory story (p. 1) to review what happened.

What really happened, of course, was that Marsh's handlers and the technical executives in New York persuaded Mr. Marsh that Ben had to go. And, in the end, it took a personal visit from Mr. Marsh himself and a direct order that Ben take the new corporate job of Safety Director. It also turned out that Ben downright refused to move to New York to take the job. He hated the place. So, as Ted would put it, The Company exhibited unusual "flexibility" and came up with some good reasons why the Corporate Directorship for Safety should be set up at Portsmouth. ("Portsmouth represents the manufacturing future of The Company, and we want our Director for Safety to be right there getting hands-on experience with safety problems." Not that Portsmouth is *unsafe*, of course.)

In one sense, Ben had been cooled out, but in another he hadn't. Ben knew what had happened to him, and he made no attempt to deny it. But then, for a mill hand, he hadn't done too badly, and The Company had been good to him. No, the coolout was for students of The Company bulletin board.

In some ways Ben's story is unusual, though in others it isn't. So let's try a more typical problem. Take a look at what Kerry Drake has been doing out at the Research Laboratory. And here's a secret: The Company isn't happy about it. The stories that follow are going to depart a bit from their usual format. The problem will be set up for you as The Company sees it, and then the story will finish with three alternative scenarios. In that way you'll be able to see The Company coolers at work and get a better understanding of what is possible in the art of the play.

It's not quite accurate to say that Kerry Drake was a problem for The Company. Kerry was one of the original engineers in The Company's modern history and had a long, successful, and distinguished career—first as an inventor and then as a technical manager. It's actually misleading to speak of Kerry as a technical manager. He never had much interest in supervision, but he exercised leadership through example. Kerry led his technical people with helpful ideas and a sharp sense of where new developments in the field were going.

Sounds pretty good, you say? How does someone like that get in trouble? He gets in trouble when The Company changes and he does not. When The Company was small, Kerry would invent something or cause it to be invented, and it was usually good. Then The Company would market it. That strategy worked out pretty well when The Company was small, and it is largely responsible for the fact that The Company is no longer small.

With growth came the development of new functions and new specialties. For example, Ted Shelby became Corporate Director for Financial Plans and Controls. New products were planned by a marketing organization peopled by specialists who had only a glimmering of knowledge as to how the product might be designed. But that was the game: long-term planning, market development, recovery of capital investment, and planned obsolescence. All this, of course, meant that product development wasn't nearly the fun it once was. And it was this fact that Kerry Drake refused to accept.

Stories about Kerry's "misunderstandings" with executives were legion. Yes, Kerry was admired greatly by less resourceful counterparts throughout The Company. There were stories about executives making that time-consuming trip from New York to the West Coast, having a no-nonsense, this-is-it confrontation with Kerry, then getting back as far as Chicago before realizing they'd been had once again. One apocryphal tale even had it that the executive, upon reaching Chicago, turned around and went back for another session, all to no avail. Kerry was also master of the art of long-distance passive resistance. Directives from New York would state that work on such and such a project would terminate and would commence immediately on such and such a project desired by Corporate management. Dutifully, the paperwork would be put through, and it would look for a time as though the skirmish had been won. But those close to the Laboratory could tell you that, although the project numbers and project descriptions were different, you would find the same people working on virtually the same problem under that different title and project number.

Wait a minute, you say. Aren't you stretching it a little? No one can get away with plain insubordination.

But that isn't exactly what I said. Kerry never flatly refused to do what he was asked. As a matter of fact, he was always very careful to comply with exactly what was asked. It's just that, well, who's to say what the final shape of a product design will look like, and who's to say that something quite different won't emerge along the line, something that may be better than what management is looking for? And sooner or later the Corporate executives will get the thing they wanted (usually later).

It's not that Kerry was doing an *unacceptable* job. He wasn't. But Kerry was a burr under the executive saddle. He had aroused the suspicion that perhaps a manager who was more flexible in his thinking, more sympathetic with modern planning techniques, might be considerably more productive from the standpoint of return on investment.

So, you say, that's the point. Who's running The Company, anyway? Dump Drake and bring on someone who is, as you say, more "flexible."

Wait a minute. You sound as though you haven't learned very much from our stories. You can't just dump someone who's responsible, at least in part, for making The Company what it is today. That is, you've got to dump him in the right spot. Kerry's got a lot of friends in The Company, many of them people The Company needs badly, and they will take a great interest in what happens to Kerry. He's been productive in spite of Company wishes, and there have been occasions when he's been right and The Company wrong. You can't forget that either. All this adds up to the fact that he's got to be carefully cooled out. So there's the crux of the problem. Kerry likes that Research Laboratory; he's independently wealthy; and there's not much The Company can give him that he hasn't got. Well—almost nothing.

NEW YORK

People at the plant locations held New York in awe. Oh, it wasn't that they thought New York was always right, they knew that wasn't so. New York asked for some pretty stupid things now and then. But the people in New York all had fancy titles and an awful lot to say about what went on in The Company. They were obviously the cream of the crop. Not many people ever made it to New York, or so it was thought.

Stanley had spent a little time in New York himself, which gave him a faint aura of success. But what Stanley had seen there didn't square very well with the prevailing image in the provinces. Far from being an Olympus inhabited by superhuman beings, the people in New York were a pretty common lot. Oh yes, Mr. Marsh was there and some of the others, but, then, how many executives were there? Twenty, thirty, forty? And there were a hell of a lot more than forty people in that New York office. Maybe ten times forty. Stanley had never thought about how many people you can get in the top twenty stories of an office building. Well, of course, they weren't all executives, but a lot of them were. Corporate Directors of this, that, and the other thing. Vice Presidents, Assistant Vice Presidents, Assistants to Vice Presidents, and a mystifying abundance of Senior thises and thats. Where did they come from? What did they do? Yes, they all were doing something. That much could be seen. So in one of his tours there, he compiled an informal occupational history of the denizens of 711 Gotham Avenue. And that history, he has since found out, was typical of what was now happening to Kerry Drake.

The Vice President for Research and Development was speaking. "And we think you're the man for the job, Kerry. It's still wide open, you know. You can shape it pretty much the way you want to. But we've got to have someone who can pull our development picture together and give us a planned approach to new technical applications."

The position being offered was that of Corporate Director for New Technical Applications. As Kerry had been told, it was a new position, created out of the recognition that The Company needed it in order to remain in the forefront of modern technology. The Vice President had been very persuasive. It would be a sizable promotion with increased benefits and a good hike in salary. Only trouble was that Kerry didn't want it.

Kerry had been around long enough to know what was going on. He didn't have to take the promotion, and they weren't going to fire him. He also knew that they wanted to get a new Laboratory Manager. But then, that would change: the new line of Expandrium applications they were working on would change all that.

"John, I'm very flattered that you've thought of me first for this job. But really, I think my work out here comes first. Listen, I know of three or four young people around The Company who can do that job better than I. And it would really be a good opportunity for them. Take . . ."

With that Kerry rattled off the names of a few people he thought might like a job like that for a few years. But no one was fooling Kerry. The Company didn't want that job done nearly as much as they wanted Kerry to do it. And that is the way a lot of those New York positions came into being. It's a good coolout for most. But then, Kerry wasn't interested in that play. So move on to the next attempt. Parenthetically, it's a funny thing how those positions created for special purposes became permanent needs.

EDUCATION

"And in today's age of rapidly exploding technology we can't afford to let ourselves become obsolete. What this means, gentlemen and ladies, is that every ten years or so we owe it to ourselves and The Company to get a technical retread. Oh, it's expensive all right, but not nearly as expensive as not doing it."

Ted, using his best concerned/sincere tone, was outlining his latest innovation, the MAnagement TEchnical Sabbatical program—MATES. The basic notion was that at least every ten years all middle and executive managers would be required to spend six months in an outstanding university program in their specialty, chosen by The Company. It could be in finance, marketing, engineering, or any other specialty. The basic purpose would be to "come abreast of the latest technical thinking in business." As usual, Ted was quite pleased with the MATES program, seeing in it one answer to the continual challenge of being *Number One*.

The challenge, however, was presented to Kerry Drake in a different way. "Now hold on, Kerry, I am *not* trying to say that. It's just that, well, none of us has the time anymore to keep up with all of the developments in our field. You can't hold down a full-time management job in The Company and keep up with everything else. You just can't. Hell, I'd snap this up in a minute myself if they'd offered it to me."

What was being offered was not just six months, but a year at full pay at The University. Kerry would have the chance to take some courses in the latest technological applications and be able to give some seminars himself. And if that wasn't enough, he was also programmed for some short stays at European and Japanese universities specializing in Kerry's field. It was very tempting.

"I don't know, John, I just don't know. Let me think about it a little. I want to go home and sleep on it."

"Certainly, of course. There's no rush—take a week if you want. But we do want you to do this, and we'll have to start making arrangements soon to be ready by the fall."

It was thinking about what "the arrangements" might be, that kept Kerry from getting much sleep that night. This was to be a full year, not just six months. And no, you couldn't run a laboratory for a full year without a manager. Maybe you could do it for six months but not a year. And, of course, if you brought in someone else to run the Laboratory for a year—well then you just couldn't let him go when Kerry came back, could you? Oh, no. You'd say, "You know we never really intended it to work out this way, Kerry, but young so-and-so here, he's really into this new project, and we just can't afford to interrupt leadership on this thing. Tell you what, now that you've got a fresh look at the latest technologies, we could really use you in New York as Director for New Technical Applications."

And so, as the next day dawned, a sleepless but resolute Kerry prepared for his meeting with the Vice President.

"John, this has been one of the toughest decisions of my life, but I feel that I just can't take your offer. I probably would at any other time, but right now we're in the middle of developing this new line of applications. I don't think we can risk a change in leadership at this point."

DISTINGUISHED SCIENTIST

Not long ago, Mr. Marsh became concerned about what was happening to the technical people who, in such great measure, were responsible for The Company's success in the marketplace. He knew (and he was right) that there were a number of these people who, if they never again lifted a finger on behalf of The Company, would have more than earned their salary until retirement. Well then, shouldn't there be a way to recognize this and, in doing so, perhaps even tap the well once again?

So it was that the Distinguished Company Scientist program was born.

Now the immaculate conception of the program didn't prevent some of its appointments from being conceived in original sin. The operators in The Company knew a useful play when they saw one. And so a number—well, it would be more honest to say a few—of these Distinguished Company Scientists were distinguished less by their record of accomplishment than by their current unpopularity with the corporate powers that be.

So, having lost the game twice to date, our Vice President for Research and Development has "studied his game films" assiduously and is preparing his final assault on Kerry's stronghold. First, he requires a stream of progress reports. Then he institutes a new technical progress accounting system requiring in-depth monthly reports directly from the Laboratory Manager. Then a new appointment: a bright and shiny financial planning type is assigned to the new position of Laboratory Manager of Plans and Controls. His assignment requires that he work directly with the Laboratory Manager to secure complete financial accountability and "demonstrate optimum resource allocation to program effort." Oh yes, and he reports directly to New York, *not* to Kerry.

You guessed it. This is the kind of harassment that Kerry can't stand. So pretty soon he calls for a meeting with his Vice President. "John, you're making a shambles of this Laboratory. We are so tied up getting the *approval* to do something that we never get the chance to do it."

"Sorry, but you might as well get used to it, Kerry. This is the wave of the future. You need to know that we are taking a hard look at all our research and advanced technology efforts to see whether they've got the kind of payoff that warrants the investment. The old days are gone forever." And then as though a wistful afterthought, "I guess I'd have to say that the only ones who can have the kind of technical freedom we used to have in the old days are the people lucky enough to qualify for one of our Distinguished Company Scientist appointments." Then quickly, "But that's neither here nor there."

"No, as a Laboratory Manager you are going to have a lot more controls on you now. Look, while I'm here we might as well go over a few of the new monthly report forms." John thumped a big briefcase on the desk and withdrew a sheaf of forms that must have been an inch thick.

Kerry blanched. "Wait a minute. I got you out here to talk about cutting out some of this nonsense, and what do you do, bring me more? Looks like enough to stuff a paper elephant."

"Kerry, that's just not in the cards, and you didn't think I came all the way out here just to listen to you bitch about it, did you? Here, let's look at the first one: The Technical Personnel Resources Allocation report. This one is relatively simple. All it requires is that you identify the type of effort and average hourly project allocation by type and *document* it satisfactorily. Now then, here . . ."

Kerry didn't sleep much that night; John did. Kerry's thoughts kept turning on the old days in the warehouse at Pawtucket. Things were so much simpler. Fact is, nobody even asked them what they were doing. So long as a good product idea or two was delivered every year, nobody asked any questions. Why couldn't it be that way now?

Yes, and by now you've guessed it. John let the situation ripen for a month or so, and then one day Kerry got a letter informing him that he was one of three nominees for the position of Distinguished Company Scientist. Did he want to be considered? So Kerry thought it over, and well, there was nothing to lose by just being considered.

Other details of the program were attached to the letter. It seemed that each Distinguished Company Scientist, in addition to a handsome "stipend" would be provided with physical plant and personnel resources of their choosing (limited, of course). The only requirement was that the work of the scientist be somehow related to a potential market area of interest to The Company. And of course, that was almost anything. A lifelong license to play in the technical sandbox!

So what do you thinks? Did Kerry take the bait and become the eleventh Distinguished Company Scientist?

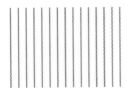

Conclusion

Commenting on the nature of organizations, T. J. Watson, Jr, then Chairman of the Board of IBM, had this to say in the early 1960s:

> I believe the real difference between success and failure in a corporation [is] how well the organization brings out the great energies and talents of its people . . . despite the many rivalries and differences which may exist among them.[1]

Watson certainly knew what he was talking about. He'd had plenty of opportunity to observe firsthand. Rivalries and conflict "come with the territory," so to speak. Watson also feared the slackening of drive that might accompany success. He pointed to those top "Fortune 500" companies at the turn of the century who were there no longer at midcentury, and surmised that complacency, a failure of will, was to blame.

What Watson had observed was that the human culture of an organization plays a crucial role in its success. And to his dismay, he has seen his own organization come to grief, not at the hand of strife, nor of complacency, but from the inability to abandon that hugely successful culture when it no longer fit the changing environment.

RATIONALITY IN ORGANIZATIONS

What is an organization? No definition is really needed here, but what is needed is some discussion of the metaphors that people use in trying to understand organizations. The first of these is the machine metaphor. Organizations are seen as systems of purposeful activities embodied in functional units arrayed in a hierarchy. The functional units are thought of as parts of a machine. If a part is not functioning properly it must be repaired or replaced, or possibly redesigned. Behavior is either functional and desirable, or dysfunctional and undesirable. Earlier, I termed this the technical/rational perspective on organizations. However, the technical/rational aspect is only one part, and not necessarily the most important part of organizational behavior.

In contradistinction, the cultural metaphor understands organizations as systems of meaning and interpretation. In his discussion of organizational cultures, Andrew Pettigrew makes the following observation,

> In the pursuit of our everyday tasks and objectives, it is all too easy to forget the less rational and instrumental, the [culture] . . . that gives those tasks meaning. Yet . . . to function within any given setting [people] must have a continuing sense of what that reality is all about in order to be acted upon. Culture is the system of such publicly and collectively accepted meanings [which] interprets a people's own situation to themselves.[2]

Thus, the cultural perspective is about understanding how an event, situation, or behavior comes to be perceived, interpreted, and understood for what it is commonly accepted to be. For example, when someone tosses off the observation that so-and-so is "not motivated," we seldom ask what that means. Rather, we call upon our stock of "things taken for granted" and agree—or perhaps disagree. But our interpretive frameworks are the same.

Similarly, participants in a common organizational culture will interpret crispness of manner in like ways. And the attribution of leadership efficacy will have a common basis. If the machine metaphor is about technical rationality, about efficiency and effectiveness, then the cultural metaphor is about meaning and interpretation, about the maintenance of the structures of authority and organization and a commitment to "our way of doing things."

Actually, the pages of *The Ropes* reflect both these perspectives. Many stories illustrate how things go awry, and for predictable reasons. But the fact remains that many things that are also predictable are not rooted in the logic of technical rationality, but rather in the cultural interpretive processes of giving meaning to human activity. Furthermore, I argue that if the maintenance of the organization as a human construction is necessary, then these processes are equally as important and significant as the technical ones.

ORGANIZATIONAL CULTURE, CORPORATE CULTURE

I would like to turn now to the distinction made earlier between organizational and corporate cultures. Corporate culture is the broader term, denoting the interpretive framework shared among all corporate organizations in "Western" countries. Organizational culture is a more specific term, used here to refer to the particular cultural attributes of a given organization, say, a General Electric or IBM.

Let me give an example of the workings of corporate culture and the interpretive framework. In the late 1960s, before current notions about "Japanese organization" became popular, I had a group of Japanese students make a presentation to my MBA class about organizations in Japan. Despite some minor language problems, things went well until the discussion turned on the Japanese system of seniority in determining promotion upward in the management hierarchy.

Several of my American students became agitated. But that will never work, they protested. What reward is there for superior performance? What is there to motivate managers to do the best possible job? But there was consternation on the other side as well. What do you mean, won't work? the Japanese replied. It does work! In retrospect, I'm not sure that either group learned very much that afternoon. But the point should be clear enough: you can't understand the workings of Japanese organizations without understanding the Japanese corporate culture—nor, in this case, without understanding the group-centered culture of Japanese society.

Here's a further example. At the organizational level, one of the things you should know about IBM (at least the IBM I knew as an employee) is this: although IBM is in the hi-tech sector, its culture, its dominant interpretive framework, is a marketing one. Crisp, hard-hitting, no room for doubt, for-it-or-agin-it decision-making styles are favored. Because of this, I believe, top management always harbored some doubts about the executive qualities of its top technical people. Their not-quite-so-crisp style, bred in the uncertainty of the development laboratory, was likely to be interpreted as indecisiveness, most definitely not an IBMmanagerlike quality. I also believe that this characteristic of the IBM culture played a key part in preventing IBM management from recognizing the depth of the change to be required of them. No place for nay-saying here.

MYTH, RITUAL, AND SYMBOL IN ORGANIZATIONAL CULTURE

Anthropologists distinguish among many different elements of culture. *The Ropes* primarily makes use of these three. Myth is the most comprehensive, containing beliefs about specific cultural practices as well as a more all-embracing set of beliefs that root the reasons for current practices in the past. In doing so, myth offers explanations for, and conveys legitimacy upon, those practices. The truth or falsity of myth is not the issue at all: most myths convey at least a dramatic reconstruction of "fact." The crucial issue is what myth does to facilitate the continuity of the human organization. I'll expand on that in a minute.

In addition to myths, cultures contain several other types of narratives about past events, handed down by word of mouth from generation to generation. Sagas are one such form—tales of the accomplishments of past heroes and how their deeds affect the shape of things today. These are exemplary tales, pointing out directions for those who would also like to "make a difference."

Legends are another narrative form, but about events that serve to define the spirit, the ethos, of the organization. For example, that story about IBM maintaining full employment during the Depression of the 1930s, and the subsequent consequences for the organization of having kept that faith. The important thing about these narratives, of course, is not what they say about yesterday, but what they imply about the organization today.

Then what are the functions of culture in organizations? Basically, these:[3]

- **Integration.** Culture carries with it a framework of meaning and interpretation that enables participants to integrate themselves and their activities into a meaningful whole.

- **Commitment.** Culture provides reasons for participants to be willing to devote energy and loyalty to the organization. It provides reasons for sacrifice and investment of self in the future of the organization.

- **Control.** Culture legitimates the structures of authority and organization that control activities within the organization. Myth, ritual, and symbol provide explanations for activities and thus help to reconcile differences between ideals and actual behavior.

Let me elaborate on this last point. As argued in Part 1, human beings are still the same folks who not too many centuries ago were painting themselves blue and dancing around bonfires. And we're the same folks who could accept the "divine right of kings" as the legitimating myth behind royal authority (at least for a while.) As our stock of knowledge has grown, our myths may have become more technical and less metaphysical, but the human impulse hasn't changed at all. And so in modern organizations, the legitimating myth is one based on performance and its attendant rituals of performance appraisal.

Do not misunderstand this argument to mean that, therefore, performance appraisal is a charade. Far from it. From the technical/rational perspective there is good reason to believe that performance appraisal is a useful, if imperfect technical tool. But from the cultural/interpretive perspective, the question of whether or not incumbent authority actually represents the most technically qualified candidates is simply beside the point.

The issue to be understood is how the cultural practices of the human organization foster the belief that the structure of authority is effective, or perhaps, why in some instances they fail to promote that belief.

APPLICATIONS OF THE CULTURAL PRINCIPLES IN *THE ROPES*

In the few remaining pages of this conclusion I would like to outline briefly the ways in which these ideas might be applied to the various parts of this text. As we do so, I would like you to go back and select cases that you believe incorporate these ideas. In that way I believe you will be able to integrate your own learning experience here.

Socialization, Perception, and Attribution

Part 1 addresses the issue of how you acquire that stock of knowledge of "things taken for granted" in the culture of The Company. There were at least several occasions where you saw Stanley learning, somewhat painfully, what everyone else knows. In fact, it is very much like learning a new language, a language of symbolic meanings. But don't be mistaken—there is more to this language than mere form. Things that may work for Faust, or Kerry, or even Ted, will probably not work for Stanley at this stage of his career. Can you think of an instance?

This part also involves a few ritual occasions. Rites would be the more correct term, actually. There are Company rituals for the renewal of commitment, and those that foster integration. Still others address the need to reaffirm the legitimacy of structures of control. Try to identify at least two.

The second section of this first part now goes on to show you how this newly acquired stock of knowledge comes into play in the processes of attribution. And, by interpreting behavior and events within this framework, you become yet more comfortable with its evident truth. An example I particularly enjoy concerns the movie hero John Wayne. Wayne's stock part was the military hero (often in the Old West). So identified had he become with this role, that upon his death a former leading lady, oblivious to the fact that Wayne had never actually served in the military, urged that he be awarded a Congressional Medal of Honor!

The lesson here for the attribution of leadership qualities ought not to be lost on you. But Lesley and Claude face the reverse problem. The interpretive framework for accounting for the lack of females and minorities in leadership positions works to make it even more difficult for them to attain those positions. Furthermore, attribution processes work to preserve what everybody knows by accounting for the occasional female or minority executive as the exception. Then how do things change? Slowly. But they change when the observed "facts" contravene "what everybody knows" to such an extent that revision is necessary. And this is why, at least in my view, Equal Employment Opportunity regulations are crucial to bringing about change. Examples in this section should be easy to find.

Motivation and Decision Making

In Part 2 you read about motivation and decision making. You began with a very simple framework for understanding motivation. This poses the question, so why the mystery to motivation? Why the search for motivational panaceas? One answer is that most organizations don't act on what we know. And this is in part a technical/rational problem. But it is also a cultural/interpretive one. Problems officially labelled as ones of individual motivation are often problems that would more accurately be termed problems in the structure of authority and organization. But the use of rituals such as "motivational programs" identifies them within the interpretive framework as problems of individuals, and thus aids in sustaining existing structures of control. You should be able to find several examples.

Dog yummies aside, you should be well aware that motivation isn't simply a matter of material reinforcers. Commitment-building rituals play a large role in creating the "energy and loyalty" and devotion to Company projects. You saw at least one such ritual in this part. And then you went on to see some examples of where the concerns of motivation and decision making blend, especially in managerial decision making. As our people learned the ropes, they found themselves in positions where taking actions that would benefit their own unit would probably be a long-term detriment to the larger organization. So there is a dilemma, and not an uncommon one. Pentagon officials work like the devil to win increases in the military budget. But someone at a lower level has to spend it...or else. So little wonder that the occasional "whistle blower" is reckoned a villain, not a hero, by his superiors. I'm certain that you can find an example.

You saw several decision-making rituals as well. And you also saw Stanley in a situation where he violated expected ritual behavior, with interesting consequences. Finally, there are at least several occasions that demonstrate how the interpretive framework can be set up to assure that the reasons for decisions or outcomes will be interpreted (incorrectly) in a more favorable context. (Hint: Stanley is directly involved in both situations.)

Leadership and Communication

In Part 3 you read that leadership and communication are kindred topics. And this is so not only because the leader must be an effective communicator, but because corporate culture must communicate necessary ideas about the efficacy of leadership action. Because these topics are so interrelated, I will review these sections together.

In saying that organizational communication helps to sustain the myth of leadership, you should understand this to mean not only the dissemination of information, but its restriction as well. There are in this part three examples of the principle of restriction of communication. Two involve occasions of attempts to get around those restrictions. And both end rather badly. Another is a tale of successful . . . ah, "information management." (Hint: Ted Shelby is involved in all these).

Management controls information, its release and the timing of the release. As in the primitive men's hut, the importance of this information is likely to be exaggerated by subordinates. But who can know? The information kept secret by the practices of the men's hut may be inconsequential, or even nonexistent. Yet subordinates can only imagine that those inaccessible secrets hold the key to understanding the most important actions taken by the hierarchy.

In this way the myth of leadership is sustained and nourished by ritual and symbol. In their turn the "communications people" (the shamans of corporate culture, the spin doctors?) are entrusted with the maintenance of the leadership myth. Facts are "massaged." Transmotions are put in their proper light. And the myth of performance is invoked to maintain the legitimacy of the existing structures of authority and organization. (There's a prime example in Section 5.) And ask yourself, what was the function of "Leadership Now"—a communications program.

Section 5 also has an example of a Company saga in the making—but it doesn't end well and will probably soon be forgotten. Sagas also serve a purpose. They are invoked symbolically to communicate to the faithful of The Company that it can be done. Sagas are exemplary narratives that invoke the myth of leadership to spur renewed commitment to The Company and its high purpose.

There are two more stories in Part 3 that deserve attention in review. One of these describes the incredible amount of attention given to the deployment of symbols of leadership status. So it's not only the communications people who are in the communication business. (No hints needed here.) The other is an example of an act of degradation. Most cultures have rituals of degradation. Individuals who are to be discredited as authorities are forced to participate in formal rites in which their status is symbolically removed. Examples are ripping the epaulets from an officer's uniform, defrocking a priest. In the Soviet Union in recent times past, those fallen from favor were forced to recant their errors publicly. An act of degradation, although not a formal rite, serves much the same purpose: the maintenance of control.

Power, Stratification, and Managerial Mobility

In the final part of *The Ropes* you looked at organizations as systems of social stratification into various levels or ranks of management and nonmanagement. The initial assignment into these ranks begins with a credentialling ceremony called receiving a college degree. Those with the proper credentials are entered into the mobility tournament, others are not.

The myth, ritual, and symbol that attend the mobility tournament, for both participants and nonparticipants, all serve the maintenance of the structures of authority and organization. The myth of performance supports the ritual exercise of managerial power. Superiors are empowered to criticize and order the revision of the subordinates' work. The opposite is not the case. In consequence, subordinates can only make the assumption that superiors "know what they are doing. They wouldn't be there if they didn't." An instance of the effect of this assumption is dramatized in Section 7.

One source of formal managerial power lies in subordinates' desire to move ahead in the mobility tournament and a complementary desire not to lose out in the competition. As noted, Ted Shelby's superiors don't have to ask twice. But that much should be evident. Perhaps what is not so evident is the informal power that accrues to nonmobile people. These include the so-called lower organizational participants who were not invited into the mobility tournament in the first place, as well as certain nonmobile managers.

Within the corporate culture, lower participants are understood to be less able or less ambitious than "management," or perhaps both. For this reason, and because their activities are generally regarded as not significant enough to warrant close management scrutiny, lower participants can wield considerable informal power. Furthermore, being only lower participants, they can count on the fact that it's often easier to get forgiveness than permission.

Certain nonmobile managers are in a similar position, those who are nonmobile by choice, but who otherwise would have been winners in the tournament. Because of long tenure in their positions, they too can build extensive informal power networks. However, they are subject to management scrutiny and occasional displeasure because they can be difficult to deal with. The examples in this section should be obvious.

On the other hand, there are also the losers in the mobility tournament. These can be individuals or entire classes of people.

Let's take the last group first. A harsh reality of organizational life is that there is limited room at the top. For this reason, it is important for organizations comprising mostly professionals with high-mobility expectations to change social definitions of success and failure. By arranging for alternative mobility structures and defining these as success, management makes it possible for all participants in the organizational culture to enact new statuses collectively for those who otherwise might be reckoned as failures. Again, you should have no trouble with examples.

The treatment of individuals is similar, though it is tailored to the situation. Especially when service has been long and honorable, organizations will go to great lengths to construct a positive social definition of what has happened. Harsh treatment is reserved only for those who have transgressed the fundamental values of the culture. Appropriate myths and the various rites of the coolout will be invoked for the primary purpose of maintaining commitment. And interestingly, the ritual here is more for the benefit of observers than for the "mark."

A NOTE ON THE IMPROVEMENT OF ORGANIZATIONS

Human beings are great tinkerers. From the first genius who replaced the log roller with the wheel, through the sewing machine, the transistor, and the space shuttle, the impulse has been much the same. We've constructed gadgets that people a few generations earlier would never have dreamed of.

Yet, from the dawn of recorded history, organizations don't seem to have changed all that much. Someone from early Roman times would have recognized all the topics in *The Ropes*: still the same problems of motivation and decision making. Greater and lesser leaders, to be sure, had difficulties in "getting the message across." And once you had explained the idea, the ancients would have had no problem understanding the process of attribution. Hail, Caesar! Even today the sagas of Alexander and Hannibal are part of our schooling.

But even more, these early people would have been thoroughly familiar with the ideas of power and social stratification. Can it be that the tinkering impulse hasn't been at work where human organizations are concerned?

Well, I'm not so sure about that. Maybe it's more a case of the tinkering not having changed the fundamental aspects of organizations very much. For, from a technical/rational standpoint, a very good case can be made that there has been lots of change, and generally in the direction of improvement. We do understand a great deal about motivation. And there are many useful techniques to improve managerial decision making. Ditto communication. And despite what I've said in a different context, we have a number of techniques to enable people to become better leaders. And our performance appraisal (don't snicker) and managerial selection techniques have unquestionably improved—from a technical/rational viewpoint, that is.

But have organizations changed much from a cultural/interpretive standpoint? That I really don't know, though my guess is not much. The old issues of power, stratification, and territoriality seem to be inherent in the species Homo Sapiens. Not that this daunts the tinkerers, mind you. Today there are not a few people advocating techniques of power sharing and status leveling essentially to reshape the basic culture of organizations. One authority has put it quite baldly: *An End To Hierarchy! An End To Competition!* is the title of his book.[4]

But there is nothing new at all about this idea. In his philosophical ideal, Karl Marx advocated the classless society and the "withering away" of formal authority. And Marx himself was a Johnny-come-lately in this regard. The longing for an egalitarian form of social organization seems to be as old as humankind. As Isaiah instructs us,

> And the wolf shall dwell with the lamb, and the leopard shall lie down with the kid; and the calf and the young lion and the fatling together; and a little child shall lead them.
>
> And the cow and the bear shall feed; their young ones shall lie down together; and the lion shall eat straw like the ox.

It may take a while.

Epilogue

A minute ago we thought we were done. But a number of people who have worked with us on this text (as Dr. Faust would say, ah—our lower participants) have asked, "What does happen to Stanley?" All right, then, let's take a look at how things turn out for our people from The Company.

As you recall, Stanley had started out in Engineering and then, for a quick promotion, had gone to work for Ted in Personnel. However, as he learned more of The Company, it became evident to him that this move to Personnel was a mistake strategically. So he screwed up his courage and applied to the MBA program at The University. He was a bit surprised to be accepted.

Degree in hand, he now had to decide whether or not to return to The Company. In that process he discovered something about himself, he had developed a considerable loyalty to his Company friends and acquaintances, and to The Company itself! So he returned to what he liked best—Production.

Now the rest of Stanley's story shouldn't be surprising. In the early going he had developed a genuine respect for the people in The Company who "actually did the work." This sensitivity, combined with a technical knack and his newly acquired managerial skills (plus some hard work) paved the way for his steady climb through the ranks of middle management. And, oh yes, he'd also learned the ropes pretty well—at last—from his mentor Dr. Faust, from his buddies Kerry and Ben, and in a way, even from Ted.

So when we last heard, he had just taken over Ben's former spot as Plant Manager at Pawtucket. His only worry is that someday the call may come to go to New York, for he can't imagine a job more important than Plant Manager. Still, who knows?

Lesley's career in The Company had begun very much as Stanley's. She had also come to The Company with a technical background and then had taken that quick promotion into Communications. But when she started to see that Communications might be a career dead end, she was able to call on a network of contacts who knew her intelligence and dedication. That was one difference between Personnel and Communications. At least in Communications you got to know some pretty important people first hand. So it was one of these people who helped her land a spot in the Company's prestigious new Systems Institute. Here she spent a year combining her skills in communications and technology with some "blue sky" concepts being developed in advanced communications systems.

From there, Lesley moved to Staff Assistant, Branch Manager and, at last hearing, to Corporate Director for Advanced Communications Systems, a very new and very exciting field. And as Lesley has moved up in The Company, she seems to have lost what some people felt was a bit of a chip on her shoulder. Maybe the fact that she's very much in demand these days has something to do with that.

Kerry Drake. Let's see, when we left Kerry he'd just been cooled out of his director's job at the Research Laboratory and confirmed a Company Distinguished Scientist. Well, you know, The Company really was right. Kerry didn't have what it takes to continue in the main stream of high-powered corporate research. He doesn't have the advanced technical training that's needed these days nor the motivation to work on other people's ideas. But he's still got that creative spark and the ability to generate enthusiasm in people around him. So he gathered around him a half dozen or so hand-picked technical castoffs and went into the developing field of medical technology. He's back to his old inventing ways now, and, as a matter of fact, he's built himself something of a national reputation for the things he's done. No, that is not in The Company's line of business, but that's okay, too. For he has brought national recognition to the research laboratory and helped to establish an image of altruism for The Company. And that image helps in recruiting new people. All this for someone who, after all, has long since paid his way for The Company.

Ben. Well, Ben was understandably unhappy with the move to Portsmouth. But with typical Franklyn determination he decided that if this was his job, he would do it the best he knew how. No matter that he would be retiring in three years. That was three years from now. But a surprising thing happened (maybe, knowing Ben, it isn't really surprising). Ben became completely absorbed in safety. And he was good at it, too. You see, his years as a mill hand were not wasted. He knew production and its problems from all angles. And now, for the first time, he could look at safety as a human problem, where before it had been a management problem. It was a different matter when it was a question of a human being losing, or not losing, a hand or an eye. There was some personal satisfaction in that.

By the time retirement rolled around, he had become so good at his work that he went into partnership with a Portsmouth safety consultant. It was an ideal setup. Not that he needed the money, but this was an opportunity to travel up and down the country touring different manufacturing plants, talking with management and the mill hands. And he loved it. He worked only when he wanted to (all the time) and couldn't help wondering now and then why he hadn't gone into the safety business a long time ago.

Then there's Claude Gilliam. Oh, yes—for various reasons Claude made up his mind to attend law school after several years with The Company. That was when Kerry Drake had his long talk with Claude, trying to convince him not to waste his time on law school, that he had a great future in technical management. Funny, neither could have predicted the final result of that session. For in the end, Claude wound up specializing in patent law. He's now The Company's Chief Patent Attorney, an important post in the high-technology business.

Dr. Faust. We are sure that it will come as no surprise to you to learn that, over the years, Dr. Faust had become a man of independent means. When the truth of that situation struck him, he promptly resigned his duties as Head of The Department at The University. Let someone else explain the fiscal exigencies of The University to visionary academic malcontents. And then, partly as an offshoot of his informal lectures to Stanley and other apprentices, he decided to write a book recounting his insights. No, not a technical book, but a set of revelations, as it were. Aha! Just as you suspected, you say. Well, this caused a little trouble in The Company. Ted, among others, read it and became incensed at what he felt was an unsympathetic treatment of him and his high-minded purpose. All to the good, thought Faust, for that was one less responsibility to worry about. In any event, this left him with considerably more time than he had ever had before to do the things he enjoyed doing.

Sooner or later, we have to come to Ted. In our final pages Ted was moving along quite well. He had become Corporate Director for Financial Plans and Controls. This is not only a very strategic position but a very responsible one as well. Perhaps too responsible. In any event, Ted made the mistake of backing the wrong side of a "palace revolt." He should certainly have known better than to back either side, but at the outset it looked like a quick step to the coveted Vice Presidency—and that was just too much to resist. These mistakes are costly, of course, and as a consequence he had to do time in the corporate "penalty box." This was an assignment as Assistant to the Vice President for New Technical Applications. But now, some years later, he's back to Corporate Director of Personnel. No, he'll never be President, and the chances are that he'll never be Vice President. But he keeps thinking he will. And partly because of this, he does what he's told these days, no more and no less. Once bitten, twice shy, as they say. And he's not ashamed to admit that The Company owns him body and soul. "If they tell me to eat Wheaties for breakfast, I'll eat Wheaties. If it's cornflakes, that's okay, too." But The Company—like many others these days—is undergoing several rounds of rightsizing, and rumor has it that Ted's days are numbered.

Wait, one more. Bonnie—Ms. Dell, that is. You know, it's odd how one thing can change a lifetime. One day when Bonnie was feeling particularly indifferent, the mail brought a brochure on sales opportunities in The Company. Of course, the brochure was actually sent to Ted in Personnel "to keep him informed." Bonnie didn't really mind being a secretary, she just didn't know what else to do. She had never finished college and, well, there weren't many things for girls to do, anyway. But this time, this time it was just one of those moments when everything comes together. Why not me? Why not indeed! So she applied, and waited, only to find out that a college degree was required. That was a disappointment. But then she learned that, having worked for The Company as long as she had, The Company would help her finish her education. They wanted women in the sales force, especially people who already had experience with The Company. And so off she went.

You would never know her now. She finished first in her sales class, and new confidence has brought her a new image. Next month she's to be promoted to Assistant Manager of the Portland office. She doesn't know it yet, of course.

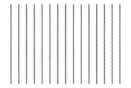

Endnotes

FOREWORD

1. *Wall Street Journal*, March 12, 1993: A3.

PART ONE

1. HARRISON M. TRICE AND JANICE M. BEYER, "Studying Organizational Cultures through Rites and Ceremonials," *Academy of Management Review* 9 (1984): 655.
2. ERVING GOFFMAN, *The Presentation of Self in Everyday Life.* Garden City, NY: Doubleday (1959): 142.
3. MERYL R. LEWIS, "Surprise and Sense Making: What Newcomers Experience in Entering Unfamiliar Organizational Settings," *Administrative Science Quarterly* 25 (1980): 226–251.
4. LAWRENCE S. WRIGHTSMAN, *Social Psychology*, 2nd Ed., Belmont, CA: Wadsworth (1977): 100.
5. ARTHUR R. COHEN, "Upward Communication in Experimentally Created Hierarchies," *Human Relations II*, (1958): 41–53.
6. PHILIP G. ZIMBARDO, "Pathology of Imprisonment," *Society* 9 (1972): 6.
7. ANDRE LAURENT, "Managerial Subordinacy: A Neglected Aspect of Organizational Hierarchies," *Academy of Management Review* 3 (1978): 220. Earlier readers of *The Ropes* might note that in 1977 Ted actually anticipated the publication of this article.

PART TWO

1. FREDERICK W. TAYLOR, "The Principles of Scientific Management," *Advanced Management Journal*, (September 1963): 30–39.
2. STEVEN KERR, "On the Folly of Rewarding A, While Hoping for B," *Academy of Management Journal* 18 (1975): 769–783).
3. ANATOL RAPOPORT, "The Use and Misuse of Game Theory," *Scientific American* 207 (December 1962): 108–118.

4. See KARL DEUTSCH AND WILLIAM MADOW, "A Note on the Appearance of
   Wisdom in Large Bureaucratic Organizations," *Behavioral Science* 6
   (1961): 72–78, for a confirmation of this reasoning.

PART THREE

1. JAMES R. MEINDL, SANFORD B. EHRLICH, AND JANET M. DUKERICH, "The
   Romance of Leadership," *Administrative Science Quarterly* 30 (1985):
   78–102.
2. RONALD HUMPHREY, "How Work Roles Influence Perception: Structural
   Cognitive Processes and Organizational Behavior," *American Sociological
   Review* 50 (1985): 242–252.
3. VICTOR THOMPSON, *Modern Organization.* New York: Knopf (1961): 70.

PART FOUR

1. FRED H. GOLDNER, "Success vs. Failure: Prior Management Perspectives,"
   Industrial Relations 9 (1970): 453–474.
2. JAMES E. ROSENBAUM, "Tournament Mobility: Career Patterns in an Organization," *Administrative Science Quarterly* 24 (1979): 220–241.
3. These characteristics are described in David Mechanic, "Sources of Power
   of Lower Participants in Complex Organizations," *Administrative Science
   Quarterly* 7 (1962): 349–364.
4. FRED GOLDNER, "Demotion in Industrial Management," *American Sociological Review* 30 (1965): 714–724.
5. ERVING GOFFMAN, "On Cooling the Mark Out: Some Aspects of Adaptation
   to Failure," *Psychiatry* 15 (1952): 451–463.
6. BURTON CLARK, "The Cooling Out Function in Higher Education," *American Journal of Sociology* 65 (1960): 569–576.
7. Ibid, 575.

CONCLUSION

1. THOMAS J. WATSON JR., *A Business and Its Beliefs: The Ideas That Helped
   Build IBM.* New York: McGraw-Hill (1963): 3–5.
2. ANDREW M. PETTIGREW, "On Studying Organizational Cultures," *Administrative Science Quarterly* 24 (1979): 574.
3. These points are adapted from Pettigrew, op. cit.
4. FREDERICK C. THAYER, *An End to Hierarchy! And End to Competition!* New
   York: New Viewpoints Press (1973).

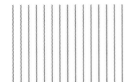

Selected Readings

For those who might want some additional reading on the topics covered in the various parts of *The Ropes*, here is a list of references. The list is not intended to be comprehensive; rather, it is a sampler of research and theory relevant to the points made in the introductory sections.

PART ONE

These readings present some of the cultural viewpoints on organizational behavior, as well as material relevant to socialization, perception, and attribution processes.

1. W. GRAHAM ASTLEY, "Administrative Science as Socially Constructed Truth," *Administrative Science Quarterly* 30 (1985): 497–513.
2. JOAN ACKER AND DONALD R. VAN HOUTEN, "Differential Recruitment and Control: The Sex Structuring of Organizations," *Administrative Science Quarterly* 19 (1974): 152–163.
3. ROLAND BARTHES, *Mythologies*, Annette Lavers, trans. (New York: Hill and Wang, 1972).
4. RAY L. BIRDWHISTELL, *Kinesics and Context: Essays on Body Motion Communication.* (Philadelphia: University of Pennsylvania Press, 1970), Part II: Isolating Behavior.
5. JOSEPH CAMPBELL, *The Masks of God: Primitive Mythology.* (New York: Viking, 1959). See Chapter 2, "The Imprints of Experience."
6. JOHN P. FERNANDEZ, *Black Managers in White Corporations.* (New York: Wiley, 1975).
7. SUSAN T. FISKE AND SHELLEY E. TAYLOR, *Social Cognition*, 2nd Ed. (New York: McGraw-Hill, 1991).
8. CLIFFORD GEERTZ, *The Interpretation of Cultures.* (New York: Basic Books, 1973).
9. ERVING GOFFMAN, *The Presentation of Self in Everyday Life.* (New York: Doubleday, 1959).

10. BETTY L. HARRAGAN, *Games Mother Never Taught You: Corporate Gamesmanship for Women.* (New York: Rawson Associates, 1977).

11. NATHAN JOSEPH AND NICHOLAS ALEX, "The Uniform: A Sociologial Perspective," *American Journal of Sociology* 77 (1972): 719–730.

12. ROSABETH M. KANTER, "Commitment and Social Organization: A Study of Commitment Mechanisms in Utopian Communities," *American Sociological Review* 33 (1968): 499–517.

13. ———, *Men and Women of the Corporation.* (New York: Basic Books, 1977).

14. MERYL R. LEWIS, "Surprise and Sense Making: What Newcomers Experience in Entering Unfamiliar Organizational Settings," *Administrative Science Quarterly* 25 (1980): 226–251.

15. ANDREW M. PETTIGREW, "On Studying Organizational Cultures," *Administrative Science Quarterly* 24 (1979): 570–581.

16. ANAT RAFAELI AND MICHAEL G. PRATT, "Tailored Meanings: On the Meaning and Impact of Organizational Dress," *Academy of Management Review*, 18 (1993): 32–55.

17. EDGAR H. SCHEIN, "The Individual, The Organization, and The Career: A Conceptual Scheme," *Journal of Applied Behavioral Science* 7 (1971): 401–426.

18. K. G. SHAVER, *An Introduction to Attribution Processes.* (Cambridge, MA: Winthrop, 1975).

19. CONSTANTIN STANISLAVSKI, *An Actor Prepares* (New York: Theatre Arts Books, 1936).

20. ———, *Creating A Role.* (New York: Theatre Arts Books, 1961).

21. VICTOR A. THOMPSON, *Modern Organization.* (New York: Knopf, 1961). See Chapter 4, "Hierarchy," and Chapter 7, "Dramaturgy."

22. HARRISON M. TRICE AND JANICE M. BEYER, "Studying Organizational Cultures Through Rites and Ceremonials," *Academy of Management Review* 9 (1984): 655.

PART TWO

These readings deal with the uses and abuses of human motivation theories and with managerial decision making and goal setting.

1. PETER BLAU, *Dynamics of Bureaucracy.* (Chicago: University of Chicago Press, 1955). See Chapters 2 and 4.

2. RICHARD M. CYERT AND JAMES G. MARCH, *A Behavioral Theory of the Firm.* (Englewood Cliffs: Prentice Hall, 1963). See Chapter 6, "A Summary of Basic Concepts . . ."

3. KARL DEUTSCH AND WILLIAM MADOW, "A Note on the Appearance of Wisdom in Large Bureaucratic Organizations," *Behavioral Science* 6 (1961): 72–78.

4. DANIEL GUTTMAN AND BARRY WILLNER, *The Shadow Government.* (New York: Pantheon, 1976). See especially Chapter 1.

5. STEVEN KERR, "On the Folly of Rewarding A, While Hoping for B," *Academy of Management Journal* 18 (1975): 769–783.

6. RICHARD J. KLIMOSKI AND WILLIAM J. STRICKLAND, "Assessment Centers: Valid or Merely Prescient," *Personnel Psychology* 30 (1977): 353–361.

7. CHARLES PERROW, "The Analysis of Goals in Complex Organizations," *American Sociological Review* 26 (1961): 854–866.

8. CRAIG C. PINDER, "Concerning the Application of Human Motivation Theories in Organizational Settings," *Academy of Management Review* 2 (1977): 384–397.

9. ANATOL RAPOPORT, "Critiques of Game Theory." *Behavioral Science* 4 (1959): 49–66.

10. ———, "The Use and Misuse of Game Theory," *Scientific American* 207 (December 1962): 108–118.

11. LEONARD SAYLES, *Managerial Behavior.* (New York: McGraw-Hill, 1964). See Chapter 12, "The Manager and the Decision Process."

12. HERBERT SIMON, *Administrative Behavior.* (New York: Free Press, 1965). See Chapter 4, "Rationality in Administrative Behavior."

13. FREDERICK W. TAYLOR, "The Principles of Scientific Management," *Advanced Management Journal* (September 1963): 30–39.

14. GAYE TUCHMAN, "Objectivity as Strategic Ritual: An Examination of Newsmen's Notions of Objectivity," *American Journal of Sociology* 77 (1972): 660–679.

15. SHELDON ZALKIND AND TIMOTHY COSTELLO, "Perception: Some Recent Research and Implications for Administration," *Administrative Science Quarterly* 7 (1962): 218–235.

PART THREE

These readings deal selectively with the formation and communication of myth, especially those involving leadership, and those involved with the role of symbols in communication.

1. ROLAND BARTHES, *Image, Music, Text,* Stephen Heath, trans., (New York: Hill and Wang, 1977).

2. JOSEPH BERGER, BERNARD P. COHEN, AND MORRIS ZELDITCH, JR., "Status Characteristics and Expectation State," *American Sociological Review* 37 (1972): 241–255.

3. KENNETH BURKE, *A Grammar of Motives.* (Berkeley and Los Angeles, CA: University of California Press, 1969).

4. THOMAS C. DANDRIDGE, IAN MITROFF, AND WILLIAM JOYCE, "Organizational Symbolism: A Topic to Expand Organizational Analysis," *Academy of Management Review* 5 (1980): 77–82.

5. CHAO C. CHEN AND JAMES R. MEINDL, "The Construction of Leadership Images in the Popular Press: The Case of Donald Burr and People Express," *Administrative Science Quarterly* 36 (1991): 521–551.

6. RONALD HUMPHREY, "How Work Roles Influence Perception: Structural-Cognitive Processes and Organizational Behavior," *American Sociological Review* 50 (1985): 242–252.

7. JAMES R. MEINDL, SANFORD B. EHRLICH AND JANET M. DUKERICH, "The Romance of Leadership," *American Science Quarterly* 30 (1985): 78–102.

8. HENRY MINTZBERG, *The Nature of Managerial Work.* (New York: Harper and Row, 1973).
9. WILLIAM G. OUCHI AND MARY ANN MAGUIRE, "Organizational Control: Two Functions," *American Science Quarterly* 20 (1975): 559–569.
10. JEFFREY PFEFFER, "The Ambiguity of Leadership," *Academy of Management Review* 2 (1977): 104–112.
11. ———, "Management as Symbolic Action: The Creation and Maintenance of Organizational Paradigms," in *Research in Organizational Behavior*, Vol. 13, L. Cummings and B. Staw, eds. (Greenwich, CT: JAI Press, 1981).
12. JAMES S. PHILLIPS AND ROBERT G. LORD, "Causal Attribution and Perception of Leadership," *Organizational Behavior and Human Performance* 28 (1981): 143–163.
13. LINDA L. PUTNAM AND MICHAEL E. PACANOWSKY, EDS., *Communication and Organizations: An Interpretive Approach.* (Sage: Beverley Hills, CA, 1983).
14. K. H. ROBERTS, C. A. O'REILLY, G. E. BRETTON, AND L. W. PORTER, "Organizational Communication: A Communication Failure?" *Human Relations* 27 (1974): 501–524.
15. DAVID SILVERMAN, *The Theory of Organizations.* (New York: Basic Books, 1971).
16. VICTOR THOMPSON, *Modern Organization.* (New York: Knopf, 1961). See Chapter 4, "Hierarchy."
17. KARL E. WEICK, *The Social Psychology of Organizing*, 2nd Ed. (Reading, MA: Addison-Wesley, 1979).

PART FOUR

These readings concern the topics of power, stratification, and managerial mobility. In particular, they concern how organizations attempt to control so-called lower participants and to manage definitions of failure and success.

1. BURTON CLARK, "The Cooling Out Function in Higher Education," *American Journal of Sociology* 65 (1960): 569–576.
2. THOMAS P. FERENCE, JAMES A. F. STONER, AND E. KIRBY WARREN, "Managing the Career Plateau," *Academy of Management Review* 2 (1977): 602–612.
3. LEON FESTINGER, STANLEY SCHACHTER, AND KURT BACK, *Social Pressures in Informal Groups.* (New York: Harper, 1950). See Chapter 9, "A Theory of Group Structure and Group Standards."
4. ERVING GOFFMAN, "On Cooling the Mark Out: Some Aspects of Adaptation to Failure," *Psychiatry* 15 (1952): 451–463.
5. FRED GOLDNER, "Demotion in Industrial Management," *American Sociological Review* 30 (1965): 714–724.
6. ———, "Success vs. Failure: Prior Management Perspectives," *Industrial Relations* 9 (1970): 453–474.
7. FRED GOLDNER AND RICHARD RITTI, "Professionalization as Career Immobility," *American Journal of Sociology* 72 (1967): 489–502.

8. WILLIAM GOMBERG, "The Trouble with Democratic Management," *Trans-Action* 3 July/August 1966): 30ff.

9. LAURA GORDON, "Bureaucratic Competence and Success in Dealing with Public Bureaucracies, *Social Problems* 23 (1975): 199–207.

10. DAVID MECHANIC, "Sources of Power of Lower Participants in Complex Organizations," *Administrative Science Quarterly* 7 (1962): 349–364.

11. JOHN MEYER AND BRIAN ROWAN, "Institutionalized Organizations: Formal Structure as Myth and Ceremony," *American Journal of Sociology* 83 (1977): 340–363.

12. JEFFREY PFEFFER, "Toward An Examination of Stratification in Organizations," *Administrative Science Quarterly* 22 (1977): 553–567.

13. JAMES E. ROSENBAUM, "Tournament Mobility: Career Patterns in an Organization," *Administrative Science Quarterly* 24 (1979): 220–241.

14. THOMAS SCHEFF, "Control Over Policy by Attendants in a Mental Hospital," *Journal of Health and Human Behavior* 2 (1961): 93–105.

15. HERBERT SIMON, *Administrative Behavior.* See Chapter 7, "The Role of Authority."

16. LINDA SMIRCICH AND R. CHESSER, "Superiors' and Subordinates' Perceptions of Performance: Beyond Disagreement," *Academy of Management Journal* 24 (1981): 198–205.

17. WILLIAM F. WHYTE, *Money and Motivation.* (New York: Harper, 1955). See Part I, "The Worker and His Work Group."